For everyone who has ever felt like they are incomplete alone.

(You're not)

There's love everywhere around me – there's love for my friends, there's love in my paintings, there's love for myself. [...] I have a lot more love than some people in the world. Even if I'll never have a wedding.

LOVELESS, ALICE OSEMAN

LOVE EXPANDED

Wren grew up in a quiet corner of Hertfordshire, where they spent a lot of time wondering why everyone else was so interested in the whole 'dating' thing. Without much of a local queer community, they turned to the internet to find their people, and to stories for their representation.

They spend their free time birdwatching, playing video and tabletop games, and over-analyzing fictional characters in everything from Shakespeare to science fiction. *Love Expanded* is their first book.

LOVE EXPANDED

HOW ASEXUALS AND AROMANTICS ARE REDEFINING LOVE, LIFE AND FAMILY

WREN BURKE

ALLEN&UNWIN

Published in hardback in Great Britain in 2025 by Allen & Unwin,
an imprint of Atlantic Books Ltd.

10 9 8 7 6 5 4 3 2 1

A CIP catalogue record for this book is available from the British Library.

Hardback ISBN: 978 1 80546 258 3
E-book ISBN: 978 1 80546 259 0

Printed and bound by CPI (UK) Ltd, Croydon CR0 4YY

Allen & Unwin
An imprint of Atlantic Books Ltd
Ormond House
26–27 Boswell Street
London
WC1N 3JZ

www.atlantic-books.co.uk

Product safety EU representative: Authorised Rep Compliance Ltd., Ground Floor, 71 Lower Baggot Street, Dublin, D02 P593, Ireland. www.arccompliance.com

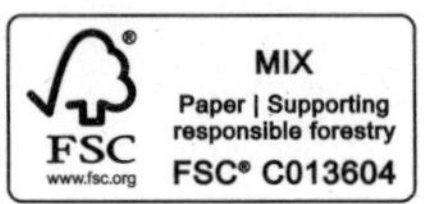

Contents

1

Love Expanded

Widening our Definition of Love

There is a page of my battered Penguin copy of *The Case-Book of Sherlock Holmes* I have turned to so often that the book now always falls open at that point. The great detective of Baker Street is crammed behind a wardrobe with his friend Watson, as ever, by his side. They are in a deserted house on Edgware Road, and they are waiting. Holmes knows that something lies hidden below the floorboards of this room; he knows, too, that a murderer is on his way to claim it.

The door opens, and Holmes's quarry, 'Killer' Evans, enters. Evans pulls up a concealed trapdoor and disappears into a basement room. Holmes touches Watson's wrist as a signal, and they pad from behind their cover to the trapdoor, guns drawn. Evans hears them coming, and in a second his pistol is in his hand. He fires two shots through the open trapdoor.

One shot misses. The other strikes Watson in the leg.

For perhaps the only time in all of Arthur Conan Doyle's stories, Holmes loses control. He forgets his stoicism, forgets his calm rationality, forgets everything but the knowledge that his dearest friend has been shot. He slams the butt of his pistol into Evans's face, sending him sprawling; he rushes to Watson's side: 'You're not hurt, Watson? For god's sake, say that you are not hurt!'

It is, fortunately, a minor injury. But in a moment of uncharacteristic fury, Holmes turns on Evans: 'If you had killed Watson, you would not have got out of this room alive.'

Holmes's intensity of feeling is not lost on his friend. 'It was worth a wound – it was worth many wounds – to know the depth of loyalty and love which lay behind that cold mask,' Watson reflects. And it was never lost on me, when I read and reread this passage. 'The Adventure of the Three Garridebs' is an unremarkable little story with a very simple mystery at its core, but this – its climactic scene – has always had a magnetic power over me.

Plenty of queer people have a fondness for Holmes and Watson. Some like to reinterpret their relationship as romantic; I, however, was enthralled by the weight the Holmes stories gave to their friendship. They have other significant relationships – Holmes has a brother, and Watson a wife – but as far as the narrative is concerned, their most important bond is with each other. This scene, perhaps the most emotionally charged moment Holmes experiences, is one that centres not a romantic love, but a platonic one.

I was thirteen when I first read 'The Adventure of the Three Garridebs', and already understood that this was unusual. In most other books I read and films I watched, romance was the most important kind of love. And yet here were two friends who lived together and loved each other; who had everything they wanted and were missing nothing. I read that one short story time and again, soaking in every word that seemed to tell me: *this can be love, too.*

In Western society, romantic and sexual attraction sit atop a hierarchy of love. We're told from an early age that a single, monogamous romantic relationship is the expected state for our future lives. Those who aren't partnered up are the exceptions, the ones to be pitied; the crazy cat lady, the forever bachelor, the relative who never has a partner to bring to family gatherings. To live without a romantic partner is to have something missing, to be dissatisfied and discontent. A partnered romantic and sexual relationship is the normal end goal of human life.

This mentality is an ancient one. In 385 BC, the Greek philosopher Plato wrote his *Symposium*, a philosophical text that posited the idea that, once, all humans resembled two people stuck together, with eight limbs, and a head with a face on each side. When the gods cut them in half, humans were left to seek their missing other piece. 'Each of us is a matching half of a human being, because we've been cut in half like flatfish, making two out of one, and each of us is looking for his own matching half.'[1] Those who had once been male became men who loved men; those who had once been female women who loved women; and those who had once been androgynous went seeking opposite-gender partners. That's refreshingly inclusive (although the welcoming of same-sex love isn't surprising for an Ancient Greek). But it also gives us a message that, although appearing to be romantic at first glance, it has another, colder, implication. All of us are fundamentally broken. We are all incomplete, until we find the one person who can make us whole.

I doubt anyone takes the *Symposium* literally. But its influence, and that of stories like it, is embedded in our brains and our beliefs. When Dr Bella DePaulo, a psychologist and author who has devoted years to studying the joys of singledom, showed a draft of her book, *Singled Out*, to an acquaintance, it went poorly. 'I believe,' the acquaintance said, 'as I think 99.9 per cent of people on the planet do, that it is human nature to find another person.'[2] This sentiment is reflected in our vocabulary: spouses refer to their partners as 'my other half'. We talk about 'finding the one'.

'There's someone out there for everyone', we say, as if a particular perfect soulmate has been predestined for every human being since before birth.

We seldom stop to consider: *does this serve us?* Do we not diminish ourselves when we speak and act as if we are all incomplete until we find that missing other half? And what is the consequence of such an assumption for those who do not experience romantic or sexual attraction at all?

*

For me, it began with an internet meme. 'If you're asexual,' it said, 'you don't experience sexual attraction. If you're aromantic, you don't experience romantic attraction. If you're aromatic, you smell nice. And if you're automatic, systematic, and hydromatic, you're grease lightning!'

Oh.

The recognition was immediate and electric. Even in primary school, I had often found myself thinking that relationships weren't important to me. In sex ed, our teachers told us that someday we would all have sex, and I was left wondering *why?* A lesson on safe sex and communication was carried out by way of a short film entitled *First Sex.* The protagonist snuck out of a party and into a shed with a girl he barely knew, and, watching, I felt as if I'd sprained something in my brain. They were going to have sex; I got that. What I didn't get was the *why.* The boy and girl had hardly spoken to each other; they'd swapped glances across the classroom, but they weren't in *love.* They weren't even friends. *Why did they want to have sex?* Was I the only one who seemed to find it confusing, who wasn't sure what was so appealing about the whole thing? In our religious education class, a speaker came in to tell our class why it was so important to her and her fiancé not to have sex until marriage, and I wondered why this should be so noteworthy. All this fuss about not doing something? Why should *not doing* be some kind of difficult sacrifice? It sounded easy enough to me.

What I hadn't realized was that my experience was different, fundamentally, from my schoolmates'. Because I am an aromantic asexual; someone who does not experience either sexual or romantic attraction.

These two forms of attraction are distinct from each other. Sexual attraction is the desire to have partnered sex with someone (as opposed to libido or arousal, which is more of a generalized desire for sexual pleasure or release – more akin to wanting to scratch an itch – rather than a desire for sex with a specific person). Romantic attraction isn't that restless urge towards sex; it's the proverbial butterflies, the desire to be emotionally closer to someone, to date and form a romantic relationship. Sexual attraction can occur without romantic attraction, something that's obvious from the existence of casual sex or sex work; and romantic attraction can occur without sexual attraction. And for some, these forms of attraction never occur at all. You can be asexual ('ace') but still experience romantic attraction; likewise, aromantic ('aro') people can still experience sexual attraction. Those who experience neither are aromantic asexuals; 'aroace' for short. This model of discussing sexual attraction and romantic attraction as largely separate things is known as the *split attraction model*. Not every ace or aro person uses it, or feels it is accurate to them. However, since it is often useful for discussions of ace and aro identities, I will use it frequently throughout this book. I will also use the term 'aspec', short for 'asexual or aromantic spectrum', as an umbrella term for anyone who belongs to an aromantic or asexual identity.

The existence of those without sexual and/or romantic desire has been little spoken about, but it has always existed. As early as 1895, German sexologist Emma Trosse wrote in her work *Contrary Sexuality* that 'mother nature herself' had created a variety of sexual experiences, including 'neutrals' who had no sexual desire.[3] She defined asexuality as 'asensuality' and added that she had 'the courage to admit to this category'.[4] In 1907, US vicar and activist Carl Schlegel argued for 'the same laws' to apply to 'homosexuals, heterosexuals, bisexuals [and] asexuals'.[5]

But perhaps the first sign of ace or aro people organizing comes in 1972, when the coordinating committee of the New York Radical Feminists created caucuses from its members, divided into their orientations. There was a heterosexual caucus, a lesbian caucus, a bisexual caucus – and an asexual caucus. It had just two members: Lisa Orlando and Barbara Getz. Together, they wrote *The Asexual Manifesto*, their position paper. Although they had yet to recognize asexuality as an orientation – they considered it 'an alternative life-style', a political position against sexist myths about sexuality – the *Manifesto*'s definition of asexuality is one that correlates with the one that aces use today:

> We chose the term 'asexual' to describe ourselves because both 'celibate' and 'anti-sexual' have connotations we wished to avoid: the first implies that one has sacrificed sexuality for some higher good, the second that sexuality is degrading or somehow inherently bad. 'Asexual', as we use it, does not mean 'without sex' but 'relating sexually to no one'.[6]

Orlando and Getz wrote their manifesto to push back against the myths they saw surrounding sexuality: that sex is essential because, if the sex drive is unsatisfied, it produces 'unhappiness and possibly illness'; that sexual excitation should always be satisfied, preferably as soon as possible; that 'sex is essential for closeness in a relationship, no relationship being complete without it'; that the need for physical affection and sex 'are basically the same'; and that 'women who have little interest in interpersonal sex [...] are somehow inadequate.'[7] (Orlando and Getz focused on women since the manifesto was intended for a feminist conference, but these myths very much affect men and nonbinary people too, as I will explore in later chapters.)

Getz and Orlando were onto something. We *do* act as if a lack of sex – and romance, too – is somehow an inadequacy. When I come out to people as aromantic and asexual, I am often met with surprise and (generally) well-intentioned concern; even from my own parents, who worried that I would grow up lacking an essential component of happiness. Strangers have asked if I don't feel like I'm missing something. Such comments speak to the assumption that underpins our lives: that *all* people, not just ace or aro people, are missing something without sex and romance.

The concept of romantic love being the most desirable state for humans is responsible for a thousand small pressures in our lives, often so ubiquitous and taken for granted that we fail to notice them. It is there in every single person who feels 'less than' because they don't have a partner, in the social studies that have found that we view married people as more mature than single people. It's in the people who hesitate to leave a relationship that isn't working for them, because you shouldn't give up on love, because love can fix all, because 'there's someone out there for everyone' and they were so sure that *this* was their someone. It's present whenever someone tells a friend or family member not to dye their hair, get a tattoo or piercing, and to shave their body hair, because 'you won't get a date like that', as if keeping your romantic prospects at their best is more important than someone's preferences for their own body and appearance. It's present in how same-sex couples were given the right to marriage long before the right to adopt.

Again: how does this serve us?

Being aromantic and asexual isn't limiting; it's liberating. Recognizing and embracing my identity shone a blinding spotlight on how I *had* no missing 'other half' to chase. I was already whole.

*

Here are two things that any aromantic or asexual person learns. First: lacking sexual or romantic attraction, or even both, does not mean we do not experience love or yearn for intimacy. Second: intimacy has far more forms than romantic and sexual love, and love is more elastic than romance and sex alone.

David Jay is one of the ace and aro community's most prominent activists: the founder of the Asexuality Visibility and Education Network (AVEN), a thriving hub where aces and aros share their experiences and connect with each other. When Jay gave a talk at Drew University in New Jersey, he titled it, 'Can asexual people fall in love?' Jay's answer was yes – but he wasn't referring to aces who experience romantic attraction (though such aces very much exist). Instead, Jay argued that when someone finds friends and companions who understand them, who share parts of their lives with them, that *is* falling in love, even though the love isn't romantic.[8]

In footage of the talk, Jay displays a PowerPoint slide in which he, represented by 'Me' written in one circle, and his hypothetical boyfriend, in another circle, are linked by a single line. 'There's an insufficient dialogue in our society about non-sexual intimacy,' Jay explains. He suggests a scenario where another person, 'Rachel' appears in his life, whom he likes and would enjoy having a close relationship with, perhaps even a shared home. But the rules of monogamy and the prioritization of romance means that he has to choose between Rachel and the boyfriend. If he chooses his boyfriend, Jay says, he loses out on this new connection and maintains only the one, dominant relationship with his boyfriend. 'But that only works if we're looking at relationships that involve sex,' Jay says. 'Otherwise, you get this.' And an interconnected web of names appears around his little bubble, including 'Rachel', and all of Jay's other close friends.

'What I realized,' Jay says, 'is that functionally, in my life, I wasn't having one person who was my source of everything.' This was his new model: one that valued equally each of the people he loved, not prioritizing one person as central, but each of them sharing something important with him: shared interests, or a shared enjoyment of non-sexual closeness like cuddling, a shared home, and so on. Developing such relationships *was* falling in love.

On paper, Jay's web of companions might seem like a radical concept. But his core argument – that love is about companionship, and that romance is not a higher form of companionship, just a different expression it can take – is something that already resonates with plenty of people, including those who aren't ace or aro. (The terms for non-ace and non-aro people are *allosexual* and *alloromantic*, often shortened to 'allo'. These terms were coined to be a useful shorthand, since 'non-asexuals-and-aromantics' is a lot to stumble over.)

Take what happened when one Reddit user shared her story of finding non-romantic, non-sexual intimacy in her life. The popular Reddit page *Am I the Asshole?* invites users to share a personal story of a disagreement or argument and ask others to judge if they were 'the asshole' in the situation. In 2020, Reddit user 'Impressive-Jaguar', who described herself as aged forty-five and female, asked, 'Am I the asshole for putting my single best friends above my married ones all the time?' She went on to describe her living situation with her two female best friends:

> We deliberately bought land adjacent to each other 10 years ago because we were sick of being chronically single and being lonely. We've since knocked down the fences on our properties so it's three houses with a huge garden in the middle which has a vegetable patch and a garden. We even have a small greenhouse and chickens, two dogs and a cat who wander around. I consider my friends to be my family, and it's been really nice over the last few years to have my own house but also have people to do activities with, buy stuff in bulk, go travelling etc and just have a good time.[9]

The problems, Impressive-Jaguar explained, had begun when married friends became frustrated that she always checked with her friends when making plans:

> I tell her, 'let me check I'm not doing anything with Alice & Claire'. I don't see what the problem with that is because she's always telling me 'let me check with Bob' (her husband) or she'll only meet me if Bob is free. If she's expected to put her husband first before her friends, then what's wrong with me saying I need to put my friends who I essentially live with and share most of my life with

> [first]? I've had other married friends complain about this too. But I never begrudge them when they have to put their husbands first. Another example is cancelling plans with me if their spouse is sick – that's super reasonable but for some reason it's unreasonable for me to cancel plans with them if say Alice is sick and Claire can't take her to the doctors.

The users of Reddit firmly voted Impressive-Jaguar 'Not the Asshole'. 'You've built your own life in what is comfortable for you and you've chosen your own family the same way as your married friends,' reads the top-voted comment. 'You've just done that in a non-traditional way and your married friends aren't seeing that. Gotta say this set up sounds pretty fantastic to me. Here's to hoping we someday get to the place that "traditional" families stop being valued higher than "non-traditional" ones!' 10,800 users voted in agreement with this comment.

Impressive-Jaguar's story reveals just how much romance is considered to have an importance beyond other forms of love and relationship. Bob's wife did not see her friend's relationship with Alice and Claire – her *love* for Alice and Claire – as equal to her own love for her husband. She had internalized a social message that plans with a spouse have an extra level of weight not present in plans with friends.

But why is this the case? Many of our friendships predate our relationships, and in ideal cases they persist if those relationships break up. Why should the presence of romance and sex necessarily add some special quality that jumpstarts an individual to the number one position in a person's life, even if they have met each other only recently, above those they've known for years or decades?

And yet living with roommates is considered a thing people do in their youth, a temporary stopgap before people move in with romantic partners, not a valid option for life companionship that might continue into maturity. It's standard to bring a romantic partner to an event as a plus-one, but bringing a close friend would likely meet with surprise and confusion. We reinforce this hierarchy of relationships with laws, with vast packets of legal and social rights being given to spouses that aren't there for cohabiting friends. Married couples can benefit from each other's insurance; they have automatic rights to end-of-life decision-making; they always have the right to be considered one's next of kin. And no – marriage to a platonic friend is not treated the same way as marriage to a romantic partner by the law. As the philosopher Sabine Hohl points out, if you marry someone from another country of origin with whom you don't have a romantic relationship, you can be charged with 'fake marriage'. Because romance is what defines 'real' marriage as opposed to a 'pretend' marriage between friends. 'No matter how important a close friend is to you,' Hohl says, 'you can't marry him to live with him here.'[10]

This hierarchy of love can be immensely damaging and distressing to aromantic and asexual people. It is alienating to feel that society sees you as inherently incomplete, and it can also devalue the relationships that often mean the world to us. For me, my platonic friendships are my most significant relationships. Part of the reason I latched on so closely to the Sherlock Holmes stories as a young teen was that *I wanted what Holmes and Watson had.* I wanted – and I still want – to be able to share a home with a friend who I am committed to, who is my life partner, my *person* in the way that Watson and Holmes were to each other. I want to share my home with someone, and consider them family, and not have that relationship seen as 'lesser' for a lack of romance or sex. I believe that this should not be treated on any level as less important, less valid or less loving than a romantic marriage.

And yet – this privileging of romance can be damaging for allo people too. Many of the most basic structures of our day-to-day lives expect everyone to partner up. Couples can meet the demands of childcare more easily than a single parent, with one parent able to care for children while another is working, or else a double income allowing them to pay for childcare. Single home ownership is out of the reach of many; two people can sometimes afford what one alone cannot. Social circles may be so tightly entwined with a romantic partner's that when relationships break up, people can find themselves losing much of their former support group.

The responses to Impressive-Jaguar's Reddit post indicate that there are plenty of people out there who envied her non-traditional family. 'Your life sounds amazing and I have serious goal envy,' replied one; another, 'It sounds ideal to me.' If many of us would welcome alternatives to nuclear romantic families, it's clearly time to break down the hierarchy.

When I interviewed my fellow aspecs, I saw just how much my community has expanded the definition of love. For those of us who often have no choice but to pursue non-traditional relationships, the gates are forcibly flung open; we have had to reconsider different paths, question the prioritization of romantic and sexual relationships, and find our own routes to intimacy and companionship.

I found many of my interviewees through a survey I initially shared online, in spaces ranging from the AVEN forums to asexual and aromantic threads on Reddit, to social media sites where I knew a significant amount of aspec people gathered, including Tumblr and Twitter. I went to bed after posting it expecting perhaps a dozen responses; I awoke to fifty. By the end of the week, there were two hundred; after a month, a little over a thousand; by the time I closed the survey after about two months, there were over 1,800 responses. The first-hand accounts in this book come from both those initial survey responses and the interviews I conducted later. (Some of my interviewees gave their names, while others chose an alias or nickname. If some of the nicknames seem odd to you, remember that a lot of aspec people are used to only interacting with the community online, given how scarce awareness is in the physical world. Many felt comfortable only using their online handles, and were understandably nervous about the prospect of any people in the 'real' world learning about their identities.)

One of the questions I asked was how people's aspec identities informed and shaped their relationships. The overwhelming impression I received was that being aspec broadens people's conceptions of what a relationship can be. One of my interviewees, who asked to be referred to as Cactus (they/them), lives with two partners. Those partners are romantically and sexually involved with each other, but not with Cactus. However, they all live together, and they're a unit that wouldn't be complete without Cactus in it. When Cactus's partners get married and have kids, Cactus will be involved in raising them. It's one example of what aspecs have termed a *queerplatonic* relationship: a relationship that blurs the normal definitions of what's platonic and romantic.

Queerplatonic relationships can look like many different things to many different people. Cactus's setup – a group where some people are romantically involved and some not, but all are an essential part of the relationship – is just one example. Some aspec people might live with a best friend, even getting married, without having any romantic or sexual feelings for each other. Others, like Ace (they/them) might be aroace but have a partner who is romantically and sexually attracted to them. 'They consider their attraction to me to be romantic and consider me their primary partner,' Ace says. 'We're getting married later this year so they can benefit from my insurance and take care of legal matters if anything should happen to me. They're content with the fact that I don't see us as romantic and have no problems with [them] fulfilling their sexual needs elsewhere.' It means that their partner's needs are taken care of without Ace having to engage in sex they don't want, and they trust that they are the one their partner is committed to. 'Having a polyamorous partner is the best! And I highly recommend it if you can communicate well.'

Even outside of queerplatonic relationships, aspecs' romantic relationships might still look very different to those formed by allos. One of my interviewees, Cake (she/they) is ace, and has a romantic partner who is also asexual. For those who aren't aspec, the idea of a romantic relationship without sex might seem bizarre, but it's common and natural for many aces who aren't also aromantic.

'It's amazing having someone who understands what it's like when hormones inspire physical interest and you're just like… "can you fucking not? I have things to do",' Cake says. 'As long as I don't snore too loud, we'll never have any problems in bed! They're my best friend, and I get to see them every day now. There are no expectations, not even from ourselves.'

In just these three examples, we see three different experiences of love and intimacy. Each an individual pattern of love and flourishing, expressed sometimes through sex and sometimes not, sometimes through romance, through friendship, through intimacy both physical and emotional, through cohabiting or not, calling each other partners or not, getting married or not. These three – and so many of my other interviewees – picked and chose what felt right for them out of different forms of closeness, combining them to make relationships unique to them, that *worked* for them and their partners. They defined love for themselves.

*

Being aspec does not narrow our options for love. It expands them. It welcomes and validates forms of love outside the norm. And it has made me readier to declare my love, even outside of any one partnered relationship. All of my closest friends know that I'm aroace, and they know this means that friendships are the most important relationships in my life. That means that they don't misunderstand my intentions, and they understand just how much weight the words carry, when I tell them – again and again – 'I love you. I love you guys.' Before I embraced being aroace, I said those words rarely. Now I say them every chance I get.

Many of my interviewees experienced a similar deepening of their platonic relationships after finding the words for their aspec identity. Edmond, a bisexual aromantic person in Australia, told me of how a friend confessed feelings for them:

> My reply of 'thanks, but I don't feel romantic attraction, and don't think I ever will,' has allowed us to be closer than we were before. This clear communication makes him one of my closest confidants, and we have all sorts of discussions about gender, romance, sex and the porn industry. Then we go back to watching Pokémon speedruns.

And, like me, Edmond embraces love and declaring it:

> I don't do romance except for when I do. I daydream of romantic scenarios, I read romantic fanfiction, books, and comics. I also use the term 'love' for everything. I say 'I love you' to my friends, to a dog, to the cool bark on a tree. I yell, 'in love with this!' to art I enjoy, music and silly ideas people come up with. My existence is a rebellion against societal norms, and a problem for those who refuse to expand their view of the world. A problem for them, not for me.

This is what is so crucial: this kind of gleeful, and sometimes rebellious, aspec joy.

As I tell the stories of the aspecs I interviewed for this book, I will not ignore the difficulties, marginalization and mistreatment that we have experienced. That is part of our journey – especially when it so often bleeds into other forms of marginalization. Our society has dozens of ingrained, often unconscious assumptions about how much certain groups have sex, *how* they should have it, how often, and how desirable they are as sexual and romantic partners: disabled people, people of colour, neurodivergent people, transgender people, fat people, men, women, everyone. Part of why it is so necessary to challenge the idea that love and sex should be so prioritized in human existence is because it weakens the foundations on which these assumptions are founded; it fights the extent to which desirability is entwined with a person's worth in the eyes of others and themselves.

But this is not a book *about* suffering, although the challenges we face are everywhere and real. It is a map: a guide for what non-traditional relationships can look like in all their myriad forms, and a source of advice from aromantic and asexual people on how to form them. It's about opening up opportunities for expanded love, both for aspecs and for allos. It's for single people struggling to own a home, for those who feel that friendship is less prominent in their lives than they would like, and for people who want more social support for lives lived happily single. It's about new languages for consent that can create better, clearer communication between sexual partners; it's about different approaches to dating that focus less on seeking instant 'chemistry' and more on building friendships. It's about aspec joy.

Joy is all too often left out of queer narratives. It's easy to focus on the depressing statistics of aces and aros afraid of rejection by partners, the stories of coerced sex and awful experiences with doctors and therapists. This is understandable: it's an easy way to show the need for change. But among the sadness and frustration, we must not lose sight of what we are working towards. The aspecs I spoke to told me of how recognizing their identity helped them stop worrying about their appearance, to view their bodies as something for them to enjoy their lives in, rather than existing for another's consumption; how they dress up now for their own sake.

For me, aroace joy is lying on my back beside my best friend, my head tucked against her shoulder, talking about memes and life and knowing that this is the deepest, truest bond I've ever known. It's making a playlist of songs, and only realizing later with a laugh that I unthinkingly filled it with songs that have nothing to do with romance. It's the grin of the other person wearing an ace or aro flag at Pride. It's in being able to speak to my fellow aspecs and say *yes, you understand. Yes.*

I am so glad to be aroace. For all the difficulties we have encountered, when for all the tragic and painful stories I read as those answers to my survey came flooding in, I found myself growing more hopeful with every response. Because when I was a teenager – when I read a joke on the internet and knew it spoke to me – I had no model for my future. The familiar social script had been torn away from me and I had no idea what the road ahead might be. But now, having read almost two thousand stories of how aros and aces have carved out our spaces, built our families, and found out how to love in our own ways, I don't wonder any more about what our future looks like.

It looks like the people whose stories I am about to tell. It looks like them – and it looks like me.

2

Not the Only Story

Reconsidering the Coming-Out Narrative

We all know how the coming-out story goes. A young person realizes that they aren't straight or cisgender. They make the announcement, perhaps standing up in front of their family, perhaps telling their friends at school. They wait for the reaction, and it comes: acceptance, or rejection. Whatever the response, the teen is now officially Out, their rite of passage completed. Their time of hiding is over; they have passed the greatest milestone on the road to becoming a queer adult.

These were the stories I grew up with, and I knew I was lucky to have them; lucky to live in a time and a part of the world where coming out was an option. When I reached the point of, belatedly, being certain that I was ace (knowing that I was aromantic took a little longer), I knew what needed to follow: the declaration.

I tried the script on my brother, hoping that he would be the most receptive of my family members. He mentioned, offhandedly, that university was so full of relationship drama that it was like a sitcom, and I pounced. 'Everyone? You have to know someone who's not interested in that kind of thing.'

'I guess there are people who haven't clicked with anyone yet.'

'But some people aren't interested in relationships, full stop. Or sex. Any of it.'

He considered this. Then shrugged. 'I think anyone who says they're not interested is just making an excuse for why they can't get a relationship. Or there's something medically wrong with them. I mean – sex is such a natural human instinct. Anyone who doesn't want it probably has some kind of disorder.'

I stopped, the words I'd been planning to say sticking behind my teeth. This wasn't how it was supposed to go. This wasn't what happened in the books and films. Those had taught me that the responses to coming out were *I accept you* or *I don't.* Nothing had prepared me for the possibility of someone saying *I don't believe you.*

With my mother, I tried a different approach. I started with hints that I didn't want to get married or have a relationship. I showed her an article in a newspaper by a closeted asexual. I came out by degrees, gradually building towards explaining that I didn't fantasize about sex, or factor it into my daily life, or picture it a part of my future. The difference between asexuality and aromanticism felt too complicated to explain, but I told her I had never been interested in anyone – that I wasn't interested in being interested.

'That doesn't mean you'll never feel that way,' she said. 'You might just not have met the right person yet.'

I set my teeth together. 'If I'd told you I was a lesbian, you wouldn't tell me I just hadn't met the right man.'

'The right *person*,' she insisted, in a tone that implied this made a difference.

So I typed up and printed out a list of frequently asked questions about asexuality, and went to try my dad. This time, I was ready for *you haven't met the right person yet* and *this sounds like a disorder.* I had answers for *you're too young to know* and *that isn't a real identity.* What I wasn't prepared for was what he said.

'All right. As long as you understand that it may change in the future.'

The speech, the rehearsals, the FAQs – they were all suddenly worthless. I flailed for the crucial question. 'But you believe me?'

'Of course.'

All right. This was good. This meant it was going well. 'Okay. That's great. I was – I don't know, I was worried you wouldn't think it was a real orientation.'

'Well, it's not. It's a lack of orientation.'

'Dad. I just want you to give my identity the same respect you'd give it if I'd come out as gay.'

And he agreed. *That went well*, I told myself. *That went really well.*

A month or two later, when I brought the topic up in conversation, he frowned at me. 'Right, because you… you consider yourself to be one of those people without a gender?'

It wouldn't be long before I realized that he was, in fact, right. I am indeed nonbinary. At the time, though, I wanted to scream. I had expected my family to accept my asexuality or not accept it, I had prepared for it – but not for them to fail to believe me, or to misunderstand what I was saying, or for them to appear uncomfortable whenever I brought it up. I was out; didn't that mean I got to talk about it now? Didn't that mean I was open, able to live my queer existence to the full? Because I wasn't doing that.

I turned nineteen. University, I knew, would offer a place where no one had expectations about who I was and who I was going to be. My mum drove me to the station. As we crawled up the motorway, she said, abruptly, 'I know you think you're asexual—'

My excitement crashed somewhere on the road behind us.

'—but please don't tell anyone. I don't want you to miss out on opportunities. There are so many wonderful experiences you can have at university.'

Words seethed behind my lips. I wanted to tell her that she was wrong, that the real opportunity was the chance to finally be seen as an aroace person and not as the person my family thought I was, a straight woman who just had to get over my fear of the unknown. I wanted to tell her that I was sick of living in limbo, somehow both out and not.

I stared at the streetlights sliding by, and said nothing.

*

The coming-out story does not work for everyone.

Coming out, as we currently understand it, does not mean what it did when the term was coined. When queer subculture existed underground, a queer person 'came out' when they introduced themselves to that subculture. It was to other queer folks, not to straight and cis people, that they came out – a truth reflected in the phrase itself. *Coming out* was the term once used for a young woman's debut into society when she reached marriageable age; queer people were, like those young aristocratic women, joining their peers and starting their romantic lives.

By this definition – joining a circle of peers – I had come out long before I said a word to my parents. I was openly aroace online, the only place I interacted with other queer people, and had aspec friends through the internet. I might only have dipped a toe into the queer world, but I was definitely not standing on the shore anymore. But in my head, *coming out* meant telling the allo people around me. That was what happened in coming-out stories, and it was what I thought my story had to be.

But for many aro and ace people, coming out is rarely so simple as those stories. When a person says *I'm gay*, at least everyone knows what they mean; saying *I'm asexual* or *I'm aromantic* to an unfamiliar allo person can lead to them having visions of sad, closed-off loners. By the modern definition, I never came out to my family as aroace. There was no transition from before or after, from dark into light, from hiding to transparency. My parents' lack of understanding made that impossible. I never underwent that rite of passage – and given how much the coming-out story is presented as *the* major queer milestone, I was left feeling like I had failed. I was neither out nor in; I was not fully adult. Not authentically queer.

Queer people have long since questioned the coming-out story's accuracy and usefulness. As many have pointed out, the idea that one big declaration brings you from 'closeted' to 'open' is erroneous. We come out all through our lives: any time someone makes an assumption about our sexuality or gender that we have to correct; any time a doctor's form asks for our sexuality; any time a woman mentions her girlfriend, or a polyamorous person wants to talk about 'my partners'. And as I found out, coming out as belonging to one identity is not necessarily the end of the story. I came out, in my staggered, blurry way as ace, then later introduced being aro into the mix, and spent a year or two thinking I was done with the whole exhausting business before realizing I was nonbinary as well. I have more than one friend who identified as gay, and came out as such, before realizing they were in fact a straight trans person.

Coming out itself is not the problem. When being queer was an offence, something that had to exist underground, being out and open was a radical thing, a tectonic shift that forced society to acknowledge the presence of gay, bi and trans people in their lives and society. It was – and still is – a refusal to live in shame or concealment. It can still be these things for many people, and there is value in many coming-out stories. The problem arises when it becomes the dominant story we tell about queer people – sometimes, indeed, the only one.

For aspec people, part of the issue is that we very seldom get any kind of linear coming-out story. In my initial research survey, one of the questions I posed was about people's coming-out experiences, and I was struck, though not surprised, by how many people said that they had never come out at all; or that they had started to come out to their loved ones, and then stopped; or come out to friends but not to family. For many, the process of having to explain their identity every time they wanted to come out, correcting the misunderstandings and challenging all the assumptions – it's just too tiring to be worth it. 'I've rarely felt better after coming out,' says one of my survey respondents called Jay (any pronouns). 'I've always had to do so much explaining and justifying of my identity that any relief I might have felt from having it out in the open was immediately negated by the amount of intrusive questions and insensitive comments I had to put up with.'

Even the methods of coming out are often more limited to an aspec person. A gay person can wear a rainbow pin or wristband, and new acquaintances will know exactly what is meant by it. A woman can refer to 'my girlfriend', and just like that, she is out to her interlocutor, who may not know her exact identity immediately (she might be gay, bi, pan, or not have a distinct label), but at least understands that she is not straight. The lack of recognition of ace and aro identities, however, means that, if I were to wear my own flags into work on my clothing, few would know what the combination of colours meant. Nor can I drop a reference to my lack of attraction into casual conversation; it's the problem with having an identity that's defined by a lack of something. I can mention, of course, that I'm 'not interested in dating', but this would not be seen as coming out. People could easily think I was just on a break from dating and would continue to see me as heterosexual. This makes it hard to come out in a subtle way, without a big declaration or explanation.

Overall, even before you get to how people respond to your coming out, the actual process of doing so is often that bit harder for aspecs. This is by no means the greatest of problems, but it is significant. Things add up. The vulnerability of coming out, combined with the knowledge that you'll have to explain it all *again*, and answer the same questions you've heard a thousand times before *again*, knowing that you could wear your pride colours and it wouldn't say anything to anyone so you have to make it a whole *thing*, and still not even have someone understand at the end of the process – this adds up. This is before we consider any extra factors such as race or neurodivergence that might affect what coming out will mean for you (on which more in a moment). Plenty of aspecs decide that it simply isn't worth it.

And for those who decide to take the plunge? Many of the aces and aros I spoke to felt, as I did, that their coming-out attempts didn't result in any change in their lives, or any significant reaction from those around them. Casey (she/they) came out to their mother – and nothing happened. 'My mom and I don't talk about the fact that I'm ace, but I get the feeling she thinks I'll grow out of it. Every now and then she'll mention me having kids, even though I've made it clear that I'm never having biological children.'

For aspecs of colour, there are still more reasons why coming out may be fruitless. In an interview with Heart Radio, Black aroace activist Yasmin Benoit summarized the problem: she wasn't able to 'successfully' come out for a long time, because 'people just do not picture asexual people being like me. They do have a very [*The Big Bang Theory*'s] Sheldon Cooper-esque vision of what asexual people are like, and they do not picture minorities most of the time. They do not picture Black people.'[1] And she's right. Much of the community's most productive activism has come from people of colour, like Benoit herself, or Chinese-American author Angela Chen, or the Black activists Sherronda J. Brown and Marshall Blount. The latter, who blogs as Gentle Giant Ace, led the activism that was directly responsible for Asexual Awareness Week gaining official recognition in Pennsylvania. Despite this, the image that many outside the community (and all too many within it) have of an aspec person is white. Many of the ace and aro characters that have appeared in popular culture, like Todd Chavez of *BoJack Horseman*, are white, and/or portrayed by white people. Our online spaces are predominantly white.

If asexuality and aromanticism are consistently portrayed as something for white people, how are people of colour to know that they can even *be* aspec? And if they wish to come out to others, how likely are those others to take them seriously?

Even if you have the good fortune to be believed and respected by those around you, it's still easy to feel that, in some way, you're missing out on a queer milestone. Coming out is often likened to a second adolescence, where you get to live out all the aspects of maturation that you might have missed as a closeted teen. This is the time for exploration, making mistakes and figuring yourself out – and for finally achieving those milestones. Your first kiss with the gender you're attracted to. First time going to a party as the gender you really are. First time dating and having sex with the right gender, or as the right gender.

This is not all that a second adolescence is, of course. There's plenty of non-sexual and non-romantic aspects to it, such as figuring out your style of dress and presentation, entering into the queer world and expanding your social circle, and the emotionally exhausting process of working through your grief for all the lost time. But those milestones – kissing, dating, sex – are often the first things that spring to mind. And these are things that asexual and aromantic people might not be doing. It's easy to feel that you're missing a crucial step in the coming-out narrative.

Casey was keen to make it clear that coming out 'is not the be all and end all. You can still find value in self-identifying as aspec. I went five or so years without coming out to anyone, and I was relatively content to just have a label for my experiences.' The problem is, they say, that 'it's all well and good to have a rich inner understanding of yourself, but only by coming out does that become a part of your outer self.' For all aspecs, this sense of separation between parts of yourself can be a very unsettling way to live. 'I've been thinking a lot recently about Judith Butler's theory of performative utterances,' Casey says, 'words that make things happen in the real world, like "I pronounce you husband and wife" being a phrase that makes a marriage official. Coming out is a way of making things happen, of changing things in the real world. So if I never say the words "I'm asexual", am I really ace in any way that matters?'

Casey's question gets to the heart of the problems with aspec coming out. What do you do when, because people don't understand the words you're saying, or dismiss them altogether, your self-declaration changes nothing? When the words that, according to popular culture, are imbued with the power to alter your entire life and deliver you to a new kind of personal freedom do *nothing*? When you put yourself through all that emotional labour and end up with nothing to show for it? Except, perhaps, a sense of guilt, a feeling that you've failed to complete the queer master narrative?

As an aroace person, I never underwent many of the milestones considered to be an integral part of growing up – no first crush, first kiss, first date, first relationship, first time having sex. Now, by failing to come out in any meaningful way, I had even fumbled the one milestone for living as a queer adult that I knew of. I felt like an incomplete adult, and an inauthentic queer.

And even all of this assumes that coming out is an option to begin with, or, indeed, something desirable. Because for many – and disproportionately for people of colour – it is not.

*

Coming out was once not about coming out to straight, cis people but to your queer peers, and, crucially, to yourself. That process of self-realization can be infinitely more complex for aspecs of colour. Racial assumptions are often entwined with expectations about sex. Many of my Black interviewees spoke of living under the weight of hypersexualization: the act of viewing certain people as extremely sexual, and focusing on their sexual lives to an intrusive extent. Hypersexualization can involve, for instance, viewing people – especially girls – as sexual beings while they are still very young: an experience that many Black people know well.

'Adult men have been hitting on me since I was a pre-teen,' says Ginger, a Black asexual woman in the USA. 'And adult women – often white women – have been insisting that I've been acting or behaving sexually since the same time. I'm simply a pear-shaped Black woman. I've had a butt as long as I've been alive. There's nothing inherently sexual about my existence except that racism says so.' Ginger's experience is emblematic of a study by the Georgetown University Law Center that found that Black girls are considered to know more about adult topics and sex than white girls of the same age.[2] And even knowing that these stereotypes are, in Ginger's words, 'bad, troublesome, annoying and incorrect', being aspec can be a confusing experience for a Black woman coming up against them. 'Many aspects of Black culture that are popular in society, like music videos, play up sexuality,' Ginger says. 'So it can all combine to make you feel more broken.'

Black men receive this hypersexualization too. One of my interviewees, Vance, who is Black and asexual, is blunt about how the 'sex-crazed Black man' stereotype affects him. 'People's – mainly white people's – fantasies are destroyed upon finding out that I'm asexual. Some have even got vocally upset that they aren't able to act out their fetish of having sex with a Black person.' In *Refusing Compulsory Sexuality*, Sherronda J. Brown breaks down how the depiction of Black men as hypersexual predators of white women, rooted in the racist fear of the 'Black Brute' that led to so many being lynched on false rape charges, is still spread today through 'interracial porn' marketed at white men.[3] One porn producer said that Black men 'taking advantage of white women, seducing their daughters and wives' is ever popular. The titles of these films include 'black lives matter thug choking out white cop daughter' and 'Oh No! There's a Negro in my Wife!'[4]

And this weight of sexualization falls heavily on Latine people, too. (*Latine*, for the unfamiliar, is one of the gender-neutral alternatives to the terms Latino and Latina; it is what I will use throughout this book.) Ellie (she/they), who is Mexican, says that because of her race alone, 'I'm supposed to twerk to Bad Bunny and his nasty, nasty sex lyrics. For some reason, the world seems to like the idea of Latinos being spicy and foggy and always thinking about sex. People have a hard time believing me when I tell them that I feel repulsed at the thought of sex, no matter the context.'

Meanwhile, for many East Asians, the ideal of a sexualized woman who's available to the appetites of men comes hand in hand with infantilizing language that tries to turn them into doe-eyed dolls. 'I'm mixed Southeast Asian, physically unassuming, and for lack of a better word, cute-looking,' says Alex (they/them). 'I'm simultaneously hypersexualized and infantilized. How could I be asexual when Asian women (I'm not a woman) are all kinky seductresses? But wait – it makes perfect sense that I'm ace, because Asian women (*I'm not a woman)* are perfect, delicate, innocently feminine objects.' And white media has reinforced these tropes: Kim in the Broadway hit *Miss Saigon*, set in 1970s Vietnam, is a prostitute, fulfilling the (white) male desire for a sexually available woman, and she's also a devoted mother who pines for her American lover for years, even after he abandons her. Ultimately, Kim kills herself so that her son can have a life in the USA, dying in the service of the great ideals: motherhood and love (and America).

When these are the assumptions forced upon you, any process of realizing your asexual or aromantic identity is likely to come into collision with them. If you're from a racial background that gets hypersexualized, such as being a Black or Latine person, then how can you be certain you're not just subconsciously trying to refuse and defy that stereotype? And if you're desexualized and infantilized, as is the case for many Asian people, or if you've had the weight of the desexualized Black 'mammy' figure hanging over you, then are you playing into a harmful trope just by being aspec? Are you invalidating your community's fight to challenge those stereotypes just by existing? (This last point is also very relevant to those who are physically disabled and/or neurodivergent, as I will discuss later in this chapter, and in Chapter 8.)

In her book *Ace*, Angela Chen breaks down the way in which realizing her asexual identity threw into sharp relief how much stereotypical ideas about Asians had influenced how she felt about herself, and how she felt now about her identity. 'It was frustrating enough that Asians were boring engineers,' she writes. 'Now I had *asexual*, a term that sounded clinical and reminded me of one-celled organisms. I was already introverted and uninterested in drinking; being asexual seemed to reinforce this cascade of stereotypes, further marking me as not worthy of notice.'[5]

Taking this into account, it's easy to see how we've ended up with an overwhelmingly white aspec community, especially online. A 2021 census of the ace community saw 80.8 per cent of respondents list their ethnicity as white.[6] The 2020 Aro Census run by AUREA saw whiteness dominate even more: apart from the 5.67 per cent who identified as mixed, no minority ethnic racial group rose above 4.2 per cent of respondents.[7]

Why? Perhaps some of the issue lies in how ace and aro awareness spread, initially, via the internet, via blogs and email lists. As ace writer Michael Paramo points out, because ace and aro identities are still lesser known, 'an intrinsic level of privilege [is] required to even be able to self-identify as asexual [...] those who do not possess access or awareness of these online spaces, or an internet connection in general, are far less likely to access asexuality.'[8] This was, and is, harder for those with fewer resources, and in the Western world, people of colour are more likely to fall into this group. A 2021 study found that in the USA, Black and Hispanic people were less likely to have a home broadband connection than white people – 71 per cent and 65 per cent respectively, compared with 80 per cent of white people. A quarter of Hispanic people can access the internet via a smartphone but lack any connection at home, compared with just 12 per cent of white people. While 80 per cent of white adults have their own computer, only 69 per cent of Black and 67 per cent of Hispanic adults do.[9]

Not having your own device or method for accessing the internet can be a huge hurdle to researching sexuality. A family, school or library computer is not private enough, and may have settings where any websites relating to sex are blocked. What's more, children whose family are unable to afford separate rooms for them will end up sharing with siblings or parents, which again limits their ability to investigate sexuality in private. And all this doesn't even consider how overwhelmingly English-language online aspec resources have traditionally been, and remain. This limits the accessibility of our spaces to those outside the Western world and to those for whom English is not a fluently spoken language.

So, people of colour start out with less access to resources that could help them realize their aspec identities. They then have to grapple with racial stereotypes and assumptions, a process that Angela Chen likens to having to strip away dark paint from a wall to paint it light blue, while white people have a white wall that can just be painted over. Only then can people of colour 'determine whether we are *really* ace'.[10]

All of this work to be certain of your identity – and then what? For white aspecs, coming out can be exhausting and fruitless. For aspecs of colour, it can be all that and more: it has a higher risk of danger, and there is often much more to lose.

Afana (she/her) grew up in the Middle East in a Muslim country (she now lives in the UK). 'In the environment I grew up in,' she says, 'boys and girls don't mix. Girls learn the skills of running a house. As you grow up, you hide the changes in your body, you hide your menstruation – and you don't think about sex.'

For Afana, this last one was easy. Being uninterested in sex was a boon when it came to meeting the standards of parents and peers; she was focusing on her studies, being a dutiful child. Then she turned eighteen, and everything flipped. 'You finish school,' Afana says, 'and you go from "don't think about sex at all" to "actually, you need to have children – hurry up and get married! If you haven't produced a baby in a year, there's something wrong with you." She likens it to having been running a marathon, only to be suddenly thrown into a swimming pool. 'Everyone else is swimming, and you're still running a marathon at the bottom of the pool. Being penalized for what you were doing a minute ago.'

Afana has no intention of coming out. 'In the Middle East, coming out as queer would be punished by law. I could go to jail. And even among my family in the UK, being queer is seen as a Western fad. It's not something that would be accepted, and not something I would ever do.' She has no desire to trouble her relationships with her family in the way coming out would, nor to face exorcisms or religious attempts to 'fix' her.

Her story reminded me of the many aspecs I'd spoken to from conservative Christian backgrounds, who'd found being 'pure' easy during their teens, convinced that everyone was exaggerating how huge a temptation sex was. Then they experienced a sudden clash against their religion when they turned eighteen and were suddenly told to get married and be good Christian wives and husbands. I will discuss the experiences of conservative Christian aspecs in more depth later, but for now, it is telling that the vast majority of those I spoke to have since left the branches of Christianity they were raised in, whether leaving religion behind altogether or seeking other, more liberal avenues and establishments for their faith.

Several well-meaning but shortsighted white people have told Afana to do the same. Just leave. If her family won't accept her, then they don't truly love her, and she should walk out in favour of finding people who do accept her as aroace.

But this is unrealistic. 'In Western social depictions, if your family don't accept you as queer, you just walk out,' Afana says. 'Yet that's not how we live. That's not how it works.' For a start, it's something far more accessible to a Western culture that prizes individualism and 'being yourself' than to a more communal and collective culture like Afana's own. 'You're expected to live with your family, the larger family unit sectioned into different houses. You have family meetings. Your family is very involved in everything you do, which can be frustrating, especially when you have to hide being queer. But at the same time, you have strong family relationships to fall back on. When I became disabled, I spent several months unable to work and without any sort of income – my family supported me then. I love my mum, and I want to stay living with her for as long as she's around. So "just walk out" doesn't match the cultural values.'

Several of my other respondents echoed this feeling. Elias (they/fae), who is South Asian, points out that the narrative of the queer kid who gets rejected by the family because of their identity doesn't work for them. 'Being kicked out? That's not a thing that happens in my family.' In a culture that prizes individualism, cutting off unaccepting relatives and making your own way is a story we're familiar with – one that's understood, respected, and is at least possible, if not at all easy. But in more community- and family-focused cultures, it often doesn't happen at all.

And for those living in immigrant families and in diasporas especially, leaving or being disowned means losing more than your family. 'If you *are* kicked out,' Elias says, 'that's severing ties to your culture. So, when white people toss around ideas of leaving or saying "fuck you" to family pressures, that's just an entirely different context for them.'

'For me,' Afana says, 'walking out would mean losing my eight uncles and aunts, my siblings, more than twenty cousins, family friends who are basically siblings… I have a friend who *did* come out, and *did* end up distanced from her family, and she ended up having to assimilate into white culture. White queer culture can be so antireligion, and there's this huge pressure to never talk about religion, to give it up and hate where you came from. My friend went from being religious to not being religious at all, because that part of herself was treated like an attack on white queer people. She started going out drinking, because that's where the culture and community is. There's no attempt to reach out to you, only to make you *join.* You have to give up everything that makes you *you.*'

And this is the heart of the problem. The sentiment 'just leave so you can be yourself!' implies that Afana's Muslim identity, and her cultural identity, are things that hold her back from being herself, rather than being an essential part of who she is.

Losing one's ties to a culture is an agonizing loss – and it has a ripple effect beyond the individual. In a 2000 study of how race, class and the decision to parent affected lesbian coming-out experiences, Nancy J. Mezey found that some lesbians of colour were hesitant to parent because it seemed inevitable that their children would grow up cut off from their culture. 'If coming out to an ethnic community means losing that community, then coming out as a lesbian mother can mean the loss of an ethnic identity and community connection for her children. Not having that connection means that children lose the chance to take part in the community, learn from the community, "eat the community's food, drink its drinks and dance its songs".'[11] Mezey might have focused on lesbians, but the same is true for any coming out that risks a severance from one's community, aspecs included. Yet another extra barrier for aspecs of colour who might want to pursue non-normative forms of family.

Even being openly aroace in a more limited way – to friends, and in online spaces – can lead aspecs of colour into alienating clashes with the whiteness of the larger community. Elias says that when they've asked online spaces such as Discord servers if they could have a channel dedicated to issues faced by aspec people of colour – a place where they could discuss these very difficulties, or just a place to talk about their race and culture in an aspec-friendly space – they get nothing. 'I meet with no response, or "we'll discuss".'

And if the queer community is not making room for people like Elias and Afana, why would they want to come out? Why would Afana want to jeopardize her relationship with her family? 'The LGBT community is not a refuge for me,' she says. 'But I will always have my family on one side.'

Around her Muslim community, Afana cannot feel safe mentioning that she's ace; among queer people and other aspecs, she doesn't feel safe mentioning that she's Muslim. 'I'm resigned to sitting in the closet for the rest of my life, sticking out a hand wearing a sock puppet to talk through. And I have to switch these depending on who I'm talking to, so I don't present as threatening.'

*

Race is one factor that can force aspec people to grapple with caricatures and misconceptions before they can realize their identity. Another is neurodivergence. For many, the standard image of an autistic person is someone like Sheldon Cooper, who is childish, awkward, and emotionally illiterate. He struggles to engage in romantic or sexual relationships (though he does eventually get a girlfriend). For much of the series, he finds the idea of engaging in that kind of physical contact icky. Or there's the titular protagonist of BBC's *Sherlock*. Like Sheldon, he was never labelled autistic, but he was nonetheless portrayed as a package of stereotypical autistic traits: savant-level intelligence, a lack of social graces, a knack for spotting detail… and a cold, unfeeling nature.

If you are told again and again that you are kooky and childish like Sheldon, or a misanthrope who can't relate to other humans like Sherlock, then how can you look clearly at your own sexual and romantic orientation? Many neurodivergent (ND) people aren't expected to have any kind of sexual or romantic interest anyway. If you aren't included in conversations about sex or love, if you're never portrayed as having these feelings or relationships, how can you recognize that your experiences diverge from the allosexual and alloromantic norm?

And neurodivergence itself can also complicate the process of self-recognition. When I was seventeen, I was struck by the epiphany that sexual attraction was a physical sensation – that other people around me were genuinely feeling a physical pull towards each other. That kind of revelation can be even more delayed when your personal experience of neurodivergence means that it's harder to get into other people's heads. For Jack (he/they), being autistic and having ADHD meant that his own epiphany was a long time coming. 'I grew up with my various hyperfixations, only interested in talking and thinking about them. And that made me forget that sex was apparently something that people were also supposed to think about. My struggles with putting myself in other people's shoes made me take a long time to figure out that other people didn't feel the same way I did.'

Not only can neurodivergence make other people tricky to figure out, but it can make your own mind and body opaque as well. One trait common to many people who are autistic or have ADHD is a decreased awareness of the physical body – manifesting in, for instance, someone working for hours without realizing that they're thirsty or hungry, or really need the bathroom. Obviously, this can complicate matters when trying to gauge one's level of physical attraction. 'I have a tenuous awareness of my physical body,' says Naomi (they/them), 'so it is hard to tell whether I don't experience attraction, or I just don't recognize it.'

Even if you figure out that you have, for example, a strong sense of discomfort around sex or romance, that alone might not be enough. After all, a ND person living in a neurotypical world often has to – or feels that they have to – mask their ND traits, push past discomfort and act like a neurotypical person as much as possible. 'Masking' is exhausting, and yet it can swiftly become a reflex, since the consequences of not doing it can involve social ostracization, being labelled as weird and difficult, and being laughed at and bullied.

Such was the case for Allison (she/her). 'Growing up as a masked autistic meant I put a lot of energy into trying to fit others' social expectations,' she says, 'even if that meant pushing down on and ignoring my own distress and sensory pain. I thought everyone else was navigating life in about the same way. For example, I knew I tended to like a small number of foods and be picky about the texture of clothes, but I thought other people were also similarly sensitive and were either just better at sucking it up and toughing things out.'

Allison knew on some level that she was repulsed by sex, but after a lifetime of ignoring and pushing through her own discomfort, she did what she always did. 'I thought my repulsion towards sex should be handled the same way as other activities I did not like and did not want: by pushing down the distress, trying hard to approach it with a positive mindset, and ignoring my own mental alarm bells. I'd spent a lifetime going along with things that made no sense to me, just because it was socially expected. So when sex became socially expected, that's what happened.' She adds wryly, 'Surprise! It turns out repeatedly saying yes to sex acts that you do not like and do not want is traumatizing and a bad idea! Go figure, huh?'

So the ND aspec must pull down the obscuring veils of the Sherlocks and Sheldons, figure out what's going on in their own minds and bodies *and* those of others, and recognize their own boundaries in ways they may very well not be used to. And then there's the daunting prospect of coming out, and worrying that by doing so, you might be in some way invalidating either the aspec community, the ND community, or both. 'To be honest,' says Jack, 'having autism sometimes makes me feel like I'm playing into the sexless autistic stereotype, even though I know that's ridiculous. No one is a stereotype, and there's nothing negative about being asexual and autistic. It just makes me feel dehumanized sometimes, especially when I want to write about my own experiences through a fictional character. I end up feeling like I'm writing bad representation or stereotypical representation, even though I'm just… writing about myself.'

Coming out as aspec can be daunting enough. It's even more so if you know that people have an extra reason to dismiss your self-disclosure – or that it's something that your own community doesn't want to hear.

*

How many aspecs make the decision not to come out? A 2023 report from Stonewall, *Ace in the UK*, found that it's rather a lot. Just

10.3 per cent of ace respondents in school or university said that they were open with all classmates and fellow students, whereas for other LGBTQIA+ people, it was 26.3 per cent. At work, just 9 per cent of aces were open with all their colleagues who were of a similar or lower level than them, with the average for other LGBTQI+ people being 39 per cent. Unsurprisingly, but still startling, is the fact that *50 per cent* weren't open with any co-workers at all, in comparison with 18 per cent of all LGBTQIA+ respondents.[12]

In Chapters 9 and 10, I will discuss how we could make the environments into which people might come out – should they choose to do so – more accepting and accommodating. Clearly, that is the biggest problem here. But at present, I want to sit in the lived reality of those who decide not to come out – for whatever reason. Ultimately, *I don't want to* is the only reason anyone needs.

The problem with treating coming out as a necessary step before we can enter queer adulthood is that it can, unfortunately, lead to the infantilization of those who choose not to do it – and considering how infantilized aces and aros can often be already, this is the last thing any of us need. It's too easy to think that only kids are in the closet; kids, and those who have yet to truly enter the world or embrace their sense of self. Closeted people are those who aren't outspoken enough, bold enough, liberated enough. But coming out is so much more than a matter of bravery and confidence, and a person does not need to come out to be 'liberated'.

We must be careful not to portray this as the only way to be queer. We must be especially wary of viewing aspecs of colour (and queer people of colour in general) as repressed souls, who are kept back from being 'out and proud' by their race, religion or community. And there *is* an assumption that the real, liberated queer person is someone who is out and confident and sexually active. In the documentary *A(sexual)*, there's a scene from San Francisco's 2009

Pride, which David Jay and the early AVEN members attended. A man brushes past Jay, saying, 'I pity your poor soul.' Jay asks him why. 'Because I don't stand for what you stand for.' What did this man think Jay stood for? My best guess is: repression. A sexless existence that the man couldn't reconcile with what he understood queerness to be, something at odds with his image of Pride.

This attitude has persisted since that Pride parade. Many of my interviewees remembered, with some dread, the boom of exclusionists on many social media platforms, particular Tumblr, which until then had been something of a haven for aspec folks. These exclusionists argued that aces and aros weren't *really* queer, that they had to have some other queer identity in order to qualify as part of the community. Some of this backlash came from a completely false belief that aros and aces don't face any kind of oppression, but I saw other posts arguing that asexuality and aromanticism were harmful because they encouraged social isolation, because we weren't 'doing anything' and therefore didn't qualify as authentically queer. More than one of the aspecs I spoke to said that this wave of hatred had pushed them away from being open – and no wonder. Some of the sentiments floating around spaces such as Tumblr, Twitter and Reddit at the time were truly vile and outright threatening. (I could list examples here, but I don't have the heart.)

Again: there is nothing wrong with being a queer person who is out and proud and sexually active. Queer people should never feel we have to be quiet and palatable; that we should avoid being 'too queer' to appease those who find our identities inherently uncomfortable. The man who pitied David Jay's soul was wrong, but I think I understand what was going through his head: being sexually active as a queer person in a world that maligns your sexuality, being out in a world that would rather erase you, is a radical, revolutionary act, one that this man mistakenly thought the ace community was failing to do or was even trying to suppress. So much of the progress we have made in the last few decades was made by those who took the dangerous step of being out and proud, who refused to be invisible and faceless.

But there's a danger in *equating* queerness with sexuality. And that equation has persisted long beyond that Pride parade fifteen years ago. During my early research for this book, I came across a YouTube video called 'The Queer Erasure of Asexuality'. I put it on my 'watch later' list and, months later, tried to come back to it – only to find that the video was now no longer available. It turned out that its creator, James Somerton, a gay man who made YouTube videos analysing queerness in the media, had recently been embroiled in a scandal when it was revealed that much of his video scripts were stolen without credit or permission from other queer creators. Putting that scandal to one side, though, there was something possibly more disturbing in one of Somerton's videos.

As I looked into the story, I came across a video (no longer available) in which Somerton claimed that the reason modern gay activism focused on marriage equality rather than what Somerton considered more important milestones, such as workplace equality and legal protection, was because 'so many of the gays left [after the AIDS crisis] were, to be frank, the boring ones; the ones who knew nobody and who nobody knew.' These 'boring' gays, Somerton claimed, wanted to fit in with heteronormative culture. 'They wanted to join the army and have big gay weddings [...] because they were the good gays, not the bad gays who were sleeping around and dying of AIDS.'

I scrolled through the first several hundred comments on this video. There were, thankfully, a handful of commenters pointing out the inaccuracy of Somerton's claims: there absolutely was a big push for workplace equality and legal protection in the 1990s, lesbians were involved in it just as much as gay men, and part of the push for marriage equality was *because* so many had lost their partners to AIDS. They were not acknowledged as their romantic partners, and not given the right to be with them when they died. It is inhuman to write this off as a desire to assimilate. Unfortunately, these comments are by far outnumbered by those who apparently didn't notice the awfulness of this claim, or if they did, didn't feel it was important enough to remark on. (There are valid criticisms to be made of the fact that marriage equality has come before so many other rights, but let's focus that blame where it is due: on lawmakers who pass some rights while denying others.)

Apart from those sparse few comments, this claim was not challenged in any major way by the community until the scandal of Somerton's plagiarism broke. The video had over 400,000 views. That's a lot of people who heard him make these claims and didn't question them, at least not aloud. A lot of people who didn't interrogate the idea that both art and the legal battle for rights declined in the 1990s because the only people left to pursue them were the 'boring' gays who didn't have sex, and who apparently didn't see a problem with it.

In Somerton's vision, the right way to be gay is to be sexually active and to be out. You can't be someone who 'knew nobody and who nobody knew', someone who isn't immersed in the community. And you can't be the kind of person who doesn't get laid. If you're not out and having sex, you're trying to assimilate to the cishets and betraying your community, not making a valid, personal choice.

It's worth noting, too, that in Somerton's view, the 'interesting' gays were the ones who *died.* Is that what you have to do to be a real queer: suffer?

*

If we say that being out to the world is necessary for being a queer adult, who are we saying that *for?* Too often, 'the world' in this case, is synonymous with 'cishet allo people'. The thing about coming-out stories are that they centre the *otherness* of being queer; the way the queer person is announcing their difference from 'everyone else'. As Chinese-American author Lillian Li writes, popular culture has a habit of 'completely flooding many LGBTQ+ characters' story arcs with shame-filled closeted life, dramatic declarations, homophobic families, and the like [...] when LGBTQ+ characters are only shown overcoming adversity at the hands of homophobic people and navigating finding acceptance within society, it suddenly becomes the only thing they are valued for and capable of.'[13]

In 'The Queer Erasure of Asexuality', Somerton angered many aces by claiming, wrongly, that there is 'no specific persecution for asexual people in the way that gay people have faced' and 'there isn't really any conversion therapy directed at asexuals'. Quite aside from the fact that this is – provably – factually untrue, his point seemed to be that ace people didn't experience an axis of oppression in the way that gay people did.

Even if ace people somehow got to exist in a world where no one attempted to put us through conversion therapy... that is not a milestone we'd need to reach to be included, or to have our issues, and our push for rights and equality, be considered as important as everyone else's. To suggest otherwise only pushes queer people back into the image of queer life as defined by struggle and suffering – queer existence defined by the pain of clashing against a cis, hetero, allo world. As long as we accept this image, we cannot be liberated, because our sense of self will still be written by the picture that others have of us.

I want to be clear, here: a lot of coming-out stories are both valuable and necessary. Such stories can do a lot. *Loveless* by Alice Oseman is a novel that follows an aroace protagonist as she realizes her identity and shares it with those around her. It is in part a coming-out story, and it hit so many beats I recognized from my own attempts at coming out that I felt more seen than I had by any other work. Just the simple act of seeing your experiences reflected – including the bad ones – can be huge. It tells you that someone sees your pain, believes in it, and agrees with you that it should stop.

But this is not the only story. Suffering *must not* be the only story. The interest in queer suffering can often feel fetishistic, a desire to see us in pain; we cannot accept this.

In her famous TED talk, 'The Danger of a Single Story', Chimamanda Ngozi Adichie says, 'If you show a people as one thing, as only one thing, over and over again, that is what they become.'[14] We see this fact reflected in the desire to necessitate that aces and aros reach a certain level of suffering or experience a certain level of struggle before we can be *really* queer. Aroace activist Yasmin Benoit, when interviewed along with a group of fellow aces for a BBC Three documentary, found that, despite the aces talking about all the happiness of their ace lives, 'the producers would be like, "So. The struggle. Tell me: dating, how hard is that for you?"' Benoit and the others pointed out that plenty of them were aromantic, or were in perfectly happy relationships. 'And they were like, "uh huh, uh huh… how bad is it, though […] sex: how bad would it feel if you *had* to have it?" What kinds of questions are these? Just let us say that we're happy!'[15]

When I was a teenager, trying and failing to come out, my family's confusion came from never having heard any story about people like me. There were no stories where people like me could be happy, whole and fulfilled. The stories they had been told about people like me were stories of loneliness and inhumanity, and those stories did not match with who they saw me as, or what they wanted my life to be.

Part of the problem is that aces and aros have not had much in the way of representation in popular culture or in the media, and, without such representation, few will encounter stories of aspec lives. As Alice Oseman put it when I spoke to her, 'there's no very famous people who are openly ace and aro', which can put an immense amount of pressure on the few who, like Oseman, are public about their identities.

'I feel a certain amount of pressure to be vocal – insightfully and eloquently vocal – about my experience,' Oseman told me. 'I've never seen myself as an activist – I'm not a great public speaker and I often struggle to express myself outside of the written word – but because there are so few public figures with a sizable audience who are openly ace or aro, I end up thinking, "well, *someone* has to do it." I'm not sure I'm very good at it, but I'll keep trying, even if it helps just one person. We're never really going to see much cultural change in terms of awareness until a big celebrity comes out as being asexual.'[16]

There are a handful of public figures who are openly aspec, including the singer Cavetown and the author T.J. Klune (*The House in the Cerulean Sea*), but as of yet, there's no one who's a household name. The most well-known figure to hint at an aspec identity is the US TV personality Tim Gunn, presenter of the show *Project Runway*. Gunn has described himself as 'kind of asexual', and has been open about not having had sex in decades. 'Do I feel like less of a person for it? No! I am a perfectly happy, fulfilled individual.'[17]

Gunn's contentment with his celibacy suggests his having some variant of asexual identity. However, since it's unclear whether he used the term 'asexual' to align himself with the community, or just as a term to describe his disinterest in sex – as many of my interviewees once did, coming up with the term on their own, before knowing it was an official name for an orientation – that is where I will leave things. I don't want to dig any deeper into the sexual orientation of a living person, and Gunn is absolutely not obliged to identify with any particular label. What is notable, however, is that the rest of the world doesn't seem to take much note even of the indications that he *might* be asexual. Most news articles about Gunn describe him as gay. A *Los Angeles Times* report about his declaration of long-term celibacy features a psychologist declaring that his celibacy likely stems from fear: 'It's not a natural sort of decision, nor is it biological or physiological – we are not wired that way.'[18] And this is the problem. Because there is so little aspec visibility, the world does not know that many of us *are* 'wired that way'.

And we have always been here. To name just a handful of the historical figures who might have been aspec: Emily Brontë (1818–1848), author of *Wuthering Heights*, showed no inclination towards romance throughout her life. The Irish playwright George Bernard Shaw (1856–1950) and his wife, the activist Charlotte Payne-Townshend (1857–1943), never consummated their marriage, which was by all accounts a happy one. Artist Andy Warhol (1928–1987) had romantic relationships with men and did have sex with them, but didn't seem especially interested in the physical parts of his relationships. In a 1979 interview by *Forum* magazine, he showed an obvious disinterest in sex: 'I'd rather laugh in bed than do it […] I find that sex is much more exciting on the screen and between the pages than between the sheets anyway.'[19] In his biography, he talked about how he could never 'let [his] mind go blank and fill up with sex and not-think-about-it', and how he often found himself 'not really attracted' in the moment.[20] To me, this smacks of someone who likely experienced romantic attraction to his partners, but was not 'really attracted', sexually speaking. It is very likely that Warhol had sex because his partners wanted it, because he didn't know that not having sex was an option in a relationship, because that was just what happened in the contemporary gay scene – but that he didn't have any strong feelings about it or desire for it, and didn't get the same level of satisfaction from it that his partners did.

We'll never know for sure how any of these people might have identified if they were alive today, and the point is not to 'claim' any of them as aspec. It's to be aware of the possibility, and to prove that aroace lives have always been present and vibrant – and it's to offer some kind of template for aspec people for what our lives could be. Others have come before us. They found their ways to experience love and family.

We need to tell their stories.

This chapter is called *reconsidering* the coming-out story, not *erasing* the coming-out story. We need to tell different stories, side by side. We need to acknowledge that people *need* different stories. Some people want the sense of validation that comes with seeing a fictional mirror of yourself face the same things you have been through. Some people want stories where there's no hardship to overcome, no need to come out, as a symbol of what our world could be.

We need to tell aspec coming-out stories, so that people can understand our experiences and so we can all work towards making things easier and better for those who *do* wish to come out and currently do not have that option. When I spoke to Alice Oseman, she pointed out that plenty of people still don't realize that aro and ace folks *need* to come out. 'Most people have no concept of what it's like to be an ace or aro person – they are unaware that it can be even vaguely similar to discovering that you're gay. Happily and openly aro or ace characters are great, but they don't necessarily help people to understand how it feels to be an aro or ace person. We've seen a wonderful uptick in queer stories of self-discovery in recent times, but I'd love to see aroace ones – an aroace version of *Love, Simon*, an aroace *Moonlight*, an aroace *God's Own Country*. I often yearn for a highbrow, award-winning drama film about an aroace experience. Maybe we'll see one someday.'

Coming-out stories are still important. This chapter is not a condemnation of coming out, and I am not telling people that they should stay in the closet. I am telling people that they *can* choose not to come out, and that that decision does not make you repressed or suffering; it can simply be what you want. You might not come out because it isn't important to you, because it wouldn't benefit you or for any other reason at all.

(Of course, there are also some who cannot afford *not* to come out; for many trans people, staying in the closet means never getting to live as your whole self, at significant risk to one's mental health. There are no blanket statements that can be made here. There are too many nuances.)

But we also need to tell more than one kind of story. We need to tell the stories of historical figures who lived their aspec lives, even if they did not have the words for what they were. We need the kinds of new queer stories I'm starting to see all around me. Where once most queer stories I knew of were about coming out or facing oppression, I now encounter more and more stories in which queerness is simply present and unquestioned. There are TV shows like *She-Ra and the*

Princesses of Power, with its lesbian leads, or *The Dragon Prince*, with its gay and nonbinary characters. There are books such as Becky Chambers' *Wayfarers* and *Monk and Robot* series, or Tamsyn Muir's *Locked Tomb* series. In these works, queer people simply exist, never facing oppression for their identities and never having to come out.

If these stories about other queer identities are being embraced – and they are – we can tell these stories about aces and aros too. We *are* telling them. And in doing so, we expand the possibilities for how we see ourselves, and what we can become.

3

'Something So Cold About Him'

Compulsory Sexuality and Amatonormativity

It is the worst day of Sophie Whitehouse's life. Her husband James, a high-flying Conservative politician, has been accused of raping his parliamentary aide. The story has just broken in the *Daily Mail.* The Prime Minister dispatches his director of communications, a man called Chris, to Sophie and James's house to perform damage control, and Sophie sits numbly watching Chris sneer over the article.

In this scene, one of the opening chapters of Sarah Vaughan's bestselling 2017 novel *Anatomy of a Scandal*, Sophie observes Chris with disgust. She does not trust him; cannot bear him. He has a 'ratty' face, 'dulled by the grease of too many takeaways', and he is 'single, without children, but apparently not gay [...] politics genuinely appears to consume him. He is that unfathomable cliché; married to his job.' And then Sophie finds an explanation for his 'unfathomable' lack of a partner, his cold nature. 'It strikes her that perhaps he is asexual. There is something so cold about him; as if he finds human frailty inconceivable.'[1]

Reading this for the first time at eighteen, I hurled the book across the room.

In that moment, Vaughan's words stung because they were careless, insulting and embodied every way in which people misunderstood what asexuality was and therefore who *I* was. It hurt to be reminded that this was how the world saw *me.* But what haunted me most after reading this passage was the feeling that Vaughan had somehow left me behind. In publishing these words, Vaughan appeared to assume that no aces would be reading the book. She didn't need to worry about anyone being hurt by that depiction. All her readers would be allo, and would all view asexuals as an unfathomable 'other'.

Perhaps worse was the implication, however unintentional, that Chris (and I) did not deserve the same sympathy and respect as the allo characters. The novel's framing is very much on the side of James's victim, and rightly so. Vaughan makes sure the readers understand that it did not matter that she had consented to sex with him before, nor that she had kissed or touched him in the lead-up to his sexual assault. She did not now consent to sex. And everyone has the right to say no; no one should ever assume a yes. No one should be forced or coerced into sex they don't want, not the aide, not Sophie, who has made concessions for her husband's sexual appetite before – and yet Chris's assumed lack of sexual interest is 'cold'. Abnormal. Everyone has the right to say no to sex – but they *should have sex*, the book seemed to say. Those who might *always* say no to sex are suspect.

I do not believe Vaughan intended any of this. I doubt she was even aware of asexuality as a distinct orientation. That ignorance does not excuse her – it was irresponsible to portray *any* group so negatively without taking the time to do further research and make sure she was not perpetuating harmful stereotypes – but her depiction of Chris did not happen in a vacuum. It was influenced by a social assumption that is everywhere in Western society, and yet barely ever remarked upon. It's reinforced in our sex education, in our daily conversations and by popular culture. That assumption is this: every normal person is sexual. Therefore, any non-sexual person is abnormal, and those perceived as abnormal are non-sexual.

Pop culture has another bad habit: spreading the idea that sexual gratification for those who want sex is more important than honouring the wants of those who don't. In *Small Island* by Andrea Levy, one of the main characters, Queenie, is miserable in her marriage, in part because sex with her husband is such a passionless affair, something he seems disinterested in. Of course, I sympathize with her situation. She has married, like many real-world women of her time period, because she had so few other life options, and having a mismatch of sexual needs within a partnership can be a very painful thing. My frustration is not with Queenie (who, after all, doesn't exist), but with the framing of her situation: a framing that, I feel, paints her husband as blameable for not having the inclination to fulfil her desires.

When I watched the stage play adaptation of the book, the audience was encouraged to laugh at the husband, and laugh they did. His sexlessness was a joke. I was clearly meant to sympathize with Queenie's frustrated sexual desire and see her husband as a ridiculous, selfish person for not giving her the passion she craved. Queenie's husband *is* ridiculous and selfish, but because he is racist, sexist and self-centred, not because of his lack of passion. I had no sympathy for anything else about the character; I did have sympathy for how he was seen as immature for not giving his wife the sex life she wanted.

Welcome to what ace activists have termed *compulsory sexuality*.

Part of the difficulty with discussing ace issues is that we very quickly become bogged down by lengthy, academic-sounding terms. But I promise: you don't need to be an academic or a queer theorist to understand what compulsory sexuality ('compsex') is. It's a phenomenon that's everywhere in our everyday lives, something that affects how we are educated as children, how we are expected to form relationships, how we act in sexual situations.

You may have heard of similar terms: *compulsory heterosexuality*, or *heteronormativity*. Very simply, heteronormativity (from the words 'heterosexual' and 'normative') is the assumption that heterosexuality is the 'normal' state for human sexuality. Crucially, when a thing is considered normative, it is *perceived* to be normal, regardless of whether it actually is. Consider how often children are assumed to be straight by default; they only have to declare their sexuality and 'come out' if they find that they are *not* heterosexual. Straight people do not have to come out, because they are considered the default setting. All sex education I received in school was about straight sex. Parents will coo over two different-gender children having 'puppy love' in a way they never do over children of the same sex. This is heteronormativity. There is no 'normal' for the myriad variations of human sexuality, yet straightness is *treated* as the norm.

And when society as a whole incentivizes people to be or pretend to be straight, and those who aren't face social or legal repercussions, you get *compulsory heterosexuality*. Where gay marriage is not legal, for instance, the only way a gay person can attain the financial, legal and social benefits that straight people enjoy is to enter into a heterosexual relationship. Or when someone cannot be openly gay or bisexual without risking threats, violence or ostracization, they may have to feign heterosexuality for their own safety. In these situations – still, sadly, too common – heterosexuality is not just an assumed norm; it's a structure that people are being forced into, forced to mimic, for fear of the consequences of doing otherwise. Hence *compulsory* heterosexuality.

From here, it's a short step to understanding *allonormativity.* It's the assumption that not just heterosexuality, but *sexual attraction in general* is the default for being human. More than that: sexuality is inherent in a healthy existence, and necessary to one. Any normal person is sexual, and anyone who isn't – well, they must have 'something so cold' about them. They are consumed by their soulless work. They are unfeeling, repressed or ill. There is something less than human about them.

Take this a step further, and you have compulsory sexuality: a society in which there are repercussions for not being allo. On the most basic, practical level, if you don't want romance, you go without the financial support that having a partner or spouse can provide. On a social level, being openly ace or aro, asserting our own wants and desires for sex and romance, and building relationships in a way that suits us, can be so difficult that we can find ourselves forced to feign being allo.

Take what happened to Gwyn (they/them), who was fifteen when their first relationship began. Their home country of Macedonia was and is, in their words, 'still pretty conservative', and they had never heard the term *asexual.* They knew, however, that they didn't seem to experience sexual attraction to anyone; they also knew that they were open to having sex with their new girlfriend. Even though they weren't sexually attracted to her, they loved her, and sex seemed like an enjoyable way for the two of them to be close to each other. (I will expand in later chapters on the many reasons an ace person may want to have sex. For now, if you are unfamiliar with the concept, consider how a person might have an active libido and want to have sex, while not experiencing attraction to any particular person at that exact moment. *Wanting sex* and *feeling attraction towards a person* are not the same thing, and can happen independently of each other.)

Gwyn wanted to be open with their girlfriend from the start. So they made sure she knew about both their lack of sexual attraction and the fact that they were willing to have sex. And, at first, all seemed well. But even though they were having sex, Gwyn's girlfriend soon made it clear that she wasn't satisfied. 'She saw it as her fault; that she was somehow defective for not making me attracted to her,' Gwyn says. 'And she saw it as a fault on my part too, for not loving her enough.' Unfamiliar with the idea that a lack of sexual attraction could just be a normal, healthy, innate part of her partner, Gwyn's girlfriend assumed that it meant something, somewhere, was wrong.

Feeling guilty, Gwyn tried to force themself into a model their girlfriend would understand. They would be best described as a biromantic asexual – experiencing romantic attraction to multiple genders, without any sexual attraction – but for a time, Gwyn tried to identify as bisexual instead. 'I was forcing the attraction to fit the label,' they say. But, of course, it didn't work. And neither did the relationship.

This is compulsory sexuality. Gwyn's ex assumed that sexual attraction – not just sexual activity, but the attraction itself – was something critical for their relationship. Love could not exist without that attraction. Gwyn ended up being forced into the pretence of allosexuality, trying to make attraction happen where it couldn't, labelling themself in a way that didn't suit or aid them. They tried to fit their behaviour and even their internal identity to their allo partner's needs, because the price of not doing so was guilt and friction and, ultimately, the loss of their partner. This is long in their past now, and Gwyn is happily in a relationship with a fellow aspec, but their first relationship is a sharp example of how aspecs face very tangible repercussions for being on the outside of what is assumed to be the 'normal' of sexuality.

These repercussions can be social, as in Gwyn's case, but they can be physical – and very detrimental to aspecs' health. When Anne (she/her) went for her first Women's Wellness Exam since her marriage, the form she was given asked for her relationship status and her sexual orientation. She duly entered that she was married, but there was no option to state that she was asexual; she wrote it in herself.

'Asexual?' said the practitioner, when Anne handed her the form. 'I don't think I've heard of that one before.'

Anne did her best to explain – 'fumblingly,' she says – what it meant. 'It was more than a little awkward, and it left me wishing that I'd just picked something else on the list so I could have avoided it. I'm married to a woman and often let people assume that I'm a lesbian, because it's frankly so much easier in a lot of ways.'

But the awkwardness was only the start. On all her medical records, Anne had made it clear that she had never been sexually active. That was still the case, and there had been no change to those records since. As such, those administering her cervical smear test had used the smaller speculum appropriate for patients who hadn't been sexually active. On this occasion, however, the practitioner used a much larger speculum, and before long, there was 'a significant amount of bleeding'.

Anne had tried to explain that she was asexual. Her records made it clear that she was a virgin. The only change was that she was now married. 'I have to assume that my listing my relationship status as married caused them to assume that I had been sexually active and treat me accordingly. The practitioner was taken off guard and seemed nervous, but she sort of blustered through and played it off, saying that bleeding happened sometimes. She had to give me a panty liner, though, because it was quite a lot of blood. I didn't realize until much later, when I got home, how much there had been.'

Compulsory sexuality is very often unintentional, and Anne is sure that was the case in this incident. 'I think this was an honest mistake on her part, because she did seem very taken aback by how much blood there was. But it was an extremely unpleasant experience all around, and I've put off going in for another Women's Wellness Exam since.'

And that is compulsory sexuality. The awkwardness and self-consciousness of trying to explain being asexual made Anne wish she had lied about her identity. But such pretence can only go so far. The doctor's assumption that all romantic relationships are sexual, that anyone who is married is not a virgin was so ingrained, so powerful that it outweighed what she had read on Anne's medical records and heard from Anne's own verbal testimony. Anne was subjected to careless, wrongly applied medical care *just because she was a person in a non-sexual relationship.*

The result is that she has put off seeking that yearly health checkup. These are the repercussions aspecs face for being non-allo in an allonormative world, and they are detrimental to our physical as well as our emotional wellbeing. Anne is far from the only person I interviewed whose faith in the medical system has been shaken. Cake, from Chapter 1, once found their doctor more interested in 'curing' their asexuality than in their ovarian cysts. Jacke (they/them), similarly, had a doctor recommend hormone treatments to fix their asexuality. 'I refused to go back,' Jacke says, 'even when I got a urinary tract infection so bad that I spent a couple of weeks pissing blood.' Even that was less painful to them than the idea of going back to face a doctor who thought they needed to be fixed.

Compulsory sexuality in medicine is an ancient thing. In *Refusing Compulsory Sexuality*, Sherronda J. Brown traces the pathologization of sexual disinterest right back to the thirteenth century, to the idea of *frigidity*, which Pope Greogry IX called one of the main sources of impotence.[2] Brown tracks this obsession with 'coldness of passion' through the centuries, as it became described as a sickness and neurosis: in 1855, *Doctor Teller's Pocket Companion, or Marriage Guide* discussed 'continence', the 'absolute withdrawal from the pleasures of the consummation of the act'. According to Teller, continence was 'the most miserable perversion of mind and body', and led to various further maladies. 'Mania, melancholy, apoplexy, and various foul diseases of the skin, deafness, loss of vision... Hysteria and other nervous derangements.' Continence, Teller warned, would lead to the loss of 'domestic felicity' and ultimately societal downfall.[3]

Then, in 1980, the *Diagnostic and Statistical Manual of Mental Disorders,* or DSM-5, used for psychiatric diagnoses in the USA, included 'inhibited sexual desire disorder'. Nowadays, this is known as hypoactive sexual desire disorder, or HSDD. According to the Planned Parenthood website, 'People who have HSDD have little or no thoughts or fantasies about sex, don't respond to their partner's sexual signals or suggestions, lose desire for sex while having it, or avoid sex all together.'

HSDD is not asexuality. There certainly *are* medical conditions that lower the sex drive or libido, but asexuality is a sexual orientation. A 2014 study illustrated this by pointing out the numerous differences between HSDD sufferers and asexuals: people with

HSDD tend to have experienced attraction and desire at some point before their HSDD began, whereas asexuals tend to have never experienced them at all. (There are exceptions; there's a spectrum of ace and aro experiences, and I will discuss some of the variations of our identities in Chapter 7.) In fact, *none* of the HSDD sufferers interviewed in the study said that they had never been interested in sex, whereas *most* of the aces in the study said that they hadn't. The aces were also markedly more satisfied with their sexual lives.[4]

I've had people tell me that aces are trying to invent an orientation out of a medical disorder, but the science is not on their side. Unfortunately, the differences between HSDD and asexuality are not common knowledge, even in the medical community. Too many people hear 'no sexual attraction' and fail to look any deeper at the nuanced, diverging experiences of the two communities. In 2013, after a diligent campaign from aces, the DSM-5 was finally updated to allow patients who identify as asexual not to be diagnosed with HSDD. This is a vast improvement, but it raises the difficulty that a person must *already know* they are asexual before they can be granted this 'exemption'.

The practical result of all this is that aces can be subjected to a sort of accidental conversion therapy. When a lack of sexual attraction is assumed to be a disorder, something to be fixed, medical practitioners unaware of asexuality, like Cake's and Jacke's, set out to do just that. Many, I am sure, would be horrified by the idea that they might be engaging in something akin to conversion therapy. But that is nonetheless the message they give to aspec patients. They tell us that we would be better – happier, *fixed* – if they took away our way of experiencing the world, love and relationships, a formative part of who we are, and replaced it with something they think would be preferable.

These are some of the more egregious examples of compsex at work, but it most often manifests in thousands of small moments that most allo people have no reason to question. Consider how 'virgin' is used as an insult, suggesting that someone is too unpleasant or pathetic to have sex – because any healthy, normal, socially adept person would be sexually active. (The 1995 romcom *Clueless*, for instance, has one character put down another with: 'Why am I even listening to you to begin with? You're a virgin who can't drive.') Or how it's seen as an oddity to be a virgin into your twenties and beyond. Or how advertising so often features attractive models and sexualization, telling consumers that their product can make you look like the model or have sex with someone like them. Rather like Vaughan assuming her readers were all allosexual, these adverts are expected to reach allosexual viewers. It's a common joke among aces that we're immune to such ads, but that doesn't stop them from being a reminder of how exhaustingly *everywhere* sex is, and how the world is designed for allo tastes right down to the adverts it flings at us.

Then there's how popular culture reinforces how evil its villains are by portraying them as uninterested in sex and romance, in an exaggerated echo of how Vaughan treated her asexual politician. Take Voldemort, the villain in J. K. Rowling's *Harry Potter* books. We are told, again and again, that he is not just callous: he *cannot* love. He cares for no one but himself. He cannot even conceive of his supposed minion Snape having had romantic feelings for Harry's mother, and his failure to understand that love leads directly to his downfall. (The Harry Potter stage play, *The Cursed Child*, reveals that Voldemort fathered a child with one of his minions, but it is clear that he did this to further his legacy, rather than out of any love or desire for the woman in question.) In short, he is coded as an aromantic asexual. *Coding* in fiction is when a character or group are given traits that are reminiscent of a real-world group, without explicitly stating that they belong to that group. It can be done deliberately; in other cases, it is unconscious. I imagine Voldemort's was not intentional – but neither is it flattering.

Voldemort has torn his soul into pieces to gain eternal life. He is pale, cruel and cold-blooded as the snakes he controls. And coding him as aroace is a form of compulsory sexuality. Rowling writes Voldemort as unable to desire because, in her opinion, *it makes him appear more villainous.* More ruthless, more unfeeling. A natural, whole person is romantic and sexual, and Voldemort is anything but. Harry Potter ends the series happily married and with children, as do his friends; he, a normal, loving human, has his life completed by sex and romance. Those who do not desire such things are embodied in the figure of a monstrous murderer.

Then there's *A Song of Ice and Fire* (1996), the adult fantasy book series by George R. R. Martin, and its television adaptation, *Game of Thrones*, which was broadcast from 2011. In *Game of Thrones*, we find another aroace-coded monster: the teen king Joffrey Baratheon. He never shows real interest in any women (or anyone else). When sent two prostitutes, he declines to have sex and instead has one beat the other, relishing that pain more than the prospect of sexual satisfaction. Baratheon is one of the most reviled characters in the franchise, and he, too, was coded as aroace. His inability to love or desire is there to highlight how his only pleasure comes from inflicting suffering. It makes him appear more unfathomable, more demented; devoid of any human feeling.

Voldemort and Joffrey are not flukes. They are some of the more recent examples of an ancient tradition: that of fictional villains, murderers, criminals and other amoral individuals being portrayed as disinterested in sex and romance in a way that is meant to highlight their villainy. Take the James Bond franchise. Since the publication of *Casino Royale* in 1953, Bond has been a male sexual fantasy. He is hyper-virile, hyper-manly – and so his enemies are the opposite.

As Sherronda J. Brown points out, the Bond series – both in its novel form and in its film adaptations – 'seems to have a peculiar interest in asexual and aromantic antagonism and villainy'.[5] There is Auric Goldfinger in *Goldfinger*, the gold smuggler with no sexual interest, and Rosa Klebb of *From Russia With Love*, for whom 'sex was nothing more than an itch'. In the same book, there is Grant, a 'narcissist and asexual'. And in the 1965 film adaptation of *Thunderball*, there is the villain's henchman Vargas. Dressed sleekly in black, Vargas performs the necessary rituals of a Bond villain – assassination, abduction, the torture of attractive young women – without expression and in impassive silence. He does none of the things that make Bond glamorous, 'does not drink, does not smoke, does not make love'. All he has is his stoic devotion to murder.

Why do so many Bond villains fall into this pattern? Because of compulsory sexuality. Bond was Ian Fleming's male ideal: charming, virile, with an active sexual desire and sex life. The villains are aroace to highlight their difference from the red-blooded fantasy ideal that Bond represents. Bond is what men are supposed to want to be; the aroace-coded villains are what they are supposed to want to avoid.

But this is fiction, you might say. Surely, we do not believe that real people fit these stereotypes? Unfortunately, it appears that we do. In *Singled Out*, Bella DePaulo points to the media response to the case of serial killer Dennis Rader, who was caught in 2005 after murdering ten people. *Newsweek* reported, 'Rader would seem an unlikely serial-killer suspect. Far from a shadowy loner, he is married with two grown children.' The idea of an amoral killer having a romantic partnership and loved ones was startling; we associate such coldness with single people. Marriages and families are supposed to be the secure framework that produces good members of society. DePaulo also notes how television host Nancy Grace dismissed the idea that the perpetrator of a shooting in Washington, DC, three years earlier, might be married. 'How many serial killers actually go home to a wife and a family and a dog and a white picket fence?' she protested.[6]

Perhaps that is how we should portray fictional villains, if we really want to make them seem inhuman: show that they are capable of *both* callous cruelty and real love. Show that they *can* love other human beings, and want them to be safe and happy, but that they choose not to when those other humans are not personal to them. They choose not to care when their personal gain is on the line. This is the reality of the world. When we tell the fiction that 'evil' people are incapable of true feeling, we comfort ourselves. *Oh, well,* we think, *I could never be like that politician I hate, or that celebrity who abused a child, or that awful figure from history, because I am capable of love.* In doing so, we ignore our own capacity for cruelty. All of us have the potential to do terrible things. The difference is not the capacity for romantic love; it's the conscious choices we make *not* to act in certain ways.

This is how compulsory sexuality is introduced to us in the books we read, in the films and shows and plays we watch. It is reinforced through the language of our peers, through jokes and insults. And when we try to assert ourselves outside of the assumed norms, we can find our partners accusing us of not loving them, our doctors trying to 'fix' us or making thoughtless mistakes about our care. Allosexuality becomes not just a different sexual orientation, or even a norm that we sit outside; it becomes an institution that we either have to fake being a part of or accept living with the consequences. How ironic that when Sarah Vaughan set out to write a book condemning rape culture, she ended up echoing one of its tenets: that a lack of sexual desire or interest is a flaw, a problem, some aberrant thing that needs to be fixed.

*

In Lynne Reid Banks's 1960 novel *The L-shaped Room*, the narrator knows exactly what her father's problem in life is. 'There was nothing wrong with my father except being alone,' she says. 'Everyone who is without a mate is basically alone. It's a special and very destructive form of loneliness.'[7]

Loneliness is, of course, natural for anyone who wants a romantic partner but does not have one. I sympathize with this. Where I disagree – powerfully – is in the implication that to not be romantically partnered is to have *something wrong*; that it is a destructive state of being, and that only romance prevents a person from being alone.

Consider Reddit user Impressive-Jaguar and her two committed friends living together; consider David Jay and his web of loved ones. None of these people have romantic partners, and none are alone. I am aroace, and do not for a moment consider myself alone. I have a friend who is *my person*, who understands me more than anyone. I have a network of close friends, a vibrant family, a much-loved labrador. Why should the presence of romance have some magical quality that would transform me into being *not alone*, when these relationships already fulfil me?

Because of amatonormativity.

Amatonormativity (from the Latin 'amare', *love*, and 'normative') was a term coined by philosopher Elizabeth Brake in her book *Minimizing Marriage: Marriage, Morality and the Law.* Amatonormativity, as defined by Brake, is the belief that 'a central, exclusive, amorous relationship is normal for humans, in that it is a universally shared goal, and that such a relationship is normative in that it *should* be aimed at in preference to other relationship types'.[8] It's effectively the romantic version of compulsory sexuality. Amatonormativity tells us that romance is more important than friendship or other platonic bonds – hence Impressive-Jaguar's friends telling her that her platonic life partners were less important than their own romantic marriages. It's the belief that romance is a default state that all human lives should eventually end up in. It often occurs entirely unintentionally, yet even small instances of amatonormativity can contribute to people feeling – be they aspec or otherwise – that to be single is to be lesser, and that to lack romantic love is indeed destructive.

Here are some scenarios that depict amatonormativity at work:

- You have a dear friend who has been the most important person in your life for years, with whom you share the closest bond you have. You then find a new romantic partner. Your partner complains that you don't consider them more important than your friend.
- You're considering a change to your appearance, such as a haircut, dyeing your hair, getting a tattoo, or similar. When you bring this up to a friend or family member, they warn you that 'you'll never get a date like that'. They imply by this that the prospect of getting a romantic partner should be prioritized over what you want for your body and how you'd prefer to express yourself.

- You're watching a film that isn't focused on romance, such as a thriller or sci-fi. There's a romantic subplot between two characters, but the film hasn't spent much time focusing on their interactions and as a result they have little chemistry. The romance feels shoehorned in, like the writers thought there had to be a romance somewhere, even if it didn't make any sense. (For example, take the superhero film *Captain America: Civil War* (2016), where the main character Steve Rogers shares a kiss with a female side character. It happens with little build-up, is never relevant again in this film or any other in the series, and has no bearing on anything else happening in what's otherwise an action movie.)
- You're talking to a friend or family member about a hobby you love, but which they consider nerdy or uninteresting. They laugh that you 'need to get a boyfriend/girlfriend/partner', or that 'you need to get laid'.
- You read a book in which a character is disinterested in relationships. This disinterest is portrayed as a negative trait, a character flaw to be overcome. By the end of the story they are proven wrong and end up in a relationship.
- You have a close friend with whom you are very affectionate. People assume that you are dating, even though you aren't, assuming that your level of closeness would only occur in a romantic relationship.
- Your long-term friend finds a new romantic partner. You soon find yourself seeing less of your friend; they are devoting most of their free time to their partner, and don't make time to hang out with you as much as they used to. When you mention this to others, they say it's only natural that your friend should be putting their partner first.

All of these situations have happened either to me or to friends. But for a more specific example, take what happened to Mildred Sanford and Nancy Inferrera.

Sanford and Inferrera met while living and working in Massachusetts, and when Sanford's husband died, the two friends moved in together and stayed together for four decades. In 2007, with Sanford now seventy-nine, and Inferrera sixty-nine, they moved together to Sanford's original hometown of Guysborough in Canada, where she was a citizen. In 2011, Inferrera applied to become a Canadian citizen.

It is true that Inferrera had lived in Canada for some years without declaring her presence, having travelled there on a now-expired visa. But the difference between what happened to them as a consequence and what would likely have happened to a married couple is stark. Socially, and legally, we understand that humans have the right to family life. This is why, for instance, asylum seekers in the UK who are granted leave to remain are allowed to bring their families here with them; we all generally agree it's not ethical to separate spouses, or parents and children. The same is true in Canadian law. A citizen can sponsor their spouse to become a citizen even if they are in Canada illegally, as was the case with Inferrera. Once such an application is in process, as Inferrera's then was, a citizen's spouse cannot be deported.

Inferrera was not Sanford's spouse. And she was immediately deported from Canada.

Their immigration lawyer, Lee Cohen, was quick to point out the disparity. 'Effectively, Mildred and Nancy are family,' he stated. 'But under the immigration legislation, they are not.' Sanford refused to leave Inferrera and travelled to the USA with her at the risk of losing her home and health insurance (she had a heart problem and was exhibiting signs of dementia) where they stayed in a motel in Maine until an immigration official stepped in to allow Inferrera to return. Inferrera did become a Canadian citizen, but as Cohen points out, 'Had we been able to determine that they are family in law, Nancy would not have gone through years of waiting to get to this moment.'[9] A romantic marriage, perhaps even a romantic relationship, between the two would have provided Inferrera with protection against deportation, yet a four-decade-long cohabitation did not. As ace writer Angela Chen states, 'a couple in an abusive relationship would have received more protection'.[10]

This is amatonormativity. Romantic relationships receive protections, priority and privileges that aren't given to other kinds of relationship. And when people try to build alternative forms of relationship, as Sanford and Inferrera did, they find that the world does not afford the same level of importance and respect to their relationship that they do.

Inferrera and Sanford never received a true acknowledgement of the importance of their bond. Inferrera's case was reconsidered because she was Sanford's 'carer', not because the immigration court saw their relationship as equal to a romantic one. But to Sanford, watching Inferrera finally receive her immigration papers, this was about far more than having a live-in carer allowed to stay with her; her closest friend, her family, was finally allowed to be a part of her life. 'I know she's going to stay now,' she said.[11]

You'll notice that there's no suggestion of either woman being aspec. And that's because amatonormativity, like compulsory sexuality, does not just affect aros and aces. To be sure, it is perhaps most obvious to us – we are the ones who inevitably confront the consequences of not conforming to amatonormativity just by being *alive* – but the examples I listed earlier could, and do, happen to anyone. Anyone in Sanford and Inferrera's situation might have been treated the same way. After all, amatonormativity impacts allos, too. There are plenty of allos who are contented, confident singles.

And sometimes, the consequences of amatonormativity can be far, far more dire.

*

In 2014, Ray Rice, then a running back for the Baltimore Ravens American football team, was caught on footage dragging his unconscious fiancée, Janay Palmer, from a lift in New Jersey. When the ensuing media scrutiny meant that the security video from inside the lift was released, it showed a brief fight: Rice hit his fiancée, Palmer hit back, and Rice struck her again with enough force to knock her unconscious.

The day after Rice was formally charged, he and Palmer married. Palmer spoke out to defend her now-husband, saying online that the incident was an anomaly and that 'we will continue to grow & show the world what real love is'.[12]

The backlash against Palmer was immediate. Comments on a *Seattle Times* story about the incident included: 'What an imbecile to marry him DESPITE his violence!'; 'What Rice did was inexcusable, but also the decision for this gal to go ahead and marry him is also inexcusable'; and 'She obviously lacks the personal fortitude to stand on her own two feet and tell that jerk to take a hike… I won't waste sympathy on her.'[13]

The blame had shifted to the victim, as it does all too often, and Beverly Gooden had had enough. She had escaped an abusive relationship herself, and she posted about her experience on Twitter, describing how she had been physically prevented from leaving, how her church had pressured her to stay, and how she'd believed, just as Palmer did, that real love could conquer all obstacles. Gooden tagged her tweets '#WhyIStayed'. The hashtag went viral.

In 2016, the Institute of Family Studies realized that there was an opportunity here. They used the #WhyIStayed responses as the basis for a study of the factors keeping abuse victims in their relationships, so as to examine what could be done to ease these pressures and make escape easier for victims. They categorized the tweets into eight general factors, such as fear of their partner hurting them or themself, financial instability and damaged self-worth. And looking at the study, one reason stands out as something that's likely influenced by amatonormativity: what the Institute of Family Studies called the 'saviour' reason.[14]

So many #WhyIStayed responses spoke of a belief that love could save their partner. 'I thought love would conquer all.' 'I believed I could love the abuse out of him.' 'He said soulmates didn't leave each other.' 'I would be the strong one who would never leave and would show him loyalty. I would fix him and teach him love.' Echoing Janay Rice, they believed that this was 'real love' – and having that love meant that they could persevere and grow. And many more who fell into this category in the study said that giving up on the relationship would feel like a failure – 'I didn't want to fail' – or that it was preferable to singledom. 'I was so afraid to be alone.'[15]

I was so afraid to be alone. This is what amatonormativity can do at its most insidious: it can persuade people into believing that singledom is a solitude so terrible that an abusive relationship is better.

This mentality – that a relationship breaking up constitutes a failure – is a widespread one. When Amy Gahran surveyed over 1,500 people for her book *Stepping off the Relationship Escalator: Uncommon Love and Life*, she found that many of her respondents felt that anything short of riding the 'relationship escalator' to the top – the escalator serving as a shorthand term for the traditional monogamous romantic relationship, beginning with interest and dating, progressing to sex and cohabitation, and following this momentum through to marriage and living together for life – was a personal failing. 'The only way you can be sure you've succeeded,' one said, 'is when neither of you have sex with anyone else, and then someone dies.'[16] And this sense that only living together 'til death do us part' is a true or successful relationship weighs heavily on those in abusive relationships, who often feel a sense of duty to stay in the relationship, and to 'fix' their partner with compassion and devotion.

We bestow such magical qualities upon romantic love. We tell stories like *Jane Eyre* and *Beauty and the Beast* where love changes and redeems a flawed character. It's a trope that goes back almost to the dawn of the modern novel, with Samuel Richardson's 1740 *Pamela, or, Virtue Rewarded* telling the story of a predatory aristocrat who abducts his servant-girl Pamela and makes multiple attempts to force himself on her, only to fall in love with her and be redeemed. The book was a sensation on release and, apparently, our appetite for the trope has not gone away. A recent and well-known example can be seen in *Harry Potter* (to complain about that a little more), where Severus Snape betrays Voldemort out of love for Harry's mother Lily, in a textbook example of love bringing a man back from the dark side. Thousands of fans immediately celebrated this, elevating him to one of the most popular characters in the franchise because of his tragic, redeeming love.

The 'love redeems' stories themselves are not the problem here. There are plenty of redemption stories that work, and many of these *do* involve the unexpected support or perspective given by a new loved one – friend, lover or otherwise – as part of the spark for the villain's growth. The problem is how romantic love, in these examples, excuses or forgives continued bad behaviour; how romantic love alone catapults them into being a hero. Snape, a regular abuser of his students, is 'the bravest man [Harry] ever knew' by time of the epilogue. It's in the implication that no one who can love the way Snape does can truly be bad, like the loveless Voldemort. Anyone capable of love must, at heart, be good.

It's not hard to see how such sentiments might make abuse victims feel the same way about their abusers. Their abuser loves them – therefore, they must be good, because truly cruel people can't love. And when amatonormative ideals tell us that romantic love should be given priority over other forms of love, abusers have even more ammunition with which to isolate their victims. Many #WhyIStayed respondents spoke of abusers forcing them to choose: their partner, or their family? And they felt that they had to choose their romantic partner. Because you don't abandon your soulmate. You have to find the One, and how can you simply leave once you have? Because if you don't have a mate, you're basically alone. Because all you need is love.

Even on the most basic, practical level, amatonormativity helps keep victims tethered to their partners. Like protection from deportation, marriage offers benefits that a single person lacks, be it the support of a spouse's money or something still more vital. One woman who posted a #WhyIStayed response said that she had a chronic medical condition and needed her abusive husband's health insurance in order to survive. Many more knew that if they were living alone, they would not be able to support themselves or their children. As Bella DePaulo points out in *Singled Out*, living alone can often be more expensive, more exhausting and more demanding than living together. For example, married people can pay less per person for numerous package deals, such as memberships, while single people have to pay full price. Single people are often expected to work longer hours, and are more likely to be asked to work weekends and during holidays. In this way, DePaulo points out, singles can effectively end up subsidizing married people.[17] This is annoying for any single (and aromantic) person, but it can be devastating for someone trying to escape an abusive relationship who knows they cannot afford to lose the financial benefits that come with marriage and coupledom. Individually, the financial and social drawbacks of singledom might be small, but taken together – especially for anyone with an already low income, and for someone trying to face the emotional devastation of abuse – they can be too much to risk.

We cannot ignore, here, that this particular facet of amatonormativity and compulsory sexuality is inseparable from misogyny (although these forces very much affect men too, as Chapter 4 will discuss). It's telling that all the above stories of love 'fixing' a broken person so often involve a woman putting in the emotional labour to 'save' a man. Girls and women, after all, are supposed to be nurturing and maternal, the emotional core of a family. Nor can we ignore how much more heavily the burden of isolation and financial insecurity can fall upon people of colour, whose isolation is often compounded by an inability to trust law enforcement – Beverly Gooden, founder of #WhyIStayed, has stated that, as a Black woman, she 'never would have' called the police for help with her situation – and who are more likely to have fewer resources with which to escape an abuser.[18] In the UK in 2020, 23 per cent and 24 per cent of Black and Asian families, respectively, were found to live in households with 'persistent low income', in comparison with 11 per cent of white families.[19] According to a 2023 study in the USA,17.9 per cent of Black people, 16.6 per cent of Hispanic people and 21.2 per cent of

American Indian and Alaska Native people lived in poverty.[20] Facing the financial difficulties that come with leaving an abuser, being a single parent or simply living a single life can be a much riskier prospect for people of colour.

Amatonormativity is a social force that entwines itself with these other axes of oppression. It lends weight to the doubts that make people stay in abusive relationships, and to the arguments that abusers wield against victims, and it benefits no one – no one, except the abusers.

*

So, if amatonormativity and compulsory sexuality don't benefit aspecs or allos – if they perpetuate abuse, eat at our self-worth, deprive us of rights and spread harmful misinformation about aros and aces – what can we do? One answer is: push for more aspec visibility. Because our very existence gives the lie to compsex and amatonormativity.

My friend Jan (he/him) has always known is that he doesn't want to centre his life around a single person. His ideal is to live with a collection of close ones, some of whom might be romantic or sexual partners, others dear friends. For a long time, he felt alone in that desire, in his yearning to have multiple close relationships rather than one person who was his be-all and end-all.

'In a lot of my friendships,' Jan says, 'there have been times where I felt undervalued – often a friend who I was very close to would seemingly put in far less effort as they focused on their partner, and I would always find that somewhat hurtful, as I personally always valued my closest friends equally to my partners. Simultaneously, when I expressed that sentiment to my partner, she was hurt that I did not love her more than my friends, and that was a tremendous source of guilt for me.'

Then I sent Jan an early draft of the first chapter of this book, and everything shifted. 'This idea of building a web of intimate relationships, not having someone who is your "other half",' Jan told me. 'I cannot recall the last time I read something that resonates more with me. The commonly accepted ideas of a single partner who fills all your needs who you love more than all your friends is just so unappealing to me. And having the language to describe it makes so much difference... I no longer feel like my experiences are mine alone, that I'm some sort of one-off freak who doesn't know how to love. I finally don't feel so othered when discussing my personal solutions to those problems.'

Jan is still piecing together whether he considers himself aromantic, but whatever conclusion he comes to, aspec visibility was a blessing for him. It gave him a deeper understanding of himself, and proved that alternative forms of relationship are not just desired by others too, but also possible.

Consider what *Anatomy of a Scandal* might have looked like had Sarah Vaughan written her asexual politician, Chris, as a perfectly pleasant man, and as an aromantic asexual. Vaughan's novel culminates with her narrator, Sophie, leaving her husband James after years of keeping his secrets and ignoring his wrongdoings. This is good. But what if by befriending Chris and realizing that his life was full and whole without romance, Sophie began to question whether love was a good enough reason to cover for her husband? What if Vaughan had used Chris's aroace identity to foreshadow how Sophie's beliefs about sex and romance are built on false assumptions, and were not things worth sacrificing her happiness or integrity for?

Compulsory sexuality and amatonormativity are deep-rooted constructs, but they are just that: constructs. They can be dismantled in a thousand small ways in your own life. Treat yourself to dinner in a restaurant alone. Go on holiday alone – yes, even if you have a partner. Base your appearance on what makes you feel comfortable and what you yourself like, not what others may find attractive. Bring your friend as a plus-one to an event. Challenge anyone who uses 'virgin' as an insult or who jokes about people 'needing to get laid'. And know that being single never, *never* makes you or anyone else lesser. Coupledom is not some milestone of human existence that you must reach in order not to be a failure; it is just one possible form of human closeness. You are an entire person, not a jigsaw piece waiting to be slotted together with another before you are whole.

Aspec awareness, and the defiance of compsex and amatonormativity that it innately contains, cannot fix the pressures of sexism that create the 'your love can fix him' mentality, but it can weaken them. It cannot mend the social injustices that make single living and parenting so much harder, but it can add weight and strength to campaigns to change them. And perhaps someday, an eighteen-year-old aroace can read a book about consent and know that the statement 'you have the right to say no to sex' is true – even when your *no* lasts forever.

4

Not Opting In

How Sex and Romance Set Expectations for Gender – and Why Aspecs Aren't Engaging

When my mother was pregnant with me, she knew I was a boy. It wasn't that she wanted a boy; nor was it that she wanted a girl and managed to convince herself she wasn't having one to prepare for disappointment. She just *knew* I wasn't a girl.

Or she did, until I was born and the midwife said, 'let's have a look at her.' My mum thought, *what? I'm not having a girl.*

She was right. I wasn't a girl.

It's hard to follow the thread of my disengagement from my assigned gender. Because for the most part, it was just that: a disengagement rather than a discomfort; not great pain when being treated as a girl, but simply a lack of any tie to that label. There was *some* discomfort, certainly: I resisted wearing skirts, for instance. My mum's urgings to style my hair in a more sophisticated way, or not allow my eyebrows to grow too bushy, or to 'put a little something around your neck' before going to any formal event, sparked a tearing, wounded feeling I couldn't explain. I'm still not sure how much of this was gender-related and how much of it was due to my hesitance to make myself available to the attraction of others.

But there was something subtler, too, harder to pin down: my inability to speak the language of femininity.

Girls around me during my teen years seemed to know by instinct or by reading each other what to wear, how to hold and carry themselves. *Woman* was a thing they knew how to be as easily as they knew how to be human. And whatever this knowledge was, I didn't have it. I tried to study and imitate their dress and manner, and couldn't. I couldn't live and move in that invisible connecting current they all seemed to share.

I envied them their ease of being – and at the same time, I knew I didn't want to be them.

I entered my twenties. Being openly aroace came comfortably to me now, and with the knowledge that I didn't need to or want to be attractive to anybody, I'd stopped plucking my brows or wearing jewellery that I didn't want to. I had a few nonbinary acquaintances who seemed to me to be impossibly cool, like they had everything figured out. And then, while idly browsing the internet, I found something that made me finally see that long-running thread of gender detachment for what it was.

It was a social media post made by a nonbinary lesbian – someone who said that their lesbian identity felt inherently gender-nonconforming. Gender identity (as distinct from biological sex) is a nebulous thing, but broadly speaking, it's a package of behaviours, traits and roles which might or might not align with your assigned sex at birth. And for women, a lot of these behaviours are defined around the expectation of attraction to and from men. So much of how women are expected to dress, act and present themselves is entangled with the idea that they must be attractive to a male partner. (I was reminded, reading this, of how a female friend once remarked to me that she'd happily wear a sweater and tracksuit bottoms to our college library, but not to the larger university library, because 'people see you there'.) It is easy, then, for lesbians to feel inherently somehow outside the definition of *woman.*

Gender nonconformity within lesbianism has always been here – from the women in 1800s America who dressed in men's clothes to work factory jobs, to butch entertainers in the early 1900s who dressed as men to perform in bars. These lesbians pushed against feminine womanhood, and embodied masculinity outside of manhood. Femme lesbians, too, often feel a level of nonconformity; after all, they embody a femininity that isn't meant for men. Not inviting or seeking attraction from men is, for many lesbians, something that subverts the definition of 'woman'.

I'd been only passingly familiar with nonbinary lesbians before, but the post made sense to me immediately. It was obvious, really. I knew perfectly well that a lack of attraction to men could lead to a detachment from womanhood, because—

Oh.

Everything I had read felt intuitive to me. Womanhood was not all about attraction, of course, but for a lot of people, attraction did influence the experience of womanhood; I understood this. Not being attracted to men could leave you feeling somehow on the outside; I understood this too. I understood because being aroace very much fell under the definition of 'not attracted to men', just with the addition of 'or anyone else' tacked on. So what did that say about me?

What could I point to and say, *yes, this part of me is something that makes me a woman?* Did my lack of connection to femininity have its roots in my lack of attraction? In short: was I nonbinary? Could being aroace be the *reason* I was nonbinary? But surely it didn't work that way. Everything I'd been taught said that gender and sexual orientation were different things, and that nothing caused them. They simply *were.*

I decided a test was in order. I cut my hair, first to a bob and then truly short – and was swiftly returning regularly to the hairdresser with the simple instruction, '*shorter*'. I stopped my never-very-successful attempts to imitate the dress of the women around me and adopted a more androgynous style. Androgyny can be many different things to many different people, but my version meant looser jeans, chunky boots, jackets that obscured my figure and a never-ending rotation of plaid shirts. I stopped the tedious business of shaving my pits and legs. And one day I looked in the mirror, with my hair short and my black jacket on over red plaid and thought, abruptly – *oh. There I am.*

It took twenty-two years of life to realize that I had never recognized myself before.

My reflection, suddenly, inhabited a place of neutrality, an opting-out of femininity, that felt obvious to me. Like this was what I would always have been doing, instinctively, if I hadn't been told that 'girl' was what I was supposed to be. And I was reminded of a video I'd seen by a trans activist explaining the difference between biological sex and gender identity: 'if your body disappeared and you were just a floating head, would you still be a woman?'

No.

*

Looking at gender through an aromantic and asexual lens is fascinating, startling and revealing. When a census was taken of how the ace community identified in terms of gender, women were by far the most common, at a little over 60 per cent. The next most common gender identity? Not men, but nonbinary and genderqueer people, at over a full quarter of respondents. Men came in a distant third.[1]

I found the same pattern when I examined my own interviewees, only exaggerated (perhaps the online forums on which I shared it have a larger female and nonbinary userbase). There were almost four hundred women, nearly three hundred and fifty people who gave some variation of nonbinary identity as their gender… and around fifty men. What causes this unusual gender distribution? Why are so many aspecs outside the gender binary, and why are there so few men? It seems unlikely that men are innately less likely to be aro or ace, so what social factors might result in so few of them being in online aspec spaces? And can being aspec cause, or at least influence, someone's detachment from the gender binary – indeed, from gender altogether?

Reading my interviewees' stories, one topic came up again and again: a frustration with how much our social codes for gendered behaviour are tied up with gendered expectations about sex and romance. For many aspec women, or those socialized as women, their existence seemed inseparable from an expectation of romance. 'When I was younger,' says Aura (she/he/they) who is aroace and genderqueer but assigned female at birth, 'I thought femininity meant I had to fall in love with the prince. I had to play house with Barbies.' In other words, the expectations for her gender were love and domesticity. 'But I didn't want to fall in love. I didn't want to date. And that's what I thought being a girl meant.'

Aura had reasons to think so. Look at how our society paints women who opt out of sex and romance, or who are perceived to have done so. Several of my interviewees who were assigned female at birth told me that their families told them that if they didn't find a partner, they'd end up a 'crazy cat lady'. So what exactly is wrong with the crazy cat lady? She's chosen cats over men. She fills the hole in her life where a man should be with her pets. Google 'crazy cat lady' and you'll find an action figure described as having 'a house full of feral felines and a wild look in her eye' – as if there's something feral, even animalistic, about a woman who hasn't centred romance.

Or take the 'career woman'. She's put her focus into a job 'instead' of finding a partner and having kids – and she's stereotyped as aloof and cold. If she's the opposite of the loving, nurturing wife and mother figure, the female ideal, surely she's an emotionless automaton without any true fulfilment. And this condemnation is very much asymmetrical when it comes to the genders: there's no such thing as a 'career man'.

When this is drilled into woman-assigned people right from childhood, it's small wonder that being aspec can feel for many like being inherently not-woman. 'I just don't understand girl culture,' says Kai (she/they), who is agender and was raised as a girl. 'I always felt out of place in it, and a big reason is that I've never been comfortable with "boy talk". I've never minded listening to others talk about their crushes and partners – I quite enjoy the gossip – but I can't stand it whenever I'm the subject. There's this expectation that girls will suddenly be interested in boys and all the feminine things that come with that at a certain age, but that just made me feel distant from my elementary and middle school friends, because I just didn't understand them. Being raised as a girl comes with the expectation that you'll love *love* – and I didn't ask to be a part of this culture.'

I am not a woman. But, growing up, I still internalized these gendered sexual and romantic standards. I wish I could say that, even as my teen self felt alienated and apart from my female peers, I still respected and appreciated these girls' femininity. Sadly,

I was a teenager, and one who felt pushed away from the easy young womanhood of those around me without knowing why and without knowing that it was *fine* to feel disengaged from gender. Sneering at girls for being into makeup and parties and men was a defence mechanism – if there was something wrong with them, then the failing wasn't on my part. And it was a defence I reached for because it was familiar. It was the *not like other girls* mentality – a mentality that we still allow young women to absorb. In 2009, my first year of secondary school, Taylor Swift released 'You Belong With Me': a pop song about a teenage girl pining for her male friend who's too interested in his cheerleader girlfriend to notice her. The song spread around my school like a very catchy virus. The song's narrator, especially in the music video, is portrayed as kinder, better and purer than the girlfriend. 'She wears short skirts, I wear T-shirts,' the narrator sings. 'Hey, watcha doing with a girl like that?' The narrator finally shows up to prom in virginal white while her rival wears a revealing scarlet dress, and her crush finally notices her. She gets the boy because she's modest and caring, while her rival is sexy and selfish. Because, while we'll shame any woman who prioritizes cats or career above being available for sex and love, a woman can never be *too* available; her sexuality can never be uncontrollable. Like Taylor Swift, I'd fallen into the trap of internalized misogyny – though thankfully, I kept it to myself rather than writing a hit song about it.

I learned to grow out of this judgemental attitude during my teens. But it was embracing and fully understanding my aroace identity, and with it my nonbinary identity, that really allowed me to see these sexual gendered expectations for what they were. I had never 'failed' at being a woman; I'd never been one. Now I knew I didn't have to expect sexual behaviour from myself, I was quicker to catch myself when I fell into the trap of judging others for being a way I wasn't. And so I was able to appreciate femininity so much more. Now that it's something that's not for me rather than something I'm failing to be, I can see the beauty and strength in it. It's a lot easier to compliment a woman's dress now I'm not miserably stuffed into my own.

For me, rejecting compulsory sexuality was inseparable from rejecting sexism. Taking sex and romance down from their pedestal, no longer centring them as the necessary goal of women's lives weakens the foundation that supports these sexist expectations. If romance is not necessary for a 'whole' human existence, then the cat lady stops being 'crazy' for not wanting a husband and the career woman stops being cold for prioritizing her job.

A common argument from anti-trans lobbyists is that people who are assigned female at birth and then transition are simply surrendering to internalized misogyny. They have been trained to see women as lesser, and so they 'choose' to live as another gender. Quite aside from the fact that being trans is not a choice, my own personal experience has shown me that this isn't true. If a dislike of women and being a woman had driven me to identify as nonbinary, I wouldn't have come to appreciate and value femininity *more* after I began socially transitioning. Realizing that I was nonbinary helped me to start checking the internal judgements I made about women, and recognizing them as thoughts that other people put into my head. I gained a deeper understanding and valuing of womanhood after I stepped outside its bonds.

*

Men, meanwhile, have their own slew of sexual and romantic expectations pushed upon them. Lee (he/him) met with 'questions and confusion' when he tried to tell people he wasn't interested in sex. 'If I'd just said I wasn't into relationships, they might have got that,' he says. 'But there's a certain stereotype of men always being interested in sex.' Similarly, Orion (they/them) who is nonbinary and transmasculine, found the social pressures upon them shifting drastically as they transitioned. 'Being perceived as male had the unexpected consequence that I was suddenly thought of as someone who wants to have sex all the time, and I'm accused of lying if I say I don't. When I say I don't want a relationship, people make ball-and-chain jokes. Instead of being leered at by men, I'm told that I should be the one leering.'

Our society shames men who don't 'score'. They are cast as unmanly, not true red-blooded males. When psychologist Jessie Ford interviewed university-age men about their experiences of unwanted sex, a ubiquitous topic was the fear of judgement for not engaging in sex, and the social capital acquired by men who do have sex:

> Interviewee 1: [Men having sex they don't want] is definitely there; it's a thing. Because men always 'want it' so it doesn't get looked at. People are still going to high five them when they have sex.
>
> Interviewee 2: For a guy it will always be seen as good for him. [...] If they have reservations, they always have the fall back that it will be good for them as a social status [...] it translates to 'sex will always be good for me because of the status boost'.
>
> Interviewee 3: I thought they were going to be like, *this kid's a pussy.* He can't slam.

Interviewee 4: Especially as the guy if I ever try to say 'I'm not in the mood…' if I push, it's weird, but if she wants to do it, it's really weird if I say *no, I don't.*

Interviewer: Why is that weird?

Interviewee 4: Because I'm supposed to want it all the time.[2]

One of Ford's respondents, a twenty-one-year-old college freshman named Mark, described waking up at three in the morning after a night out with friends to find a woman straddling him, trying to initiate sex. 'There's a random person in my bed on top of me. I wasn't gonna be like, *you shouldn't be here.* It would just be weird… what am I going to do? Go complain I was raped by honestly a really nice looking girl? Say "get off me" the way a girl would? If I did that to her and then she made it a thing or people heard about it, it would be insane. I would have got shit.'

These men feared, or at least anticipated, being mocked by their peers for turning down an opportunity to have sex with someone attractive, because men are 'supposed to want it all the time'. Men celebrate each other's sexual accomplishments. Men can't say 'I don't want to' because men supposedly *always* want to. Mark could not 'complain that I was raped', even though the sex was unwanted, because men are assumed to welcome sex. But Mark didn't welcome it. He was, in his words, 'passive', going along with it rather than participating.

What society have we made where someone feels obliged to allow unwanted sex purely because he's a man?

When sex becomes social capital, the consequences can be devastating. In 2021, twenty-two-year-old Jake Davison from Plymouth shot and killed five people after plunging into a spiral of despair about how he wasn't getting sex. Videos he posted on YouTube showed him bemoaning how, after years of trying to lift weights and improve his physique, he had nothing to show for it; he had 'missed out on teenage romance', and he wasn't a Chad – a slang term for a good-looking and muscular, confident man with sex appeal – and women were shallow creatures who only cared about money.

Davison is just one of many such men who have ended up lashing out with violence. Elliot Rodger, who shot six people dead in California in 2014, targeted a sorority house because women wouldn't have sex with him. Before the murders, Rodger announced his intention to 'slaughter every single spoiled, stuck-up blonde slut' – the women who would have sex with other people, but not him.

Davison and Rodger were 'incels', members of a movement of 'involuntary celibate' men whose response to feeling unattractive and alienated is to feel entitled to women and to sex. Incel ideology reduces women to givers of social capital. In a stroke of uncomfortable irony, the term 'incel' was never intended for such use. Its creator, a woman called Alana, set up the website Alana's Involuntary Celibate Project to support single people like herself who were struggling in their dating lives. Some were hampered by social awkwardness or mental illness, some by gender stereotypes or baggage from previous relationships. It was intended to be a positive place of support and connection. Years later, after Alana had left the site and moved on, she learned that the term she'd created had mutated into a misogynist ideology. 'It feels,' she said in one interview, 'like being the scientist who figured out nuclear fission and then discovers it's being used as a weapon for war.'[3]

Don't mistake me. Men like Rodger and Davison made their own choices, and their choices are inexcusable. But it is worth us examining the trains of thought, and the social messages, that influenced those choices.

This idea that masculinity requires sexuality is doubtless an influence behind looksmaxxing, a trend in which people, overwhelmingly men, try to perfect their facial appearance in order to increase their Sexual Market Value, or SMV. Some forms of looksmaxxing focus on mild changes, such as exercise and skincare; others adopt techniques that are supposed to enhance one's jawline, such as 'mewing' (holding the tongue against the roof of the mouth). Others involve plastic surgery or 'bonesmashing' – applying blunt force to the face to build stronger facial bones.

Digging into looksmaxxing spaces was a chilling experience. Some users claimed that women only wanted rich men, making them 'poorcels'; one site declared that 'women's choosiness about men's resources may have evolved from their weaker stature and inability to survive on their own in the ancestral human environment'[4]. I saw men of colour asking how they could make their skin lighter. Another site said that if a woman had children from a previous relationship, it advertised that she had 'honed her skills as a mother' and 'proved her fertility'. The book *Sexual Market Value* declares that a woman who hasn't found a partner by forty-five will never have children and 'has missed her chance at true happiness'.[5] Amazon is packed with products meant to strengthen the jaw, and clothing companies advertise their products as the perfect 'stylemaxxing' wardrobe overhaul, profiting from these men's insecurities.

And all of this to increase Sexual Market Value; to heighten your power in the dating game and allow you to date and sleep with women.

Incels are appalling people, but while we condemn their actions and beliefs, we can still acknowledge that their actions did not happen in a vacuum. They happened because sex is a 'status boost' for men, because sex is how to get your male friends to cheer for you. Why is getting to have sex with women the solution that incel and looksmaxxing influencers present to men who might be insecure about their appearances and dissatisfied with their lives? Because of the pervading societal message telling them that sex makes them men, and lacking it makes them nothing.

Consider the 2005 comedy film *The 40-Year-Old Virgin*, in which the titular character, Andy, has his male friends rally around him to help him finally get laid. The film is on Andy's side when he insists he wants love, not just sex, and his friends' centring of sex ends up creating messes of their lives. They're clearly in the wrong to consider sex the making of a man. And yet – the idea of a man being a virgin at forty is still so noteworthy, apparently, that the writers could spin a two-hour film out of it. Then there's how Andy is portrayed, as a nerdy guy who enjoys gaming and whose house is full of collectibles. The message: a man can only be a virgin at forty, or at least could only be a sympathetic or believable virgin at forty, if he's in some way unmasculine. Andy is emphatically not a Chad. He tried to have sex when he was younger, and gave up when he couldn't find anyone to have sex with; in other words, if he could have been having sex, he would have been. Masculine, attractive, socially adept men could never be virgins; only nerds and gamers.

Now that we're on the topic of gamers, I want to take the opportunity to explore how video games where a player can choose their avatar's gender can be a useful tool to examine how the same situations are handled differently when the gender of the player character is swapped. A bewildering example of men being pushed into sex occurs in the sci-fi roleplaying game *Mass Effect 3*, where a bisexual male character, Kaidan, can be pursued romantically by a male or female player character (the customizable Commander Shepard). Largely, the romantic scenes play out similarly regardless of Shepard's gender, until the climactic scene of the romantic subplot, where with battle looming, the two discuss their relationship. They talk, they share a kiss – and at this point, the scenes diverge abruptly based on Shepard's gender. A female Shepard can tell Kaidan how much he means to her, and is then given the option to initiate sex or turn it down in favour of spending time together non-sexually. For a male Shepard, however, the scene immediately segues into a sex scene following the kiss – no declaration of love, and no option to turn down sex.

What could the reasoning behind this possibly be? Did the writers assume that a man in this situation – again, an *identical* situation to that of a female protagonist – would never want to opt out of sex? Did they think male players would find that option laughable, or that they would be embarrassed by seeing their male character talk tenderly about his feelings, even though by this point the player has built a committed relationship with Kaidan over a trilogy of games? Was the decision influenced by the sexualization of gay, bi and pan men (something so widespread that several of my gay male aspec interviewees said that they felt being aspec on some level disqualified them from being gay)? Whatever the motivation, the writers apparently thought that allowing a man to opt out of sex wasn't necessary, and the scene therefore feels like a microcosm of how we're treating men. Women can turn down sex; men can't. Women can talk about their feelings; men can't.

Considering all of this, it's no surprise that men, and especially men of colour, show up in such small numbers in censuses of the aro and ace communities. Men are supposed to have high levels of desire, to always be the ones to initiate sex – and it is hard for aspec men to assert themselves against that assumption enough to realize that it isn't true of them. Multiple men on AVEN have voiced their frustrations with how compulsory sexuality made it hard for them to realize their identities and to connect with other aspec men:

> Marki: If you don't express interest toward girls, [people] will label you as gay, which in my community can draw a lot of negative attention. I don't think many men realize this orientation exists, since it goes against everything that society teaches us about being a man. So yeah, I do think that [ace men] exist in equal numbers, but women are probably less shamed when admitting they're asexual. Us men are kind of just expected to run around flailing our arms wildly while trying to have sex with anything that moves. Or so society tells us we are.

> WheelCuddle: I am thirty-one years old. Today is the one-week anniversary of discovering my asexuality [...] I felt a strong desire to 'be a man' and first had sex at eighteen because I needed to prove my manhood as an adult. I thought sex was the only way to express my desire to love someone. I see now, clearly, that I developed a straight persona, someone loud, confident, bold, and interested in sex. It was only when I came to terms with my asexuality that I realized this persona wasn't even me. I suspect there are a lot of men still trapped in their own idea of what it means to be a man.

> MisterKrister: I think that most men don't think of the possibility of not wanting sex. When I first figured out I wasn't attracted to girls, I went straight to thinking 'well, I

> guess I like boys'. And when that proved not to be the case, I got really confused. I didn't believe I couldn't be attracted to no one, and came to the conclusion that I might be a sociopath. That stayed in my head for a year until I found the term asexual.[6]

These gendered expectations benefit no one. They lead to men feeling they always have to be the ones to initiate sex, even if they don't want it, and women feeling like they can't initiate sex when they *do*. Women feel pressure to remove their body hair to be sexually appealing, even if this is not something they actually want to do. Men feel less ready to ask for certain sexual or romantic acts. Women fear being accused of prudery or frigidity if they don't 'put out'. Men expect less emotion during sex, even if they want it.

So, once again, refusing compulsory sexuality is not just for aspecs. It's for women who want to de-prioritize sex and romance without shame or judgment; to define femininity beyond attraction; for women of colour who deserve better than being treated as easily accessible sexual objects. It is for men who should never have to fake interest in sex, 'get shit' for turning it down, or feel their masculinity is defined by sexual prowess, and for men of colour who have been reduced to racist caricatures of their sexuality long enough. It is for everyone who should never feel that sex is a requirement of their gender role.

Sex is an activity that requires a great degree of vulnerability, and has the capacity to be both difficult and wonderful. It is an activity that we should all feel able to engage in if we want to – because we trust that we're going to have a good time – and never just because gendered expectations say we should.

*

There's one last thing to point out before I move beyond discussing the gender binary, and that's something that Canton Winer, a professor of sociology at the University of Illinois, noticed when he began studying gendered experiences of asexuality. When he asked asexual men about asexual erasure – the societal tendency to act as if asexuality does not exist or is not legitimate – many of them talked about how people assumed that asexuality was simply impossible. When he asked asexual women about erasure, they echoed the same sentiments. But when Winer asked more in-depth questions about people's personal experiences of erasure, the women's story changed.

'Normally, when we define what asexual erasure is, it's this idea that it's impossible to not experience sexual attraction,' Winer told me. 'But I found that's too simplistic an explanation for how asexual erasure functions, because it's actually quite gendered. Yes, for men, that is the way asexuality is typically erased. For women, it's, "how does that make you different from other women?"'

'The dominant narrative for erasure is men's,' Canton Winer explained, 'even though they're the numerical minority.' The male narrative of erasure is one where asexuality is impossible; the female narrative is one where asexuality is unremarkable, and almost expected.

This was immediately familiar to me. I remembered an occasion where I'd tried to define demisexuality to my mum, a variation of asexual identity where you can only experience sexual attraction after forming a close intimate bond with someone. (I will discuss this further in Chapter 7.) She immediately replied, 'Well, I think a lot of women feel like that.' But no; allo women do not feel like that. A demisexual person does not simply prefer to wait to have sex with someone; they *physically cannot experience bodily attraction* until they have an intense level of intimacy, which can take months or years to build. This is obviously not a standard allosexual experience; allos can be sexually attracted to strangers, to celebrities they've never met, and to people they don't even like. I'm sure my mum knows this; and yet she still instinctively felt that demisexuality wasn't remarkable, or even distinct from the usual female experience.

'The broader assumption,' Winer writes, '[is] that women are not very sexual and ultimately responsive to men's sexuality.'[7] Often, the assumption is also that women *should not* be sexual; this is especially the case in forms of purity culture: a subculture of Christianity that emphasizes chastity, the sexual purity of the individual, and abstinence until marriage. Within purity culture, men are supposed to be the strong backs of a community and household, the leaders and workers, while women are the supporters; sweet, docile, mothers and wives. In this image of ideal femininity, a woman is desexualized: she is supposed to be the housewife and the nurturer of children. She cannot be a Jezebel, a promiscuous woman who leads men astray using her sexuality (after a seductive Bible figure). The extent to which female sexlessness is prized is demonstrated by the number of ace people assigned female at birth who gave me accounts of being raised in purity culture. Many felt they were 'winning' at being a Christian woman for years, because they weren't tempted towards sex at all, and they didn't have the sexual thoughts that everyone told them were the sparks of sin. Religious leaders warned them that a woman who had sex before marriage was like a used toothbrush or piece of gum, damaged forever and impossible to want – so not having any interest in sex at all was the ideal.

Ultimately, of course, purity culture ends up compelling sex anyway. My interviewees spent their youth being told not to be sexual beings, because they might become a 'stumbling block' to men, tempting them into sin. But now they were told that they had to become wives, have sex, and produce more Christian babies.

The term 'purity culture' refers to a Christian movement, but these kinds of pressures are not unique to Christianity. Afana, growing up Muslim, was praised in her youth for focusing on her studies over boys or dating, the things she was supposed to eschew. 'I remember being told off for wearing red lipstick because it's a sexual colour and makes me seem like a prostitute and sexually available,' she recalls. Then she, like the aces raised in Evangelical Christianity, became an adult and was suddenly shamed for not wanting to engage in marriage or sex. 'Another Muslim girl told me that it is a directive of Islam that women must marry and birth children – it is fucking not – and by choosing not to, I'm committing a sin which I will suffer for.'

These experiences are an extreme form of female desexualization, but the phenomenon is not limited to religious environments. Society as a whole expects women not to have a great deal of desire. 'I was assigned female at birth,' says Jesse (he/xe), 'and I feel like that masked asexuality for me for a long time. I was a girl; of course I wasn't interested in sex. I had so many cultural messages saying that men wanted sex and women wanted connection and affection. Even though my sex drive was non-existent, I figured that was on the low range of normal for a girl.'

This sentiment came up again and again in people's responses to my survey question about gendered experiences. 'Women are considered to just be like that anyway.' 'I feel like my lack of desire is brushed aside with "women don't enjoy sex".' 'For a long time I just assumed women don't feel sexual attraction.' 'I thought it was just the way that women were.'

So men are expected to have a big sexual appetite, and women are expected not to have one: an assumption that has consequences. In cisgender heterosexual sex, women's pleasure all too often gets overlooked; a study in 2018 found that during partnered sex, 95 per cent of men achieved orgasm, compared with 65 per cent of women. (An earlier study, in 2005, put the rate of female orgasm as low as 39 per cent.)[8] And this 'orgasm gap' is heavily influenced by the belief that women have, innately, a weaker level of desire and sexual need than men.

When researchers Nicole Andrejek, Tina Fetner and Melanie Heath set out to examine the orgasm gap, they found that one of the biggest factors in whether a woman achieves orgasm is whether she receives clitoral stimulation, such as via 'hand jobs' or oral sex. So, they asked, 'Why are couples not engaging in the types of sexual activities that might reduce the gender gap in orgasms?'[9]

'I think men *need* to orgasm,' one of their respondents told them. Women, meanwhile, did not. Others discussed sex as ending when the man orgasmed, which often meant there was 'no time' for anything else after penetration. 'I honestly never orgasm,' one woman said, 'because it just happened too soon for him' – as if there just wasn't any obligation for him to attend to her pleasure afterwards.

Tellingly, the respondents' view of sex seemed fixated on penetrative sex as being the most 'normal' or 'regular' kind of sex. Other acts were unusual or special; one said that oral sex was reserved for birthdays. As the researchers pointed out, this mentality means that sex is defined 'in narrow, phallocentric terms [...] sexual behaviours that prioritize clitoral stimulation, such as oral sex, vibrators or manual stimulation [are defined as] "alternative" sexual practices'. And these practices 'are depicted as more time-consuming labour and extra work for couples'.

For some women, receiving oral sex was not just unusual, but shameful. One reported that 'It can be very pleasurable, but it feels wrong to me… it just doesn't feel natural… I feel like it's dirty sex, almost like watching porn.' Certain men, meanwhile, seem to feel shame at the idea of performing oral sex. Reading the study reminded me of an incident in 2018, in which rapper DJ Khaled was found to have claimed in an interview that he doesn't 'go down' (perform oral sex). 'I don't *do* that!' he protested, and when the interviewers pointed out that he still expected oral sex from his fiancé, he doubled down. 'It's different rules for men. You gotta understand, we the king […] I just can't do what you want me to do. I just can't.'[10] It seemed he felt that performing oral sex would somehow stop him from being 'the king'; it would damage his masculinity.

Another study into the orgasm gap put college hookup culture under the microscope, trying to figure out why women are more likely to experience orgasm and pleasurable sex in relationships than in hookups. Several of the men the researchers spoke to expressed a startling disregard for the pleasure of female hookup partners: one said that in a relationship, he was 'all about making her orgasm', but in the context of a one-time thing, 'I don't give a shit'. Men who were equally invested in their female partner's pleasure in both relationships *and* hookups were the minority. Women, however, felt that ensuring their male partners orgasmed was compulsory, with one remarking that it was the defining factor of whether something qualified as sex: 'I don't feel like I've had a sexual experience if the guy doesn't come.' Others told of participating in sexual acts they didn't like to make sure their partners achieved orgasm.[11] Female desire, it seems, is something that can be easily overlooked; disregarded as not important or compelling. Men *need* sexual pleasure while women lie back and think of England; or rather, they think of England while actively participating in sexual acts they don't enjoy.

This can be true even outside of heterosexual relationships. Just compare the stereotypes attached to lesbians versus those attached to gay men. One of my interviewees, Sam, entered into the gay community at their university, only to find that being asexual 'made me feel like an impostor in LGBT spaces'. Being perceived as gay, and as a man, Sam felt the pressure of the 'hypersexual gay man' stereotype: the image of queer men as sexually obsessed and constantly lustful. Being ace meant being on the outside of the story told about queer men.

You don't have to be ace to end up outside that story. In a thesis examining the portrayal of men in magazines marketed to queer men, Bener Eshref points out that most images in such magazines are hypersexualized, portraying men with hyper-masculine body types, often in sexualized poses, and in advertisements for sexual products, 'like underwear, male enhancement materials, and pornographic items'.[12] These magazines, Eshref found, focused primarily on younger, white, skinny men with well-muscled physiques: the most conventionally sexually attractive man, according to normative societal standards. Anyone outside of those categories receives the message that this is not what a queer man looks like. A queer man, as well as being young, white and skinny, is overtly sexual.

Queer women are absolutely victims of sexualization, too, often in a fetishistic way, as evidenced by how 'lesbian' is the most-searched term on Pornhub.[13] But at the same time, queer women are affected by beliefs that they are *less* sexual. In a now much-maligned 1983 study, the sociologists Pepper Schwartz and Philip Blumstein claimed that couples consisting of two women had sex less frequently than any other couple type, with sex decreasing more the older the couple got.[14] This study led to the creation of the phrase 'lesbian bed death' to describe this phenomenon, a term that quickly became commonplace. There are dozens of online articles about how to stop lesbian bed death from happening to you and your partner.

Critics have pointed out that lesbian bed death is based on flimsy evidence. For a start, a dropping-off in sexual activity occurs over time in a majority of relationships, regardless of gender. And, as writer Daisy Jones points out, it was a mistake for the researchers to make assumptions about all queer women based on a single question about how often they 'had sex'. 'The definition of "sexual relations" also differs from couple to couple,' Jones writes. 'For straight people, sex might mean penetrative sex. For queers, the definition might encompass a broader range of acts (a lot of straight people don't consider oral sex alone as "full sex", for example).'[15] What's more, as Jones and many others have made clear, subsequent studies have found that queer women, even if they have sex less frequently, report having more pleasurable and satisfying sex, and explore far more sexual activities.[16] And yet, as all those online advice columns demonstrate, the myth of lesbian bed death persists, with content creators making money by writing about 'What Lesbian Bed Death is and how to prevent it', and giving women '11 Tips to Fix Lesbian Bed Death'. Regardless of the evidence, women are once again being portrayed as less sexual, less desirous and less focused on sexual pleasure – especially in comparison with queer men.

One part of Andrejek, Fetner and Heath's study was particularly unsettling. It suggests that part of the reason for the labelling of oral sex, hand jobs and other forms of sex that are more conducive to female pleasure as 'alternative' or dirty is that *women's pleasure* has so often been seen as shameful. As another investigation into the orgasm gap found, we generally no longer stigmatize those who have premarital sex (except in certain religious and conservative settings). 'The older version of the sexual double standard, in which women are judged more harshly than men for having premarital sex, is largely dead. However, a new version of the sexual double standard, *in which women who seek sexual pleasure outside of committed relationships are judged more harshly than men who do so* [my emphasis], has emerged in its place [...] men are assumed to have a strong, active drive to seek sex, whereas women are viewed as more sexually passive, responding to men's desire.' As a result, the study says, 'Women [...] may not feel entitled to communicate their sexual desires.'[17] This is especially the case in sexual activity outside of relationships, such as hookups: 'Asked the question, *have you ever hooked up with someone and afterward had the feeling that the person respected you less because you hooked up with him/her*, 54 percent of heterosexual women but only 22 percent of heterosexual men said yes.'[18]

Female desire is so often shamed where it appears, whether it takes the form of people shaming Afana for wearing lipstick or Taylor Swift portraying a girl who'd wear a sexy red dress as selfish and unworthy of a good boyfriend. And yet, women are still compelled to have sex, even in secular environments. A woman should not be a prude any more than she should be a slut. She should avoid becoming the cold career woman or the crazy cat lady. Women's own desires are downplayed and repressed, and yet they must provide sex for men. It's assumed they don't want it, but they must have it.

This is how compulsory sexuality reinforces rape culture – a culture in which sexual assault is normalized and not challenged. And these gendered pressures of compsex only enforce it more. For men, compsex increases the risk of sexual assault because, as Jessie Ford's interviewees told her, they're 'supposed to want it all the time' and they would 'get shit' for speaking up about sexual assault. For women, the risk is increased because women should not have sexual desire, or at least nor too much. Their not wanting sex is expected – *but they must be sexually available to men anyway.*

*

A few years ago, Canton Winer set out to perform a comparative study of how gender and asexuality affected each other. How does gender impact how you experience asexuality, and how does asexuality affect how you experience gender? He planned to sort his interviewees into three groups: men, women and those beyond the binary. But as soon as he started conducting interviews and asking ace people about gender, that plan fell apart.

All of Winer's respondents gave him a gender identity when initially asked, some binary and some not. 'But when you actually poked,' Winer said, 'and asked things like, *What does gender feel like to you? Are you attached to your gender identity?* That was when it all began to crumble.' In his paper on the topic, Winer describes how many respondents 'felt uncomfortable with being interpreted through the lens of gender. They found gender presentation or identity to be irrelevant, pointless or even oppressive.'[19] Even those who initially described themselves as agender often said that they weren't closely attached to that descriptor; it was simply the closest word these ace people had to express the fact that they didn't feel they had a gender identity at all; that they felt entirely detached from gender as a concept.

I understood. I felt the same.

Traditional models of sexuality and gender identity posit these as discrete and separate things. But I'm not so sure. Many of my interviewees, just like Winer's, frequently told me that they felt their aspec identity had in some way caused a sense of removal from gender. 'Attraction and gender are a feedback loop, right?' says K (she/they). 'When you see someone you're attracted to, it's not just about what they look like – they resonate with your own self-concept of who you are, and who you want to be attractive *to.* If they're interested back, it closes the loop, because your interest in them validates their self-concept of being able to attract the kind of person they desire and want to be desirable to. But being ace, though – that attraction-drive just isn't there. And that means there's not much motivation to Do Gender as part of that whole apparatus. That makes the whole thing kind of vestigial. Being ace makes gender stop being load-bearing for me. It's still *there*, because it's not really worth the effort to demolish, but I could knock it down without compromising the building integrity.'

No doubt this detachment from gender is a huge contributor to the seemingly disproportionate number of nonbinary and genderqueer aspecs. But, fascinatingly, plenty of aspecs who didn't call themselves nonbinary or genderqueer also expressed this sense that gender was pointless to them. Even some who *are* nonbinary echoed this sentiment. K identifies as genderqueer now, but isn't troubled by being perceived as a woman. 'I'm AFAB [assigned female at birth], and other people do the heavy lifting,' she says. For a longtime, she wasn't 'attached enough to being female to really embrace it, but not *not* female enough to identify as nonbinary. I rounded down to female the way pi rounds down to three.' Even though she now knows that genderqueer is the most accurate word for her, 'it's still not uncomfortable enough to be worth changing anything about.'

When I asked my respondents for their gender identity, I tried to leave the question open, asking not '*what* is your gender identity' but 'how would you describe your gender identity?', trying to allow for people who might not identify with a particular label. Even that didn't take into account the number of people who had no way to describe it at all. 'I wouldn't.' 'I don't describe it.' 'Mostly, I'd just like to be seen as myself, with a disregard for gender.' 'I don't know, I just kinda vibe.' 'Ambivalent.' 'Just a vague shape floating in the immeasurable abyss.' My personal favourite: 'It's like a tangled-up ball of string. The more I look into it, the more confused I get. I think I found a few flowers in there, my favourite mechanical pencil that I lost for two years… I gave up on looking deeper a while back.' And perhaps most telling of all: 'I wish gender were opt-in instead of opt-out, and I would not opt in.'

Not opting in perhaps encapsulates the experience that so many aspec people have with gender. As Winer put it when I discussed this with him, 'We don't live in a paradigm that allows you to opt out of the system of gender categorization whatsoever, so people say they're agender, because that's the closest you can get to saying, "I abstain".' And that was my mistake when I wrote the survey: I didn't account for people who wanted to abstain altogether. I assumed that everyone would *have* a gender identity. But reading my interviewees' responses made me realize that not everyone does – and, indeed, *I* don't. Compulsory sexuality, for me, brought with it a kind of compulsory gender, even after I realized that I stood outside the binary. Refusing compulsory sexuality meant refusing that compulsory gendering too.

I still prefer to present androgynously, not because it ties me to a particular gender identity but because it helps me feel like

I'm inhabiting a space of having not opted into gender. Often, I feel like I can choose the 'best of' from binary genders. I choose plaid, jackets, purple, boots, and bird motifs for what they do for me, not for the sake of modelling a gender identity. Which was a sentiment common among Canton Winer's interviewees as well; many of the ace folks he spoke to told him that they dressed in certain ways because they'd been doing that for so long, but didn't feel like those particular aspects of self-presentation felt gendered at all; other people might read femininity into a dress or masculinity into short hair, but to the ace people who chose them, these simply felt like clothes and haircuts and aspects of presentation. They had nothing to do with gender. And I feel similarly. Realizing that I was nonbinary made me understand that I didn't *have* to shave my pits or legs or arms, or pluck my eyebrows. But I don't think I do these things *because* I'm nonbinary, or because they're considered unfeminine. Not doing these things feels like a completely neutral act. It's letting my body be my body.

So perhaps it's time to rework our models for gender and sexuality to reflect that the two are not necessarily distinct, and that the answer to both can be 'no'. My gender, romantic orientation and sexual orientation feel connected – indeed, inseparable. Calling myself an aromantic, asexual agender person is the easiest way to communicate what goes on inside of me to others – that is what labels are for, after all – but I don't feel like those three identities are distinct. I am not an equation of aro + ace + agender = me. My identity feels like a single thing. Perhaps the most accurate thing I could put on a form that asks for my gender would be *aroace.* And I believe this is always who I was, right back when my mother *knew*, somehow, that she wasn't having a girl.

5

Love Languages

Sex and Consent

When Luna met Ana, she knew she had found someone with whom she didn't need to hide. Both first-year students, roommates, both queer, sharing many of the same interests and friends – Luna had no qualms about telling Ana that she was aroace.

It hadn't always been so easy. When Luna had told her friends in secondary school, they immediately outed her to everyone. The first boy to ask her out had soon treated her to a long soliloquy about how she could clearly never love him. (Luna sat there wondering why on earth that was *her* problem.) But with Ana, it was easy. With Ana, she could laugh over how different their experiences could often be. Ana would show her a photo of a woman in a dress, and Luna would remark on how amazing the dress looked. 'Luna,' Ana would say, 'this is a horny photo.'

'It *is?* I thought it was just showing off the dress!'

'No! It's sexy!'

'No!'

Everything was easy, for both of them – until the night before Halloween. In preparation for the festivities, they got dressed up and blindingly drunk. Luna's bed was too strewn with makeup for her to sleep on it, and Ana was quick to offer a solution. 'I told her not to worry about cleaning it up,' Ana remembers. 'She could stay in my room.'

Luna laughs. 'And I thought, yeah, this is logical!'

'Ana was not being logical,' Ana says.

She hadn't fully realized her crush on Luna until that night. But it was hard to ignore when they ended up kissing, and when Luna spent the night sleeping on Ana's bed. Waking up, Ana was struck with a horrific hangover and a sizeable pile of guilt.

'I didn't really know much about what being aro meant,' she says, 'and I thought it meant that Luna would not have a romantic relationship or do anything normally considered romantic. So I felt that by kissing her, I'd violated her boundaries. I hadn't respected her being aroace.'

Luna, already awake, was oblivious to Ana's angst. Why shouldn't kissing be a thing close friends did? 'How you doing?' she asked, perfectly cheerful.

'Nngh,' Ana said.

'That was a fun night!'

'*Nnngh.*'

The incident left Luna wondering: what did she want her relationship with Ana to be? Luna didn't – couldn't – have romantic feelings for her. But she loved the idea of being Ana's person. Being in some kind of committed relationship with her would be incredible. And she knew that being aro didn't take relationships off the table – because many aromantics have queerplatonic partnerships.

Queerplatonic partnerships, or QPPs (also called a queerplatonic relationship or QPR) are hard to define by their very nature. They're intimate partnerships, though by no means limited to two people, that aren't traditionally romantic. They're platonic bonds that are somehow 'queered', in that they don't fit neatly into the expected structure of either a romance or a traditional friendship.

What Luna had in mind was just one possible variation. Luna was absolutely fine with Ana having romantic feelings for her, as long as Ana was content for Luna to love her and be her partner without having romantic feelings in return. And so she told Ana, 'I want us to have a queerplatonic relationship.'

Ana, unfortunately, did not know what a QPP was. She heard 'platonic', thought Luna was ruling out any kind of relationship, and gave her a disappointed *okay* while silently despairing.

'And I was like, great!' Luna remembers. 'We have reached a conclusion!'

Ana shakes her head. 'Ana did not think we had reached a conclusion.'

*

For some, stories like Luna's sound at first like a paradox. She's aroace, but she was okay with kissing Ana? She loves Ana platonically, not romantically, but wanted to be in a relationship? How does that *work?*

The answer to the question of why an aro person would have a relationship, or why an ace person would have sex, is deeply individual to the aspec person in question. But here's perhaps the most important thing to understand: *action is not attraction.* In other words, the behaviours you perform in a sexual or romantic scenario do not define who you are attracted to.

We already know this to be true. Imagine a gay person in a time period or country where having a same-sex partner is not an option. They might well marry and have sex with an opposite-gender partner; many gay people did, and do, exactly this. They are still gay, regardless of the fact that they're in a relationship with an opposite-gender partner. Or picture a straight person who's questioning their sexuality, explores a same-sex relationship, and eventually ascertains that they're straight. Or an aroace person who hasn't realized that they're aroace, perhaps because they don't know that being aroace is even a *thing*, and has a relationship with someone. In all of these situations, the people involved took romantic and/or sexual actions that didn't match up with their orientation.

Even when someone engages in romantic or sexual activity with someone of a gender they do find attractive, there are plenty of instances in which someone might have sex without being attracted to the person involved, such as a sex worker who doesn't have any attraction to their partner, or a one night stand between people who are just in the mood to have sex and find it enjoyable. One last time: sexual and romantic *behaviour* is not the same as sexual and romantic *attraction*.

I learned this from experience. As a teen, I felt a crushing desire to *prove* to myself that I was aroace by avoiding anything sexual. I refused to make any kind of sexual joke, terrified that it invalidated my asexuality; whenever I read romantic fanfiction and felt a thrill at reading about two fictional characters kissing or having sex, I felt a whirl of bewilderment and guilt. How could I do any of these things if I was aroace?

The answer, of course, is that none of these things had anything to do with attraction. Sexual actions and sexual attraction are often conflated; so, too, are the concepts of attraction, libido and arousal. Libido, or sex drive, is the desire for sexual release and sexual pleasure. Allo friends have described it to me as like being hungry but without having a specific food in mind, or like needing to scratch an itch. It's an urge that's not directed at anyone in particular. Arousal is the experience of getting 'turned on', your body getting excited when you think about sex, or when you start to engage in sexual activity. And attraction is the desire to have sex with a specific person, or finding that specific person attractive. To continue the food metaphor, it's craving a specific food rather than being generally hungry.

Some aces, like myself, find that their levels of libido or arousal are lesser than many allos'. My libido is non-existent, and that little buzz that comes with reading romantic or sexual content is the closest thing to arousal that I ever experience. But levels of libido and arousal vary between aces just as they do between allos. Cake and their partner, for instance, are both ace, but can both sometimes find their bodies craving sex even though that craving isn't targeted at any particular person. 'There's an understanding that bodies sometimes want things that our brains don't agree with,' Cake says, 'and that going for a wank to get it out of our systems doesn't change a lack of interest in having sex.' Other aces might have sex because they enjoy the physical sensation, to experience intimacy with their partners, to conceive, because their partner wants it and they're happy to do it for them, because they find that arousal tends to begin once they start engaging in sexual activity, or for an array of other, often highly individual reasons.

This all requires a lot of thinking about sex – not just about the act itself, but the intricacies of why we have it, what we want from sexual encounters, what sexual activity is and isn't. Not every aspec person delves into it all in this much detail, but for many of us, understanding these differences – picking apart all the things that allonormative culture tends to conflate – is often essential to understanding ourselves. Spike (it/its) found that figuring out the difference between libido and attraction was the missing link that allowed it to finally realize that it was definitely ace. 'I would read explicit fanfiction,' Spike says, 'and I jerked off, I felt arousal. All of that masked my lack of desire to actually have sex. It wasn't until I got into my twenties, had ample chances to have sex but chose not to [that] it felt absurd not to admit to myself that I had no desire.'

The result is that the stereotype of aces as clueless about everything towards sex is not just infantilizing but often wildly inaccurate. Indeed, some of the aces I interviewed felt that their asexuality gives them a deeper understanding of sex than some of their allo peers. Scout (any pronouns), for example, finds allo friends going to them for advice about things they've never examined in detail, because they've never needed to. 'I can explain to you the difference between arousal, attraction, and consent,' Scout says, 'and then I can give examples of all the various situations that can arise from the combinations of the three. Do you know how many allo people can't even explain consent?'

As it turns out, the answer is *quite a lot.* And that is a problem.

*

A few years ago, MaDha (she/her), a communications student from Colombia, reconnected with an old friend, a boy she'd had a crush on in school. They got talking, and the boy asked MaDha to his house to play some video games and watch some films. Delighted, MaDha showed up with her favourite movie, anticipating a comfy few hours sharing her interests with someone she liked. But the boy had other plans.

'In the middle of the movie, he started touching me,' MaDha says. 'I moved away. I told him I was asexual and didn't like these things. He just laughed, and after a while it started again. I had to stop him by pretending I wanted to save myself until marriage – an obvious lie. Only then did he leave me alone.'

What baffled MaDha was how many people asked, *well, how didn't you see it coming?* 'They said to me, "how did you not notice? If someone asks you to go to their house to watch movies, it's a plan to fuck, it's very obvious." And I was like, "No, if they tell me we're going to watch movies, it's... to watch the movie." From that day I understood that allo people have their own codes.'

Let's stop and consider this for a moment. What exactly was the code that led MaDha's crush to think he had been given a 'green light' to begin making sexual advances? It is culturally understood by many (though not by all) that extending an invitation to someone to come to your house and watch movies can be a tacit request for sex – how exactly have so many people learned this? And why did the boy assume that just by coming over to play games and watch movies, MaDha had somehow consented to sexual interaction?

MaDha is onto something when she says that there's a kind of 'code' that allo people understand intuitively. Hubert Izienicki, a professor of behavioural studies at Purdue University, has an exercise he likes to carry out with his classes: he asks them whether they think the patterns of behaviour that people perform in sexual encounters are essentialist – in other words, they're somehow innate and intrinsic to humans – or whether they're learned. In other words, are these behaviours spontaneous or scripted?[1]

To begin with, many of Izienicki's students vote for *spontaneous.* Isn't that what makes these encounters sexy: the spontaneous advances, the way one thing naturally leads to another in a passionate flow? And that's when Izienicki introduces the students to the idea of *sexual scripts*: the theory that there are unspoken patterns for how participants behave in sexual situations (or in situations that they hope will become sexual). He asks them how they might go about completing a sexual script that's familiar to many young people: 'Netflix and Chill'. It's a similar script to the one MaDha's crush was trying to employ, that of inviting someone over under the pretence of watching Netflix shows, with the intention of having sex. And all of Izienicki's students are able to provide a script for performing Netflix and Chill, with a typical list of steps going like this:

> (1) invitation, (2) shower, (3) turn on Netflix, (4) pick a show, (5) have snacks (not to be eaten), (6) decide on a setting (couch or room), (7) start the show, (8) lean in for the cuddle, (9) make a move, (10) take off clothes, (11) foreplay, (12) sex, (13) clean up juices, (14) shirts and undies back on, (15) restart the show, (16) actually chill and snack, (17) go for time number two.

Even students who've never participated in a sexual encounter of this kind recognized the steps and were able to make a list, and all of them tend to agree on the rough outline that the script takes. I have no interest whatever in sex and have never engaged in any kind of script like this, but I still knew the rough framework. I knew that, as Izienicki puts it, 'In a heteronormative script [...] touching comes before kissing, kissing comes before heavy petting, and oral sex occurs before penetrative intercourse. A person needs to complete each step before moving on to the next one in that culturally prescribed order.' In other words, one thing leads to another. So ingrained is this script that even UK law echoes it: oral sex with someone who isn't your spouse does not count as adultery, while penetrative sex does. It's as if oral sex is some preliminary or secondary form of sex, without the weight carried by 'real', penetrative sex.

Such scripts are not known instinctively; they are learned. We aren't born with the knowledge that if someone who's been flirting with you invites you to their home to watch a movie, it might be the first step towards having sex. We learn from the internet, from social media, from media that we watch and read, from pornography, from conversations with friends. 'Drawing on these resources,' Izienicki says, '[young people] learn what to do and how to be sexual, a process that is rarely clear or obvious to them.' We absorb cultural norms for sexual scenarios, and we emulate them.

And all too often, these scripts skip around the issue of consent, or don't include it at all.

In a 1984 study of sexual scripts, William Simon and John H. Gagnon mapped out the pattern of the traditional heterosexual sexual script: 'the male makes a move, and the female then engages in token resistance before eventually submitting to sexual activity'.[2] It's a formula we recognize from the trope of a woman 'playing hard to get'; think of 'Baby, It's Cold Outside', Frank Loesser's 1944 Christmas song, where the male singer makes advances and the woman's feigned excuses are part of a dance they're both taking towards sex. Crucially, in this script, 'sexual consent is negotiated non-verbally, or not at all'. And rejection is just a part of the script – often, as MaDha found, to the cost of a partner who *does* mean their refusal. It's easy to see the parallel between this script and the assumptions about gendered desire I discussed in the last chapter: men are assumed to always want sex, and so the man is portrayed as the active pursuer, the one who wants and initiates. Women are assumed to 'put up' with male desire, or at least to not want sex anywhere near as much or as often as men. They are the passive participant, the pursued, described as *submitting* to sex; they make a 'token resistance' because female desire is shameful. The woman cannot want it too much without being 'easy', so she has to be *convinced* into sex for her behaviour to be acceptable.

Five decades later, sexual scripts still leave out discussions of consent. Izienicki notes that his students' typical lists usually don't include asking for consent at any point. Look at that script for 'Netflix and Chill', and you'll notice the similarity to MaDha's experience. The boy reached step 9, fully expecting to move on to the subsequent parts of the script, before he found out that MaDha didn't want to have sex. Because in this kind of script, consent is assumed; if you've come over to watch Netflix, you've registered your interest in sex.

Except you might not have. You might be aspec and never have had an interest in the types of sexual, romantic media that would clue you in to the other person's intention. You might be familiar with the idea of 'Netflix and Chill' but be so unused to thinking of yourself in sexual or romantic situations that the pieces don't connect. You might be autistic or have any neurodivergence which makes it difficult for you to pick up on unspoken implications. You might just genuinely want to watch Netflix. For many aces, the idea that engaging in one form of intimacy could give unspoken permission for another is incomprehensible. '*Why* does one thing lead to another?' complains Magdalena (she/her). 'We've just been cuddling, and now you're horny? Sounds fake.'

And even for those who know how these scripts go, they are not always a helpful framework for how to proceed in sexual encounters. In the worst circumstances, they can pressure people to follow the script through to the end, even if they don't want to. In Jessie Ford's study of consensual but unwanted sex among college students, several stated that they felt that once they'd given a 'green light' for sex, such as getting into a taxi with someone, going home with them or kissing them, they had a responsibility to 'finish what they started'. 'I felt I had to go all the way,' said one. 'It was just necessary.'[3]

A study by the *Journal of Sex Research* asked students to keep diaries of their sexual relations over several weeks, and 38 per cent – regardless of gender – said that they engaged in consensual but unwanted sex. Another study, in 2005, found that 28 per cent of women said that their first time having sex was consensual, but not wanted.[4] There are myriad reasons why someone might agree to sex they don't want, ranging from a conviction that sex is essential to their gender role, to that all-too-common assumption fuelled by compulsory sexuality that when there's an unequal level of sexual wants between people, the partner with the greater level of desire – the normative level of desire – should be prioritized. And then there's the 'saving face' motivation; the feeling that going along with sex will avoid the guilt of feeling that they had 'led someone on', or the awkwardness and social tension that comes with breaking script.

Then, awful though it is, there's the fear of violence. Once you've found yourself alone with someone in a sexual situation, what happens when you retract consent? The risks of such situations are illustrated neatly in a scene from the sitcom *It's Always Sunny in Philadelphia*, whose main characters are, quite deliberately, terrible people. In one episode, they buy a boat, and one character outlines his intention to invite women aboard, and why he's certain of success:

> She's out in the middle of nowhere with some dude she barely knows. She looks around and what does she see? Nothing but open ocean. 'Aah, there's nowhere for me to run. What am I going to do? Say no?' [...] She's not going to

> say no. She would never say no. Because of the implication. […] The implication that things might go wrong for her if she refuses to sleep with me.

It doesn't have to be a boat, of course. It could be anywhere. This is the danger of sexual scripts that assume consent without discussing it, especially those that portray women as 'submitting' to sex (though anyone can end up in these situations, regardless of gender).

Even when everyone involved *does* want sex, there may be specific acts that one or both don't want to engage in, and these should be negotiated, just as sex itself should be. But some acts can become so normalized by the sources that teach us sexual scripts that people may not realize they need to ask for consent. A 2023 *Guardian* column about readers' sex lives featured a young couple named Luke and Kali, who discussed how Luke had put his hands around Kali's neck during sex. Kali hadn't enjoyed it, and Luke later admitted that he didn't much like it either but had felt it was normal and something he had to do in the bedroom. Why? Because it was something he'd seen in pornography.[5]

Increasingly, young people are learning their sexual scripts from pornography. And frankly, I can see why. I learned more from reading the odd erotic fanfiction than I ever did in my school's sexual education classes. I left school knowing a number of sexually transmitted infections (STIs) by name and what their symptoms were, but not how gay or oral sex worked, or having any in-depth discussion of consent beyond 'don't have sex with someone who says no'. When theatre director Abbey Wright asked 10,000 UK children and teenagers about their experiences with pornography as material for her play *Why Is the Sky Blue?*, which explores the effects of porn on young people, they 'universally ridiculed' the sex ed they were receiving in school, saying that porn was filling in what their teachers hadn't. This was especially true for queer kids for whom sex ed is especially lacking; one gay teen spoke of how just seeing gay porn was a 'massive relief', and a young trans man of colour said that, while he knew porn fetishized both his race and his transgender identity, it had been essential for him. 'At least it's *a* depiction. I can look and see – OK, how might I go about trying to get off with someone? [...] There isn't anywhere else I can go to learn this stuff.'[6,7]

And it's not just queer kids; in the USA, only twenty-two states mandate that children receive sex education at all, and only thirteen require that it be medically accurate.[8] In 2015, government funding for abstinence-only programmes stood at $75 million a year, a sum then matched by some states.[9] As a result, thousands of students receive nothing but abstinence-only education, and this education is profoundly lacking. A US Government Accountability Office study found that some abstinence-only programmes taught that touching a person's genitals could cause pregnancy, that condoms fail to prevent HIV transmission 31 per cent of the time (the actual figure is less than 3 per cent), and that a forty-three-day-old foetus is a 'thinking person'.[10] In her book *Pure: Inside the Evangelical Movement that Shamed a Generation of Young Women and How I Broke Free*, Linda Kay Klein speaks of people raised in purity culture not knowing what testicles were until their twenties, and thinking that a penis goes into a vagina and then 'just sits there'. Small wonder that people might turn to porn to fill the gaps.[11]

But porn often leaves out crucial aspects of what healthy sex looks like. For a start, contraception is rarely shown in porn; you'll notice that in the 'Netflix and Chill' script, there's no mention of contraception – perhaps the influence of porn at work. (This also feeds into the all-too-common assumption that women will already be on birth control, which in turn promotes the idea that contraception is in some way a woman's responsibility.) And porn generally runs true to those sexual scripts where consent is non-verbal or not a factor at all. Since conversations about what people want or about consent are considered an arousal-killer, and spontaneity is supposedly the sexiest thing there is, these discussions don't happen in porn scripts. 'Most of the young women I interviewed had experienced problems around consent,' Wright says. 'This would often revolve around young men performing sexual acts they had seen in pornography without asking.'[12] Porn frequently treats acts like choking or unlubricated anal sex as normal, without making it clear that these can be dangerous, potentially painful and vulnerable acts that absolutely must be discussed and mutually agreed to. (These discussions don't have to be anything complicated. One couple I spoke to told me that they have a 'sex checklist' of things that they're happy to do or not do during sex, and that's absolutely a good idea if it works for you. At the other end of the scale, simply asking your partner what they want, whether they want to do a certain thing, and 'is this okay' in the moment is usually all you need.)

And then there's the risk of porn giving people erroneous beliefs about sex. A great deal of porn involves women crying during sex, which can mean that less experienced partners think it's normal for a woman to cry when they're having sex with them. In one awful case in the UK, a fourteen-year-old boy accused of rape was asked why he didn't stop when the girl started crying. He replied, 'because it's normal for girls to cry during sex'.[13] It was what always happened in porn.

Just watching porn does not necessarily mean your understanding of consent is eroded. Indeed, a 2013 study that set out to examine the effects of porn consumption on sex found that there wasn't a correlation between frequency of porn viewing and a belief that consent was less important. But crucially, there was one factor that made men (though not women) more likely to believe that asking for consent would be 'weird'. That factor? Not whether they watched porn, but whether they perceived pornography to be realistic. 'Pornography as a whole,' the study concludes, 'reinforces the traditional sex script, which negotiates sexual consent through nonverbal cues or not at all.'[14]

So if sexual scripts – whether learned from porn or just from cultural osmosis – so often fail us, what motivates people to use them?

While I was writing this chapter, this question sometimes truly baffled me. I understood that people might want plausible deniability when seeking sex with others, but there seemed to be a paradox built into the fabric of scripts like 'Netflix and Chill' and I called my friend Jan to ask him for his perspective. 'Maybe you can explain this to me,' I said. 'If you ask someone to come over and watch movies as a code for "do you want to have sex", then you're avoiding the awkward question itself. If someone agrees to that, then they've registered an interest in having sex with you.'

'That's absolutely it,' Jan said.

'But there's a paradox in that, right? It can only work if both parties understand what's really being asked. Otherwise' – MaDha's story flashed through my head – 'you could end up with someone making a move and the other person not wanting it, not realizing that they'd even been asked for sex at all. So, if the whole apparatus only works if everyone involves *knows* you're talking about sex, *why pretend you're not asking for sex in the first place?*'

'Fear of rejection,' Jan told me instantly. 'Liking someone feels so good, and being desired gives you so much validation. It helps you feel loveable. So saying what you want out loud means exposing yourself to the possibility that they say *no.* And that can be devastating. So you do the whole song and dance instead. You invite them over, there's a moment where you hold their gaze, then you move in. And in healthier circumstances, hopefully there's a moment where one person says, 'Do you want this?' But I get why people don't, because just following from one thing to another, not saying it out loud… you never have to make yourself that vulnerable.'

'So these templates – they allow people to get sex and intimacy without the awkward, painful business of expressing that you want someone?'

'Exactly.'

I pondered this. 'But surely that moment of risk is inevitable in the end? I mean, eventually you're either going to have to bite the bullet and ask *do you want this,* like you said, or you make a move and risk that you're crossing their boundaries, because they don't want it.'

'Yes,' Jan said, 'and I think the latter really is less scary for people.'

This made me terribly sad. We have a society where the fear of being unwanted is so powerful and so crushing that we cannot look for intimacy without couching it in euphemism and pretending not to be looking for what we want. Confessing that you want someone is scarier than the fear of crossing someone's boundaries. It is so hard to think and talk about sexuality that we rely on scripts that help us get sex, but don't give us a template to help us ask for what we want or set up boundaries that we need.

But then Jan told me something else. 'Allos – especially straight, cisgender allos – can just assume their sexuality is the default, so they don't examine it. I think being ace actually gives you an advantage here, because you've had to think hard about your sexuality from a young age, so the paradox is obvious to you, as it might not be to other people.'

And perhaps he's right. Perhaps aspec people do have an advantage here. Because while those sexual scripts don't work for us much of the time, the upshot is: we cannot rely on them, and so we learn to build new frameworks. We know that one thing does not have to lead to another. Aspecs have had to think hard about our sexuality and about our own wants. We've had to build our own languages for sex and consent. And our tools are things that allos can use, too.

*

Over the next few months of their not-quite-relationship, Ana was panicking. Luna wanted a platonic relationship, which meant she wasn't allowed to do anything that might be seen as romantic. She had to respect Luna's aroace identity. She asked Luna not to touch her, not to sit on the same bed as her.

'I was so confused,' Luna says. 'I was going, did I piss her off? Is she afraid of me? How did I fuck up?'

'Meanwhile I was thinking, I'm doing such a good job!' Ana laughs. 'She'll never suspect I've got a crush! I had everything planned out: I'd marry a man, because I couldn't marry a woman or it'd be Luna, and then I'd just be best friends with Luna forever. Flawless strategy. No notes.'

But eventually, Luna just asked the question: 'Ana, what are we? Are we dating?'

'And I,' Ana says, 'could only think, *no! My cover is blown!*'

She tearfully confessed everything – her long-term feelings for Luna, how she'd obviously disrespected Luna's aroace identity just by *having* such feelings, how she understood if Luna never wanted her to talk to her again…

'Ana,' Luna interrupted. '*What are you talking about?*'

And so they had a conversation – a real one, this time. With Luna explaining what kind of a relationship she wanted, and both of them working together to figure out exactly where Luna's boundaries lay.

It's an ongoing, constant conversation. Once they agreed to a relationship, Luna quickly found herself flirting with Ana in the way she'd seen people flirt in books and films. 'And when I got a reaction, I'd think, aw, that was cute! I'm such a great girlfriend!' And Ana had to explain, '*Luna, flirting with me turns me on. Constantly. This makes me want to have sex with you.*'

'It was a whole hour-long conversation,' Ana remembers. 'Flirting genuinely can make your level of attraction go from 0 per cent to 100 per cent, whereas Luna thought it was putting me in maybe the top 50 per cent. The thing about being in a relationship with an aspec person is that you have to keep explaining things you assumed would be instinctual – on both sides. Because a lot of it feels instinctual, and it *is* for allo people. There's so much secret context that I didn't think I'd have to explain.'

'That's what I think the difference is between us and a standard relationship,' Luna says. 'As time went on, I felt I needed the label QPP less; we're honestly not too far out of what people would consider a "normal" relationship, even though I don't experience attraction. The difference is conversation. We have to communicate more.'

What both wished they'd had, in the early days of that communication, was a guide: anything that could have clued them in to what they would need to have conversations about. Something to help them navigate that 'secret context' that Luna would be surprised by and that Ana had never realized she'd have to explain. 'A lot of existing ace resources tell ace stories and tell you what asexuality is,' Ana says, 'but they don't give any advice. *Here's what sex could look like for you and your ace partner, here's what you're going to have to talk about.*'

I could never possibly address every issue that an aspec person might encounter where sex is concerned. Again: every aspec person and every relationship they might form is entirely unique. What works for one person or dynamic will not work for another. But when I asked my interviewees for their advice on navigating sex, consent and relationships, several broad themes emerged.

While this advice is largely intended for aspecs and their partners, it is by no means unique to us. Much of it is a response to the lack of consent discussion built into sexual scripts, and these can affect anyone. Differences in the levels of sexual desire that partners have can occur between allos. Sex can mean more to one partner than another in any relationship. If any of the advice here speaks to you, then it is yours. (Though I use the term 'your partner' in much of this advice, it can apply regardless of how many partners are involved, such as in a polyamorous relationship.)

1. Work out, and discuss with any partners, what sex means to you – but understand that it may mean something different to each of you

For every aspec person, sex is something different. It might be a *never*, a hard line, something you have absolutely no interest in engaging in. It might be an intense form of intimacy, something you might not particularly desire but which you're happy to engage in for your partner, or it might be no more special to you than folding laundry. You might know it will never be for you, just as you wouldn't need to roll in mud to know you're firmly averse to the idea of mud-rolling; it might be something you've never done but are curious about trying to see if it's pleasurable, or something you're sure you'd enjoy and want quite actively to have. All of this is fine.

But, at the risk of stating the obvious, your partner cannot possibly know where you stand unless you tell them, even if they themself are aspec. After all, sex to them might mean something very different from what it does to you.

Many aces find the language of 'sex stances' useful for communicating their feelings on the subject. These aren't political positions about sex; rather, they're used to describe a person's feelings toward sexual interaction:

- A **sex-favourable** person feels positive and favourable towards the idea of engaging in sex. For example, Gwyn, who enjoys sex as a way of bonding with their partner, is a sex-favourable asexual. (Not to be confused with sex-positivity, which is a political stance about generally embracing people's sexual freedom.)
- A **sex-indifferent** person doesn't have strong feelings about sexual interaction. They aren't opposed to engaging in it, but neither are they actively favourable. A sex-indifferent person might, for example, not seek sex under their own initiative, but be happy to have it if their partner asks, seeing it as just one more fun activity they can do together.
- A **sex-repulsed** person is repulsed by the concept of sexual interaction.

- A **sex-averse** person is averse towards *personally engaging* in sexual interaction. This is where I fall on the spectrum. I differ from a sex-repulsed person in that, while I absolutely do not want to have sex, my discomfort only extends to the idea of myself, personally, having it. Talking about sex is completely comfortable, as is engaging in sexual jokes, as long as it's with friends I trust; reading sexual content is fine too.
- A **sex-ambivalent** person has mixed feelings towards engaging in sexual interaction.
- A **sex-oscillating** person might fall into any one of these categories at any given moment, as their position and attitude towards sex shift with time.
- A **sex-drained** person is averse towards sexual interaction because of trauma or exhaustion.

The terms for most of these stances have existed in the ace community for years, although their exact source isn't clear; we have a Reddit user, AnoymousHermitCrab, to thank for compiling them and coining the latter two.[15]

It's important to remember that these stances aren't meant to be identities, or boxes to fit into. They're intended as language to help us understand our own feelings towards sex, and communicate our wants and limits to others. (It took learning the label 'sex-averse' to realize that I didn't have to be repulsed by anything sexual to qualify as ace.) Neither are these stances monoliths. While I am best described as sex-averse, there are certain situations where I will be more sex-repulsed. Reading sex scenes is (usually) fine for me; watching any kind of sex scene that goes beyond a fade-to-black is often uncomfortable. Similarly, an otherwise sex-repulsed person might be more comfortable with certain sexual acts or concepts, while a sex-favourable person might be repulsed by others. All such experiences are unique to the individual – which is why it's so important to figure out where you and any partners you have stand.

Sex stances can tell you or a partner how you feel, generally, towards sex. They cannot express, however, how important sex is to you and what it feels like for you. 'If your partner's ace, know that having sex might not mean the same thing to them as it does to you, and talk about that. Ask them what it means to them,' Ana says. 'For Luna, it's on the same level as, say, playing a video game – a fun thing you can do to pass time, but it's just one option of all the stuff you could do, not some incredibly important thing.' (The same goes for aromantics in romantic relationships or QPPs. 'For alloromantics, saying *I love you* for the first time is a big deal,' Ana says, 'And Luna just said it to me offhand one day! I was just…' She makes a stunned expression, then laughs.)

The sentiment 'it's like playing a videogame' or 'it's like watching a movie' were echoed by many aces I spoke with; other sex-indifferent aces told me that sex feels more akin to doing a household task like washing dishes. It isn't interesting or enjoyable in itself, but they want to do it for their partner all the same, and find satisfaction in making sure that their partner's needs are taken care of.

All of this means that if you're an allo person in a relationship with an asexual-spectrum person, it's highly likely that they will not put the same importance on sex that you do. It's entirely okay to see sex as the peak of intimacy while your partner puts it on a level with reading a book or even washing dishes – as long as *you* are okay with that. Be honest with yourself: are you happy to have sex with someone who is not physically attracted to you?

Will you enjoy having sex with a partner for whom sex just isn't next-level? 'If you're allosexual and sex is an important part of a relationship for you and the ace person you're with is on board with doing it, be certain that you can enjoy having sex with a person who isn't sexually attracted to you and doesn't find you physically appealing in a way that arouses them,' said one of my interviewees, who chose to stay anonymous. 'There are lots of reasons they might choose to have sex with you, but you being hot isn't one of them. Make sure your ego is ready for that.'

It's okay if the answer is no. A mismatch of desire, or a disparity in what sex means to you and a partner, is a valid deal-breaker in any relationship. Just make sure you never suggest there's something *wrong* with your ace partner for feeling the way they do about sex. 'I'm very confident,' Ana says. 'If I weren't, I'd feel unease about Luna not being attracted to me. And that makes sense. It *can* make you feel unattractive, and there's nothing anyone can do about that. You need to remember that often, your partner won't understand how you're feeling instinctively. You've got to talk to them. Be clear, and be honest. A lot of the usual assumptions don't work here.'

2. Rethink consent

If you're anything like me, your education on consent told you not to have sex with someone who'd said no, and left the matter there. But this model of consent is incomplete. The absence of a *no* does not equate to a *yes* automatically. It does not mean that a person wants, benefits from or enjoys sex.

Take what happened to Jules (they/them), who is asexual and who spent five years having sex with their partner – sex they consented to but didn't want. 'He never felt satisfied with our sex life,' they say. 'In the beginning we had sex more regularly, but it decreased a lot, until in the end I just couldn't do it anymore.' He urged Jules to go to therapy, and while it helped them in other ways, it didn't change their disinterest in sex. He recommended they come off the pill; they did. No change. They got their blood tested; nothing.

'I started doing him favours by masturbating him,' they say, 'but it always made him want sex even more. So often I just gave in. I really was trying to "be better" and be more sexual; I accepted and tolerated and forced myself to perform in so much sex I didn't want, because I thought it was my duty to give sex.' Jules did not say 'no' to sex, but their 'yes' was given not because they wanted to, but because they felt they *had* to. In this case, clearly, the lack of a 'no' didn't make the sex healthy or enjoyable.

Or consider the situation of those young people who said they had to 'finish what they started'. Let's imagine a person – we'll call them Ash – who begins a hookup with someone they've been flirting with. They go home with this new person; they kiss; their partner begins to initiate sex. Ash realizes that they don't want to have sex, but feel that they can't say *no* now; they've given so many reasons for their partner to expect sex. And their partner goes ahead, under the assumption that Ash's lack of a *no* is the same as a *yes*. The mentality of 'one thing leads to another' can mean that just engaging in the first few steps of a sexual script can be interpreted as a *yes*, even if one has taken those steps by accident or decides not to 'go all the way'. As Angela Chen puts it, 'If two people fool around and one of them becomes aroused, the other person (usually a woman in heterosexual contexts) can feel responsible for helping the other person "finish", lest they be considered a tease or a killjoy [...] a lack of consent is built into the system.'[16] Thanks to compulsory sexuality, the needs of the partner who does desire sex are prioritized over the needs of the one who doesn't.

Here, some would offer up the model of *enthusiastic consent* – consent that seeks the presence of a 'yes' rather than the absence of a 'no'. This is a step in the right direction, but for many aces, another problem presents itself: what if you're sex-indifferent, and you'll never really give an enthusiastic yes? What if you're the type of ace person for whom sex feels like washing the dishes? Your consent might never be *enthusiastic*, but that doesn't make it nonconsensual or unwanted if you have sex with your partner because you love them and want to take care of their needs.

'I think there's a strange repulsion, especially in the younger ace/aro circles, to the idea of doing something that you may not personally be *psyched* about, but are okay with,' says Kosatka (they/them). 'We have successfully highlighted enthusiastic consent as a pillar of good, healthy, moral relationships, but I feel like this is not a realistic standard. No one should ever be forced to perform an action they find painful or repulsive, of course, but life is about balance, and sometimes, giving way is an act of appreciation, not surrender.'

So our model of consent has to allow for this nuance: for aces (and allos) who, in Kosatka's words, might not be 'psyched' to do something, but are also happy to do it for their partners. One model for consent that a lot of aces have found useful is by sex researcher Emily Nagoski, in her book *Come As You Are: The Surprising New Science That Will Transform Your Sex Life*. Rather than a binary of 'yes' and 'no', Nagoski creates more categories for consent:

ENTHUSIASTIC CONSENT

When I *want* you

When I don't fear the consequences of saying yes OR saying no

When saying no means missing out on something I want

WILLING CONSENT

When I care about you even though I don't desire you (right now)

When I'm pretty sure saying yes will have an okay result and I think maybe that I'd regret saying no

When I believe that desire may begin after I say yes

UNWILLING CONSENT

When I fear the consequences of saying no more than I fear the consequences of saying yes

When I feel not just an absence of desire but an absence of *desire for desire*

When I hope that by saying yes, you will stop bothering me, or think that if I say no you'll only keep on trying to persuade me

COERCED CONSENT

When you threaten me with harmful consequences if I say no

When I feel I'll be hurt if I say yes, but I'll be hurt more if I say no

When saying yes means experiencing something I actively dread[17]

The benefit of this model is that it identifies the key difference between situations like Jules's and that of aces who might never consent enthusiastically but still have sex that's consensual and wanted. Jules began by giving unwilling consent, saying yes because they felt they *had* to. As they attempted to pull away from the sexual aspect of their relationship, he began pressuring them, making them feel there was something *wrong* with them for refusing. Jules's ability to make a free choice was compromised, and they were giving coerced consent. But a person who isn't afraid of the consequences of saying no, and who knows that they *can* say no, can give a truly free-willed *yes* to sex even if they don't happen to be eager to have it. Nothing is influencing their desire to say *yes* except their own wants and reasoning.

The uses of this model are absolutely not unique to aspecs (in fact, it wasn't even created for us). Many allos may find that their sexual desire is more *responsive* than spontaneous. Someone who experiences more spontaneous desire is likely to experience desire before any sexual activity has been initiated; they might favour and appreciate unplanned sexual advances. People with more responsive desire might not feel a spontaneous 'I want to have sex' urge, but find that once sexual contact begins, they become aroused and desire begins. This tends to look far more like the 'willing consent' option than the 'enthusiastic consent'.

Here, then, are some questions it may be helpful to ask:

- Do you feel comfortable with the idea of having sex?
- Do you feel confident that you can freely give a yes *or* a no?
- Do you feel like you're able to stop or change your mind once sex has been initiated?
- What is your *intention* in having sex? ('I love my partner and want to show them that', 'I want to tend to their needs',

'I want to feel desired' or 'I'll enjoy the physical sensation' might all be healthy intentions. 'I want my partner to stop pressuring me' or 'I'm avoiding the tension and awkwardness of saying no' or 'I don't have any intention; it's just something I have to do' are not.)

For allo partners, remember that even if your partner doesn't find sex interesting or special, as long as they are freely agreeing to sex because they want to give you pleasure, that's absolutely okay. They are doing it because they care about you, just as you might take on a particular household task for their sake, or set time aside to watch their favourite show with them, because you care about them. Enjoy yourself – because that's what your partner *wants.*

Of course, just as they're taking time to do something just for you, you'll need to take time to do things for them. Find out what gestures of intimacy they like, whether that be cuddling, shared activities, or something entirely different, and make time to do them. Sex may be your time to have something that's all about you; make sure you make equal time that's all about them.

One word that came up a lot when I talked about this with my interviewees was *compromise* – and absolutely not in a negative context. Compromise in this case does not mean allowing anyone to cross your hard limits or the boundaries of what you're comfortable with; if sex in general, or any specific sex act, is a 'no, never' for you, then do not budge, and do not ask anyone else to budge on their firm limits. Healthy compromise is about a balance, about making sure that both party's physical and emotional needs are taken care of. Some examples might be:

- 'I'll have sex with you because that takes care of your physical needs, if you attend to *my* physical needs by cuddling me.'

- 'I don't want to try that right now, but maybe I will another day.'
- 'I don't want to have penetrative sex, but I'll have oral sex with you/help you masturbate/use a sex toy on you.'

And that final suggestion brings us to our next point.

3. Break down the hierarchy of sexual acts and types of intimacy

The idea of sex being at the top of the hierarchy of intimacy – this is artificial. So is the idea of penetrative sex being the most real or complete form of sex. There is no innate structure to sex, nor any rule that says you have to do certain things in a certain order or at all. You may not want to engage in certain acts. You may want to attend to your partner's sexual needs but not engage in 'traditional' sex. And that is fine. Penetrative sex, and indeed any sex act, is just one option from a much bigger buffet.

'Being sexually intimate doesn't always mean being naked and receiving,' says Key (she/they). 'There's a lot of intimacy and joy in helping your partner masturbate. The focus is entirely on them, and you're just a helping hand, so to speak – you get to choose how much you want to be involved, whether it's just kissing them while they do the work or something more.' Interviewees discussed holding their partners while they masturbated, masturbating mutually as their preferred form of intimacy, or as something they engage in when they don't feel like partnered sex at a given moment.

Or they pursue totally solo sex. 'A large realization for me was realizing that masturbation and having sex with oneself isn't lesser than partnered sex, and it's absolutely okay if it's the kind of sex I prefer,' says Theo (they/them). 'It really feels like masturbation is seen as the sad lonely option. It's a shame! Because I am quite enjoying exploring my own pleasure and kinks even though it's by myself – or even because it's by myself. My attempts at partnered sex were clearly not for me, and that's so okay. I'm glad to know this, and I'm not missing out.' For many aces I spoke to, masturbation was a way to take care of libido, provide themselves pleasure, and explore their own wants without the discomfort of having another person in the mix, especially for those who are generally sex-averse or sex-indifferent. If it's your thing, then enjoy. (As a side note, it's also completely okay to have no interest in masturbation whatsoever.)

Another pattern among my interviewees were the several aces who said that, while they were uninterested in sex itself, or averse to receiving sexual attention, they *were* interested in giving their partner sexual pleasure and gratification. If this is the case for you, you might find it worth exploring the concept of being *stone*. This was a term first used in lesbian communities to describe lesbians, usually butches, who would touch their partner sexually but without being touched.[18] The term has since gained traction among the wider LGBTQIA+ community. For many stones, there's a great deal of intimacy and pleasure in making another person feel good, in watching their pleasure and focusing wholly upon their needs.

For partners of stones, or anyone who likes to give but not receive sexual attention, it can be a struggle to fight the feeling that you need to reciprocate. But if this is your partner's preference, you are not doing anything wrong; indeed, by respecting their desire not to be touched, you are doing a lot right. Just because you are receiving doesn't mean your partner isn't also having fun; indeed, your pleasure will be a big part of their enjoyment.

And finally, you might find that sex is a hard boundary for you. If this is the case for you, then non-sexual intimacy is no less valuable. There are all kinds of forms of physical touch or shared activity that are fulfilling and beautiful, and you deserve to have partners who understand and respect the importance of these things to you.

4. Know that your feelings – or your partner's feelings – about sex and/or intimacy may be subject to change

It may be that some days you're okay with having sex, and some days you are not. Sometimes you may want to have one form of sex but not another; you might want to give but not receive or vice versa. And this applies to other forms of intimacy as well. Some aspec people told me that they have days when they're not okay with being kissed, cuddled or touched at all – and this is fine. 'Just tell your partner,' Luna recommends, '"I'm not okay with doing this specific thing today. It's not you."'

For partners: if your partner isn't open to a particular form of affection at the moment (or, indeed, at all), then find other translations for love. Kiss their hand or their forehead rather than their lips; hug them. Compliment them on something that isn't anything to do with 'sexiness', like their intelligence or creativity. Spend time with them. Find a way to tell them that you care in a language that they understand, and are happy to hear.

5. Kink and BDSM might be worth exploring

Many of the aspec people I spoke to said that they had found validation, a home and a form of sex that was meaningful and comfortable in the kink community. *Kink*, in this context, refers simply to non-normative and unconventional sexual practices, which can include a huge array of activities. BDSM is one aspect of kink: a subculture that involves the use of bondage and discipline, dominance and submission, and sadism and masochism.

To many, aspec or allo, the appeal of BDSM is that nothing can happen without negotiation. While outsiders' idea of BDSM is of something dehumanizing and abusive (an impression not helped by inaccurate portrayals of BDSM in the media, in works such as *Fifty Shades of Grey*), when practised properly, it can be a way for many aspecs to engage in a form of sex that asks for consent about *everything.* (Although, as many kinksters will tell you, sex isn't a necessary part of any 'scene', and it might not even be in focus at all. 'Actual sex plays a surprisingly small role [in kink],' says Timmy (she/they), 'and you might find something in the non-sexual bits that might just blow your mind.')

When BDSM partners engage in a scene, the unspoken scripts of 'vanilla' sex are abandoned. Players know that when someone is making their body so vulnerable, engaging in power plays or involving pain in sex, you cannot make assumptions; their bodily autonomy and control over the scene are paramount. Kinksters discuss their limits and boundaries in advance as a matter of course. They agree on a 'safe word', which, if spoken by any participant, immediately causes all involved to stop. (Those who ignore safe words are summarily ejected from the community.) And every aspect of a scene is discussed beforehand, with clear communication about what is going to happen and what the hard limits are. And the nature of a scene itself can be very helpful. The obviously orchestrated, choreographed nature of scenes helps participants remember that this is not something they would do in 'real life'; that these are personas they are adopting for a time.

That separation from reality is appealing to many aces, for whom sex really can feel like putting on a different persona. And 'after-care' following any scene is absolutely essential.

Perhaps most importantly, for many BDSM aficionados and kinksters it often isn't really about sex. It's about trust. It's about the safe surrender of power to someone you know will not cross your boundaries, and having a person put such entire trust in you. And it's about performance, about taking and surrendering power in a safe environment.

In short: no assumptions, only clear negotiation and constant communication. The act of sex itself decentralized to focus on trust and sensation. An expectation that boundaries will be discussed and honoured, that a 'no' will be respected instantly. Is it any wonder that so many aces find such an environment appealing? In a BDSM club, no one will assume that saying yes to one sexual act means you also consent to another; one thing does not lead to another unless everyone has agreed that it does. Saying no is not an awkward mess, but an expected part of the safety tools in place.

If you're curious about kink but not sure where to start, there are apps made specifically to connect you with like-minded people. The most popular, Feeld, asks you for far more information than the standard 'age, gender, sexuality' combo. You can enter what kind of relationship you're looking for – casual or committed, monogamy or polyamory, and so on – as well as whether you're into group sex and what kinds of groups you're interested in, and what kinks you have (with a long list of suggestions). You can invite a partner so that you can search jointly, too.

Even if kink and BDSM aren't for you – and you absolutely shouldn't do them if they're not – you can still take a lot away from this model. Extensive discussion of consent and boundaries before anything sexual occurs, clear communication about your wants, and evaluation of what you enjoyed, what you didn't, what you'd like to explore and try again – these are powerful tools to increase comfort and trust in any relationship, regardless of whether ropes and blindfolds are involved.

6. It's okay if you can't make it work

Again: it's okay for sex to be a dealbreaker. It's okay for an ace partner to want sex less often than an allo partner, including if that means not at all. It's okay if they're uncomfortable with the way a partner wants to express intimacy. And it is okay to see sex as unappealing, trivial, a chore, or just not particularly important to you.

This goes both ways. Sometimes an allo partner will feel unattractive or less loved because you aren't attracted to them, and even if they know objectively that this isn't the case they may not be able to reconcile what they know with how they feel. Or you might feel that you can make certain concessions for your partner, only to find that you can't. You may not be able to deal with how much importance they place on sex, even if you know it isn't their fault or yours.

All of this is simply human.

You do not need to exhaust every possible avenue or solution before deciding that the relationship just won't work out. If you're not comfortable with mutual masturbation or having an open relationship (where partners are free to date and/or sleep with other people), then don't try to force it, and don't pretend to yourself that you can. If you can't be happy when sex means everything to you and your partner is indifferent, be honest with yourself about that. Sexual lack of compatibility can occur in any relationship, whether between aspecs or allos, and the difference in desire is not anyone's fault. As long as no one coerces another or tries to paint their lack (or possession) of attraction as a fault, then no one is to blame. It's just an inevitable consequence of the variation in human experiences of sex and desire. And that's sad, but it's okay.

*

Even now that Luna and Ana know far more than they did when they were first starting out – even though communication is now their norm – Luna still has moments of uncertainty. 'I do worry about not loving Ana the way she loves me,' Luna says, 'I don't feel a *pull*, the way she describes it.' But a crucial part of their relationship now is trust. She trusts that Ana means it when she says she's thrilled with the relationship she has. Luna knows that her own way of loving is real and true; she trusts that Ana feels the same way.

'Being with Ana felt normal, it felt natural. It felt calm,' Luna says. 'And as long as I've found my way of love, I don't care. Ana loves me, and all she cares about is that I love her in *my* way. I want her in my life. To allos, that might translate to a romantic relationship. To me, it's like I've found the world's biggest bestie.'

Yes, there are moments when she worries, because she is human, that Ana might care more than she lets on, or wish that Luna were attracted to her, or be happier with someone who loves the same way she does. But in those moments, all she needs to do is voice that uncertainty aloud. 'That's when I just tell her… no, darling,' Ana says. And she looks at Luna with a world of fondness in her eyes.

6

Home

Non-Traditional Families

When I was eight years old, I was set a task in school: to draw a timeline of my future life, marking out along it the various responsibilities I would have throughout the years. Coloured pencils arrayed around me, I set about my work. *Responsible for going to school. Responsible for working hard. Responsible for going to university.* As a joke, I skipped to the end, drew a body lying down, and added: *Death: responsible for going to heaven.* Then I stared at the broad gap in the centre of the timeline, wondering what to fill it with. What was the next checkpoint, after education? What filled the space between that and death?

I drew a picture of me holding hands with a smiling man. *Responsible for getting married.* A baby in a cot. *Responsible for having kids and looking after them.*

That, I already understood, was the expected norm. That was the only model for life I knew.

It's hard to pinpoint when I realized that this wasn't what I wanted. I remember, as a young teenager, feeling vaguely annoyed by the thought that I would have to get married, because there seemed to be too many inconveniences attached to the whole thing. Sharing a bed or a room with someone would mean losing the wonderful, cosy privacy of having my own bed and my own room that I could decorate as I chose and live in how I wanted. Nothing about the concept of having a partner was appealing enough to outweigh that. Kissing didn't seem all that interesting. None of it did.

Realizing that I was aromantic was a crushing relief. So many things that had felt like bleak and boring inevitabilities were lifted away from my future. I had no regrets about being aromantic and no hesitation over using the label.

I wasn't troubled by the prospect of living alone. I knew I didn't want a romantic partner, and I didn't mind the idea of being single at all. Solitude has always meant comfort to me; I had always dreamed of having my own place, being able to do what I wanted at times of my choosing. Being single sounded *amazing*, frankly.

With time, though, I realized that even if I didn't want romance, I wanted companionship. I wanted someone to watch shows with in the evening, to go to with my problems, to be another human voice. I wanted closeness, to be known. I wanted my own space, but I also wanted people I cared about close at hand.

But I was aro, and having a romantic partner I didn't want would hurt worse than being alone. So, I decided I would live alone. I should reiterate that I was happy with this conclusion, and if I do live alone for parts or all of my life, I have no doubt that I will thrive. For many people, myself included, single living is its own kind of joy.

I had made a mistake, though: I had assumed that romance and singledom were the only options, and that being aro meant I would always be living solo. But I was wrong. I was as wrong as I had been when I was eight and it was all about marriage. There are a thousand ways to make a home.

*

For Ace (they/them), the world used to be a small place. They grew up in a conservative family in the USA, and were homeschooled. They were rarely allowed to go out, like other teens. One of their only points of access to the world was the internet – and it was through the web, in 2008, that they met Petra.

'We were bringing our laptops to bed to talk to each other all night,' Ace remembers. 'I guess at first, it was a replacement for what I used to have with my sister [who had moved out] but eventually I started telling Petra things I was way too scared to tell my sister. And they were… well, they were kind about it. They've really done a lot to show me that the world outside of the house I grew up in is so much bigger than I thought, and so much more loving than my conservative parents made it seem.'

The two often joked about someday moving in together. Then one of Ace's siblings needed to move back home unexpectedly, and Ace had to move into the converted garage apartment next door. At the same time, Petra was looking for an art school. 'I joked that the local community college near me had affordable art classes,' Ace says. 'So, by 2016, Petra had moved twelve hours away from where they grew up to move into a garage. With me.'

During their time rooming together, Ace and Petra began doing things that might, to an outside observer, have appeared romantic. They went to a diner together every Wednesday. They went to concerts together for the first time. 'It was all kinda, you know… date-y,' Ace says. But they never thought of their outings as dates. Petra was dating other people, and while Ace was aroace, Petra was allo and polyamorous. It wasn't until three years after they began living together that Ace asked Petra if the two of them were in a queerplatonic relationship.

It took Petra some time to understand what that meant, and at first, they weren't sure if that was how they considered their relationship with Ace. 'They have had what they'd considered a crush on me on and off in the past,' Ace says, 'and putting it under the QPR label helped put those feelings into context.'

The plan had been for Petra to move back home once they graduated, 'but that came and went, and neither of us could let go'. A few more years passed. Petra's family insurance was running out, but Ace had recently got a new job and, for the first time, got benefits from it. 'So, thinking purely from a practical perspective, I asked Petra if they wanted to get married so they can use my health insurance from work.'

At first, Petra appeared to balk. 'I kinda worried that I'd offended them,' Ace admits. 'Marriage means very little to me, and I think I assumed that was true of them too, but after that I felt, *of course it's important to them. They're alloromantic. They should marry someone they're in love with.*'

Then Petra took Ace on a day trip. On the way to an attraction that Ace had wanted to visit for some time, the two stopped in a small lakeside town. 'We took a walk on the pier – and out of nowhere, Petra does a whole down-on-one-knee, custom ring box public proposal. They explained to me that, even if we're not "in love", they still love me, and want me to feel as important as a romantic partner. They said that I'll always be a pillar in their life, and they want to prove how strongly they care about me. We both had a cry about it, and proceeded to have an irresponsibly expensive celebratory day trip.'

They've had to make the arrangements in secret. Ace's family isn't accepting of 'gay' marriage, and they met with no luck trying to explain their asexuality to their mother: she told them that the Bible told humans to be fruitful and multiply. But Ace and Petra are working on building their own family, and they won't be alone. One of Petra's long-distance romantic partners is planning to move in with them. The trio are saving money to buy a house together. 'And when we do have that home,' Ace says, 'that's when I'm gonna tell the rest of my family that we're *extremely* married.'

Nothing about this relationship fits the expected template for how a home is made. But it is, nonetheless, a family.

*

What does a non-normative family look like?

There's no one answer to this. Part of the whole point is that these relationships are designed to fit the needs and desires of the individuals in them; as a result, they will look entirely different between one set of partners and another. A queerplatonic relationship is anything that defies or refuses or blurs the rules of the amatonormative, monogamous, romantic-sexual relationship, which means it's more defined by what it *isn't* than what it is. Every respondent to my survey who had a partnered relationship described something subtly different from everyone else. Here are just a few of those responses:

- Coral (they/them) has a best friend whom they plan to marry and live with. 'We don't have any romantic feelings for each other. I don't want to date them; I just want to be their friend,' Coral explains. 'My best friend is my soulmate that I want to spend the rest of my life with. I want to experience life with them and grow old together.'
- Cas (they/them) has two queerplatonic partners. Both of them are in committed platonic relationships with Cas, but not with each other, though the two are friends.

They currently live apart and are unsure what their plans for the future are, but they're open to seeing what shape things take.

- Kei (he/him) has what he calls a 'fake relationship' with a close friend. He is a gay aromantic-spectrum man, his girlfriend a pansexual woman. They're not romantically or sexually interested in each other in any way, but neither of them enjoys discussing their relationship status with others in general, so having this relationship means they're able to say 'I have a boy/girlfriend' to sweep such questions away. 'It doesn't feel different from my previous "real" relationships,' Kei says. 'Our relationship is largely to support each other through life – and to confuse everyone around us. I'm a gay man with a girlfriend. It's so much fun.'

Non-normative families can, if desired, involve parenting. Growing up, AVEN founder David Jay always wanted to be surrounded by family, and to have the permanence that a romantic couple might have. He also knew that he wanted kids. But as his friends and roommates found spouses and moved out, he decided that he would have to pursue a family of his own making. When his two friends Avary and Zeke married, they told Jay that they wanted him to be a part of the family when they had kids, 'as close to an equivalent third parent as possible'.[1]

Now, the three have a daughter to whom Jay is a legal parent. And there's a lot to gain from the arrangement; all three parents get a family with the permanence and companionship they wanted; Jay provides an extra caregiver and income; the parenting work is less heavy when split three ways. Talking to the news station WBUR when their daughter was an infant, Zeke discussed how having Jay on hand to take a shift feeding and looking after their daughter during the night meant that he and his wife 'get a lot better rested and we also get to spend a lot more time together as a couple'.[2]

This is good for all involved. You might not need a full village to raise a child but having extra caregivers to provide an extra pair of hands and split the responsibilities more than two ways can ease a great deal of stress on the parents. And that can only be healthier for the child. 'I think that raising kids in community,' David Jay says, 'and raising kids in community that you really take the time and energy to build, is as old as human history.'[3]

Platonic co-parenting, like what Jay created with his friends, is something intuitive for many aros and aces, but it's by no means limited to us. Sites like Coparents.co.uk, Modamily and PollenTree.com now exist, aiming to match people with co-parents or sperm donors: Coparents has 120,000 worldwide members, Modamily 30,000 and PollenTree 53,000. Platonic co-parenting has long existed between same-sex couples seeking a child who want their donors or surrogates to be involved in the child's life. Increasingly, heterosexual people are also recognizing it as an option for forming a family; indeed, two-thirds of Coparents users identify as heterosexual.

Like queerplatonic relationships, every co-parenting arrangement can look very different. In 2013, *The Guardian* interviewed a trio of co-parents, a gay man who wanted a child but whose partner didn't want to look after a child yet, and two women in a relationship who wanted to have a child but for the biological father to be involved in raising them.[4] Other co-parenting relationships are between two single people who have come together with the express purpose of having a baby. Co-parents might live together or apart, with children based in one home or another.

Not everyone welcomes co-parenting. Many people have an ingrained assumption that the best environment in which to raise a child is that of a romantic couple – specifically, a married couple. This is the argument of the marriage movement, which arose in the USA in the 1990s in response to the growing levels of single parents, births outside of marriage and declining marriage rates. The government agreed, with President George W. Bush allocating $1.5 billion to spread the marriage movement's message, particularly to the poor. Improving marriage rates among the poor, the movement claimed, would lead to fewer teen pregnancies, fewer school dropouts, less poverty. It was going to fix America's morality.

(Note that it was the poor who needed 'fixing'. And remember, again, the statistics of how much more likely people of colour are to live in poverty. Rather than fixing the systemic issues that created that poverty, President Bush and the marriage movement told the poor to just get married, and washed their hands of the issue.)

Of course, a two-parent household often has more income than a single parent, and that can certainly increase stability for children. But that does not make marriage a 'quick fix' to all problems. Children are happier and emotionally better off when raised by a single parent than by two parents who regularly fight, and behavioural issues in the children of divorced parents do not spring from the divorce – they can arise as early as twelve years prior. The friction in the marriage is the original cause, not the divorce itself.[5]

So marriage is no magic pill. If there is one, it might actually be extra caregivers outside married parents. For example, when Bella DePaulo analysed rates of teenage drug use in the USA, to interrogate the claim that a married, two-parent duo is the best environment in which to raise a child, she found that the lowest rates of substance abuse in teens between twelve and seventeen happened in families where another caregiving relative – usually a grandparent, aunt or uncle – lived in the household as well. Interestingly, the highest rates of substance abuse happened not in single-parent families, but in families consisting of a father and stepmother: another clear sign that marriage does not automatically give children a more stable home, and that even the financial boost of another partner isn't enough on its own to create total stability.[6]

There's no reason why a romantic relationship or a marriage is necessary to create that stability. Indeed, for many co-parents, part of the appeal is that, by its very nature, co-parenting requires an immense amount of necessary discussion and negotiation to make sure their child's life *will* be as stable as they can make it. Co-parents discuss many things in advance that conventional parents might not: what are their values for parenting? What if one of them finds a new romantic partner? How will they make sure their child is prioritized if things don't work out further down the line? As journalist Nicola Slawson writes on her decision to co-parent with her gay friend, 'We talked about how we'd support each other if we had a miscarriage. We discussed how we would tell the child about how they were brought into the world. We researched childcare options and even how we would share Christmas day [...] we like to joke that no baby has ever been discussed or considered as much in advance.'[7]

If anything is going to give children stability, it isn't their parents having a marriage certificate, but having that level of clear communication. It is having a plan for worst-case scenarios, and a commitment to putting the child first.

There are plenty of options for those looking to co-parent. Some, like Slawson, opt for their friends; others use those online services, some of which even offer concierge services to match you with someone who shares your values and parenting goals. It's wonderful to see such a framework devoted to helping create this kind of non-nuclear, non-normative family. Still, it's disheartening to see how little, in contrast, is out there to help people who might want to find a committed friendship, a QPP, or an 'intimate tribe' (a group of people who share a sense of being a cohesive, committed unit).

Some apps do exist that aim to match people with friends, such as Bumble for Friends, or Feeld, which has an option to state that you're looking for friendship or connection. Neither app allows you to state your romantic orientation, or has any way to indicate that you're looking for a QPP.

Even ACEapp, an app designed for asexuals to find each other, isn't ideal for the task. For a start, it's, well, *ACE*app. The profile-building questions assume that you're asexual, which immediately excludes allosexual aromantics. It then asks you what kind of relationship type you're open to: monogamy, polyamory, both, none or 'ask me'. No option to say that you're looking for a queerplatonic partner. Then you're asked if you're seeking one of three options: chat, relationship or friendship. Again, no queerplatonic partnership option.

I have no idea how effective or, indeed, useful any kind of app or website for non-romantic partnerships could be. Queerplatonic relationships generally arise out of pre-existing relationships, either friendships or romantic relationships whose members realize that romance isn't for them, but a close relationship is. 'You should be friends with someone before entering into a QPR,' says Cas. 'If you have that expectation from the start, you might try to force something that's not there.' Both Cas's QPRs arose from their friendships, in one case without either of them realizing they'd formed that kind of a relationship until they were in the middle of it – just as happened between Ace and Petra.

Non-nuclear, non-normative families form in this way all the time, naturally and often accidentally, both among aromantics and alloromantics. Take Reddit user Impressive-Jaguar and her two friends, or Mildred Sanford and Nancy Inferrera. Or take the case of the seven women in Guangzhou in southeastern China, who always joked that when they were sixty, they'd buy a home together. As time passed, they began to take the joke more seriously. Why wait? In 2019, they moved into a home together, pooling their resources to buy and renovate it. They have a communal living space, a tearoom and their own private spaces. Some of them share rooms; they joke that they're all trying to learn a different skill so that they have every possible need catered for, from traditional medicine to growing vegetables. 'Sometimes, we're even closer than siblings,' one of them, Jun Di, told the news group Yitiao. 'We're independent, but we can communicate with each other.'[8]

The seven women's situation bears some similarity to the concept of the 'intimate tribe' or 'urban tribe'. In *Stepping Off the Relationship Escalator*, Amy Gahran describes these as a 'persistent network of overlapping relationships [with a] level of group awareness and cohesion, expressed through mutual care, respect, attention and support'.[9] The typical image of an urban tribe might be the tight-knit group of twenty-somethings seen in sitcoms such as *Friends* or *Will & Grace* – people whose primary relationships are with each other, who celebrate holidays together as a matter of ritual, who are each other's confidants and support network. Like any non-normative family, though, there's no template for an intimate tribe. Tribes might live together, but many are spread across different households. Some might come together for holidays or when one of them needs additional support; others might be a permanent group living together and even raising children together; and others might see members join and leave over time.

Some tribes may arise organically out of polyamorous relationships, where multiple partners might live together. Polyamory is a branch of 'consensual non-monogamy', a relationship type where partners agree that the other has their blessing to have romantic and/or sexual relationships outside of them. Being inherently outside of the script of an amatonormative relationship, they're extremely freeform. For some, it can be a 'triad' or 'quad' of people who are all involved with each other; for others, one person might be a 'hinge' between two or more partners who aren't involved with each other. They might be 'solo poly', living alone but being visited by multiple partners. It's entirely down to what fits best for the individuals involved.

Consensual non-monogamy is often stigmatized. Non-poly people's kneejerk reaction can be to liken it to cheating – remember, it's called *consensual* non-monogamy – or to accuse poly folks of just wanting to have lots of sex. As Gahran points out, the latter assumption is a problem in itself, as it 'presumes that sex for its own sake is somehow wrong or inferior'. Having lots of sex is fine. And it's not even something that happens in all poly relationships: there are plenty of polyamorous asexuals. Polyamory might involve casual sex or group sex, or it might not.

The key thing is: members of a poly relationship discuss their relationships and their boundaries with each other. Like any non-conventional relationship, their intricacies and the preferences and limits of those involved often end up discussed more often and in more detail than happens in a traditional romance.

For many of my aspec interviewees, consensual non-monogamy is an absolute boon. Take Petra and Ace. Ace is aroace; Petra is pansexual. But because Petra is also polyamorous, they can fulfil their sexual and romantic needs elsewhere without Ace having to get involved in any of it. Rather like David Jay forming his network of intimate relationships rather than having his 'one person who was the source of everything', Petra sources romantic and sexual needs in their other partners, and their need for a permanent companion in Ace. Similarly, H (she/her) is an asexual person who's also on the aromantic spectrum and has two partners. One of them is ace, and the other is allosexual. 'But because she is also poly,' H says, 'I don't feel that she's giving something up to be with me and building resentment about it. She has other relationships where her sexual needs are met, and our relationship can just be what it is.' Having this kind of open relationship means that H and her allo partner both get their physical needs (and lack thereof) met.

For H, the appeal of her relationship is all about the closeness and the community. 'I would be fine without a partnered relationship. I sought one out because I do want the kind of permanent supportive relationship where we know each other best, we take care of each other in hard times, and have each other's back against the world. And cuddles are nice.'

*

Talking to Ace, H and others in similar relationships, set me thinking again about David Jay's relationship web, particularly about what his PowerPoint slide looked like when he limited the relationships to only those that were romantic: just two bubbles, himself and the hypothetical romantic partner, linked by a single line. When one relationship is your 'source of everything', as Jay put it… that's a lot of weight and responsibility placed on one person. The line connecting the two bubbles is holding up an immense amount. Perhaps too much.

This idea quickly came up in conversation with another of my interviewees, Theo (see Chapter 5), who formed their current QPR accidentally. Their previous romantic (though very non-normative) relationships had just come to an end, and while that end had been amicable, and Theo was still close to their former partners, they weren't interested in starting anything new. Then they met someone new, and felt their empty social world coming back to life. 'And I was like, "Am I seriously having platonic feelings for someone now? Am I wanting a platonic partner right after deciding I wasn't going to have a relationship?"'

Theo knew they had to confess. 'I can't do pining. It's the worst. I know I wanted to hold onto my relationship with this person; we were already talking about ourselves as 'partners in crime'. I realized I was just going to have to ask if they wanted to be in a queerplatonic partnership with me. I was going, *I can't handle the pining! They might be able to, but I can't!*'

So Theo asked what their friend thought about queerplatonic relationships. The friend said that they liked the idea of having one, so Theo asked: 'Would you like to be in one with me?'

'They just let a flood of love loose,' Theo remembers. 'They're much better at repressing their feelings than I am, so they'd been holding a lot back. It was a little overwhelming at first. But we'd already been together, in a way.'

The two have decided not to cohabit, and they maintain a long-distance relationship. To some alloromantics, having a primary relationship without moving in together might seem odd, but Theo points out that every human has different needs – and considering this, it's odd that we prescribe the framework of monogamous romantic marriage for everyone. Why should we assume that one size fits all in something so complicated as love and relationships? And, crucially – why do we assume that one person can fulfil all of those complex needs?

'We're a social species,' Theo says, 'and we all have varied, unique needs. It seems unfair to me to designate one person as the person who fulfils all your needs. You can lock yourself into just being emotionally and physically close to just one person.'

The single, load-bearing monogamous relationship is a keystone of what's known as 'the relationship escalator'. This term describes the social script, the package of norms, that defines the shape of normative romantic relationships. As defined by Gahran in *Stepping Off the Relationship Escalator*, 'Two (and only two) people progress from initial attraction and dating, to becoming sexually and romantically involved and exclusive, to adopting a shared identity as a couple, to moving in together and merging their lives – all the way up to marriage and kids, 'til death do you part.'[10]

For plenty of people, this dynamic works. There's nothing wrong with escalator relationships themselves, any more than there's anything inherently wrong with monogamy or romance itself. The problem comes when the escalator is treated as something that everyone *should* do, or the only framework in which a healthy relationship can exist.

It's worth looking at just how much we put on romantic partners. Because romance is so often presented as the greatest possible joy in a person's life, we can easily fall into the trap of thinking that romance is what will make us happy. 'I think a lot of people,' says Jan, 'focus on getting a romantic partner because they think they'll be happy once they have one, and they don't look closely at the things that might be making them unhappy right now.'

So we expect romantic partners to be the source of our happiness. And then we start withdrawing from other people who might provide sources of happiness themselves. In *Singled Out*, Bella DePaulo points out a pattern of sociologists encouraging couples to fix their romantic partner as the centre of their life, and relegate or discard other relationships, such as columnist Maggie Gallagher writing that 'a man or a woman should put his [sic] spouse first before the demands of parents, friends or other family members,' and sociologist Pepper Schwartz claiming that the ideal form of a couple is one where romantic partners 'give priority to their relationship over their work and over all other relationships'. Such a couple should socialize with other 'like-minded couples' only so they can get good advice about their relationship.[11]

Amatonormativity, then, encourages romantic partners to view their partner as their first port of call for everything. What does that mean in practice?

It means that your partner is often your main source of emotional support, the person you turn to when you're in distress. They're your primary source of day-to-day companionship. If you're allosexual, they're likely the one meeting your physical needs (which can cause trouble if your sexual needs are markedly different from each other). They're the one who affirms you and makes you feel loved. If you have children, they're usually the other parent by biology or adoption, or at least a parental figure, and they're the person with whom you share childcare responsibilities. They're often a huge source of financial support, and a general social support – if they come with you as a plus-one to a party, you know you'll have someone there you'll always be able to talk to, even if you don't know anyone else. They help you with the most practical parts of your existence: cooking, household chores, getting taxes paid. They'll support your health, too, whether it's by sharing health insurance with you (as Ace and Petra plan to), or by taking care of you when you're sick. And finally, if they outlive you, they'll take care of your post-life decision-making.

That's an incredible amount of support expected to come from just one person.

So non-normative families can do a lot to split the weight more evenly. Let's imagine a family – a hypothetical one, but one I've created by combining the various real stories that my interviewees shared with me.

> Seth lives with his non-normative family: Mateo, Ava and Rowan. The four of them pooled their resources to buy their house, and this is one of many financial benefits that arise from them sharing a home. Ava has a disability and is unable to work, but the rest of the family make sure she's always supported. Thanks to having two regular incomes on top of his own, Mateo is able to pursue the career he's always dreamed of, even though it's not well-paying.
>
> Mateo and Seth are in a queerplatonic relationship. Seth's primary source of companionship and affection is Mateo, but Seth is aroace and sex-averse. This isn't a problem for Mateo, who loves Seth deeply and gets his physical needs fulfilled by Ava, who's his romantic and sexual partner. Ava and Seth aren't together, but they're close friends and trust each other deeply.
>
> Rowan is aromantic but wants to be a parent and to have their child's other parent involved in their life. Seth agrees to be their co-parent, and Mateo and Ava are both involved in bringing up the child too. Mateo and Ava don't want kids of their own, but they're happy to help ease some of the burden on Seth and Rowan by babysitting, cooking,

and generally making sure Seth and Rowan have more time to be parents.

If Seth dies before the rest of his family, he trusts Ava to take care of end-of-life decision making; they share the same traditions and opinions about what they want to happen after death.

Overall, the group benefit each other in many small ways. Rowan dislikes cooking, but their family are happy to take care of that task while Rowan adopts doing laundry as their responsibility. Seth has a lot of common interests with his QPP Mateo, but it's Ava who shares his love of gardening and joins him to plan their garden and spend hours outdoors. Though Rowan isn't in a romantic relationship or QPP with any of the other family members, they always have someone to bring to events, and are comfortable in the knowledge that while they're romantically single, they won't be alone.

Rowan's and Seth's child also benefits: all of her caregivers have more energy, and she has activities she loves to do with each of them individually – art with Rowan, outdoor activities with Ava and Seth, reading with Mateo.

Such a dynamic would not be for everyone. But for these hypothetical partners, their various needs, be they physical, financial, social or emotional, are spread out over multiple people. No one bond is load-bearing.

I had this hypothetical family live together, but they do not need to. This quartet could easily live in adjoining but separate houses, or even farther apart. And even in monogamous relationships, or in QPPs between two people, there's no rule saying that partners have to live together. Many want to, of course.

But, as Theo points out, there's no reason not to 'custom build your perfect relationship. You can date forever and not move in together.' There are plenty of reasons for an individual to feel that living separately is more comfortable for them than nesting together with a partner – you can have the privacy of your own space, not have someone else constantly around, decorate your home space how you like, invite friends over to see *you* rather than the couple, and have the freedom to travel when you like and cook what you want. You don't have to blend finances if you don't want to. You can make life decisions without needing to run absolutely everything past your partner. Valuing your own space and autonomy doesn't mean that you don't also treasure the time you spend together with your partner.

Another decree of escalator relationships is permanency. And don't mistake me; there are plenty of reasons why a couple might very much want to expect permanency from a relationship, whether to provide stability for a child (should they choose to have one) or as a commitment to working at the relationship. But equating the worth of a relationship with its longevity can have its drawbacks. 'I think we need to push back against that instinct to say, *I need to make this relationship last forever for it to be worthwhile*, or that a breakup means you've somehow failed,' Theo says. 'You won't be the same person you were in ten years, and it's okay if you change to the point where the relationship doesn't fit anymore. It's okay to say, "I have loved you a lot, but our lives are on different paths now." My former relationships were very valuable and meaningful, even though they didn't last. I learned things from them about what I want, and what I will and won't do, that I could only have learned by trying.'

That feeling that the end of a relationship is a failure – it's a sentiment in which the weight of amatonormativity is plain. The end of a romantic relationship means a return to singledom – a state that's seen as less mature, less adult – and it means losing out on all the benefits of a relationship, be they social, financial or even legal (of which more in Chapter 9). The loss of a person whom you loved and whose company you enjoyed is a sorrow in itself, but the societal pressure to have one enduring lifelong relationship, and the shame associated with doing otherwise, can enhance the sense of personal failure.

'Loading so much onto any relationship can trigger considerable fear, uncertainty and doubt,' Gahran writes. 'If you don't manage to get and keep an Escalator relationship, will you suffer from lack of support? Will you have enough resources to realize your goals? Will your life have meaning? Might you die alone and unloved? Will you "lose" at life, or at least at adulthood?'

Considering how much we might heap on a single person – our sense of security, our hopes for the future and even a sense of our life having meaning – it is no wonder that some breakups can be so messy and devastating. You have lost not just a person and an intimate relationship, but a safety net against being meaningless, unsupported, unjudged, unsuccessful and unloved.

Land so much on one relationship, and it's no wonder that many end up buckling. So, for those for whom non-normative families are a good fit, it's time to shed the idea of a single, central relationship, and start spreading out our emotional load.

*

There's one more type of non-normative household that deserves discussion: the household of one.

According to the Book of Genesis, when god had finished making the world, he declared it good. Except for one thing. 'It is not good for man to be alone,' he declared, looking at the first man, Adam. And so he set about the task of making a woman to be Adam's life companion.

People have been agreeing with God for centuries since. When people talk about someone without a romantic partner, they might call them commitment-phobic, a loner, a crazy cat lady. There are innumerable reality TV shows dedicated to finding partners for single people, from *Love Island* to *The Bachelor.* Self-help books exist to help people escape singledom and find their romantic partner as soon as possible. Singledom is seldom looked at as a desirable way of life; it's always the way that people live because they couldn't find The One, or because their relationship fell apart.

Princess Anne once remarked that living alone is 'plain selfish' and means that 'you don't understand the impact of your life on other people's lives, and how you depend on other people all the time. It's no good.'[12] In 2023, Melissa Persling wrote an essay in *Business Insider* about how, when she first got married as a young woman, she hadn't wanted kids and didn't see herself as a mother. After her divorce, Persling spent a period of her life single; now she is thirty-eight and ready to become a mother. (Persling also blamed feminism for stopping her from realizing she wanted a family. While I don't consider this a particularly healthy attitude, it's not my focus here; the important part is how people responded.)

Persling faced a vitriolic backlash when she voiced her experience, with online commenters declaring that she was 'too selfish to be a mother' because she hadn't prioritized kids at first, and because she'd lived single for years. 'There was one word I read over and over and over again that I felt forced to confront – selfish.'[13]

A similar thing happened that same year to the twenty-nine-year-old Californian Julia Mazur, after she posted on TikTok about her single, childfree life. In the video, Mazur celebrated that she had been able to see Beyoncé the night before without needing to pay a babysitter; and able to stay in bed that morning without anyone to make her get up. She realized she could spend the morning going to the grocery store and learning to make shakshuka for breakfast. She was making the video, she said, to remind herself that she didn't need to be 'further along' in her life. 'The effortlessness and ease of my life, just kind of focusing on myself and the shakshuka I wanna make, or the Beyoncé concert I wanna go to, really pays off when I'm hard on myself for not being where society tells me I should be in life.'[14]

Unfortunately, the video – which initially met with a positive response – made its way into the hands of the right-wing influencer Matt Walsh. 'Her life doesn't revolve around her family and kids so instead it revolves around TV shows and pop stars,' he complained. 'Worst of all she's too stupid to realize how depressing this is.'[15]

This kind of criticism falls disproportionately on single women, but single men face it too. In 2017, the UK Conservative politician Iain Duncan Smith accused single men of being 'dysfunctional' at a Conservative Party event, calling them a problem for society. Single men, he claimed, 'no longer having to bring something in for their family, so they can be released to do all the things they wouldn't normally do and shouldn't do, so levels of addiction, levels of high criminal activity, issues around dysfunctional behaviour, multiple parenting – all those things are as a result of the un-anchoring of the young man to a responsibility that keeps them stable and eventually makes them more happy.'[16] Similarly, in *Singled Out*, DePaulo describes an interview on the political TV show *Hardball*, where host Chris Matthews asked independent presidential candidate Ralph Nader about his personal life. When Nader called George Bush 'irresponsible' – quoting something Bush had said about himself – Matthews protested. 'Why do you say he's irresponsible? He's raised two daughters; he's had a happy marriage. Isn't he more mature in his lifestyle than you are?'[17]

'Married meant mature, single meant immature,' DePaulo writes. 'No amount of scholarship or public service on the one side, or debauchery on the other, could pry the equation apart.'[18]

These stories encapsulate how society too often talks about single people: Persling, Nader and the unmarried men of the UK were called selfish and irresponsible. Mazur – despite making a video rejoicing in her personal freedom, the fact that she could go out and enjoy culture and nightlife, then spend the morning learning a new recipe – had her life labelled as 'depressing'. Without a spouse, her life was empty. Wouldn't they be happier if they just got a partner?

According to the research, quite possibly not.

At this point, I must state that I will lean heavily on Dr DePaulo's work for this section. We have her to thank for much of the existing advocacy for single people, and for the research about them; without her, this section would be far less informed. If any of this section resonates with you, I urge you to go and find her work.

In *Singled Out*, DePaulo points out that a lot of the research that purports to show married people as happier than singles is often misleading. In one study, people were asked to rate their happiness levels from zero (unhappy) to 5 (happy). Married people rated themselves, on average, a 3.3; the highest average for any group. But to conclude that this means marriage leads to happiness, De Paulo points out, is to ignore the rest of the results. People who had always been single rated themselves at an average of 3.2, just a 0.1 point behind married people, and ahead of those who *had* been married but had divorced or been widowed (both at an average of 2.9). Marriage obviously was not a key to happiness for those who ended up *unhappily* married.

When sociologists Linda Waite and Maggie Gallagher wrote their book, *The Case for Marriage: Why Married People are Happier, Healthier, and Better off Financially*, they cited this research to show that marriage did indeed improve happiness. But they were using, as DePaulo calls it, 'a cheater method', setting aside all the people whose marriages had ended in widowhood or divorce, and only counting those who remained married. What was more, 'when other life factors were considered, the people who were happiest were those who were most satisfied with their household finances, and the next happiest were those who had good health. Marriage came in third.'[19]

A more reliable study is the one that studied 30,000 Germans for (at DePaulo's time of writing) eighteen years, asking them every year to rate their happiness levels from 0, 'totally unhappy', to 10, 'totally happy'. The results? People did, the study found, become a little happier after their wedding, but a few years later they returned to the same general happiness level they'd had before marriage. Once again, the unhappiest group were those who married and divorced, whose happiness averaged at a low point of 6.3 a year before divorce, before recovering afterwards. For these people, singledom was obviously preferable to being married.[20]

Which brings us back to that amatonormative message: that romance is the natural, default state of human existence, the state we should all strive for. But humans are varied. Humans are unique. A romantic partner, and a household shared with them, is the ideal way of life for some people. But for others, aromantic or otherwise, a single life suits them better. And we should trust people to know what they are suited to and what they prefer.

DePaulo has a term for people who are single by choice because it is how they will live best: 'single at heart'. 'People are not single at heart because they have rejected marriage,' she writes. 'Instead, they have chosen single life.' As one of her interviewees puts it, 'Being single isn't a matter of not wanting to be married, any more than I became a professor because I didn't want to be a surgeon, or a pilot [...] I became a professor because I wanted to be a professor. And I'm happy being single because that's who I am.'[21]

I have always thrived in solitude. It's not just a matter of being introverted, although I am. I love deciding exactly what I am going to eat and when, without anyone there to tell me I can't have breakfast at ten o'clock or lunch at three. I love cooking for myself and having leftovers to last me several days. I love not having to cater to anyone else's tastes when I decorate the spaces around me. I love doing things because they bring me joy, and not holding back because it's not what's 'normal'.

For people who prefer a household of one, all the scare stories about coming home to a lonely, empty home are inaccurate. Happily single people come home to a space that is catered to their preferences, where they can be their most authentic selves, and don't have to curb or limit any of their behaviours to account for other people being around. When they go out, they are not doing so as a sad loner who couldn't find anyone to come with them, but as someone confident to go places alone. And the social benefits are measurable. In one study of 10,000 Australian women in their seventies, researchers compared those who had always been single with those who were married and those who had previously been married:

> In later life, the lifelong single women were not just keeping up with the other women but surpassing them in many ways. They were the most optimistic and the least stressed. They had larger social networks than the married women. They were more likely to be active members of formal social groups. They were strikingly healthier: they had the fewest number of diagnoses of major illnesses [...] they were least likely to be smokers and most likely to be non-drinkers [...] the researchers concluded that far from being a 'problem' group, their 'life experiences and opportunities had prepared them for a successful and productive older age'.[22]

What stands out to me here is how these women had 'larger social networks'. I'm not surprised at all. Part of the problem with the weight we put on romantic partners is that it can lead to your partner being, in David Jay's words, your 'source of everything'. But if you're aromantic, or 'single at heart', then you aren't relying on the prospect of a romance to fulfil all of your social needs. As DePaulo writes, rather than relying on a Magical Mythical Romantic Partner to show up and take away all loneliness from our lives, 'we didn't count on a real or imagined future spouse to be our caretakers, fixers, or financial backstops. Instead we invested in ourselves, we invested in The Ones (instead of The One), and we prepared for a single life that would last for life.'[23] By 'The Ones', DePaulo is referring to the networks of close relationships that many single people form. We are less likely to regard our friends as 'just' friends, and more likely to invest time and energy into them. We spread our social nets wide.

Who will take care of you if you live alone? some protest. *Who will look after you when you age, or when you're ill?* For starters, that's no reason to pursue a relationship. If you prefer single life and feel happiest and healthiest that way, then starting a relationship just as a safeguard against being alone with your illnesses in decades' time is going to make you and your partner miserable. And having a relationship is no guarantee that you'll never be alone with your problems. Partners leave; spouses die. Unless you happen to die on the exact same day as your romantic partner, romance is no guarantee that you'll never have to cope with life's slings and arrows alone.

And besides – who says we'll be alone? We will have our friends. We'll have the people we've spent years nurturing close, caring relationships with, the people we have never relegated to second place just because our relationships with them are not romantic. We'll have friends who'll drop everything to be with us and support us.

Who'll be there for you if you don't have a spouse? Maybe that's the wrong question. The right question is one that Bella DePaulo asks in *Single at Heart*: 'Who will be there for you, if you make your spouse or romantic partner the centre of your universe, demote everyone else, and then that person is gone?'[24]

7

Friendless

The Problem with the Decline of Friendship

'The thing people don't realize about sex work,' Bug said, 'is that maybe 50 per cent of it is just holding people while they cry.'

I looked up, my interest leaping. I was at a gathering with some friends, one of whom had brought Bug (it/its), his partner, along. As the conversation continued, I sat quietly, reflecting on what Bug had said about its work. It made sense to me immediately, and I wanted to understand why.

Later, all I had to do was Google 'sex work people crying', and I found my way to a Reddit page entitled, 'Sex workers of Reddit, what's the saddest experience you've had with a client?' And there were dozens of stories. Sex workers talked about clients with crippling social anxiety who hired them because it was the only way they could have a conversation with someone. Clients whose families didn't support them in their mental health troubles and who, in one case, 'paid $3500 just to have a sleepover with me'. People going through bereavement and desperate for some kind of affection and comfort; closeted people aching to be touched by someone of the gender they were attracted to as they couldn't be elsewhere; touch-starved men who felt that affection was inaccessible to them. Plenty, like Bug, reported clients breaking down in tears, not wanting sex at all but just needing to be held. 'Many of my appointments actually don't involve any sex,' one of the Reddit users reported. 'They involve companionship. Almost all involve cuddles.'

The general impression I got was that a lot of people were going to sex workers because they wanted a space where they could allow themselves to be vulnerable, and receive love. People were lonely, starved of physical and emotional connection, and in desperate need of company.

Loneliness is about more than just being alone. You can be in solitude and not be lonely; loneliness is the state 'that results from a discrepancy between the quality and quantity of relationships we perceive we have and the quality and quantity of relationships we want to have'.[1] It's about our social and emotional needs not being met. And our entire planet seems to be going through a loneliness epidemic, one so serious that the World Health Organization has dubbed it a 'global public health concern'.[2]

They're right to do so. Loneliness *is* a health issue; about 50 per cent of people who say they are lonely also say that they are depressed – and depression itself can increase loneliness by causing people to 'isolate themselves from people around them, and hold more negative perceptions about their relationships'.[3] People living in social isolation are as much as 50 per cent more likely to experience dementia, as well as being more likely to suffer from strokes or heart disease. So it should be a concern for all of us when loneliness increases – and it *is* increasing. In a video called 'the friendship recession', Richard E. Reeves, a senior fellow at the Brookings Institution, states that '15 per cent of men today say that they don't have a close friend. That was just 3 per cent in 1990.' Reeves also points out how men today say that they would confide in a parent over a close friend.[4] A study by Cigna Healthcare found that as many as three in five Americans felt lonely in their lives. Almost half of UK residents feel lonely 'occasionally, sometimes, often or always'. Dr Vivek H. Murthy, former Surgeon General of the United States, published an intensive study into the loneliness epidemic in 2023, pointing out that Americans' trust in their community was declining: 'In 1972 [...] roughly 45% of Americans felt they could reliably trust other Americans; however, that proportion shrank to roughly 30% in 2016.' The report also found that people were spending, on average, 20 hours less every month interacting with friends. Unsurprisingly, anyone who's marginalized is more likely to suffer from loneliness: disabled people, LGBTQIA+ people, people of colour, those with mental or physical health issues, single parents and those with fewer economic means. Older people, especially those in homes, as well as teens and young adults, are also at especial risk.[5]

Psychologists and sociologists point the finger for this crisis at everything, from the Covid pandemic to political polarization distancing us from our communities, from increased social media use to our mental health and work environments. I don't doubt that all of these have a part to play. What I want to look at, though, is that friendship recession: the growing number of people who, in Reeves's words, 'lack a certain number of close friends [and] have fewer people to turn to'. The friendship recession is entangled with amatonormativity, with the relegating of friendship to second place, with the social assumption that maturity comes with romance, not friendship, that life partners are romantic. And this is devastating to those of us for whom friendships are not just important, but the closest, most beautiful relationships of our lives.

For me, there is no such thing as 'just' friends. There can be nothing *just* about friendships. My friendships are the closest, most intimate relationships I have; the people I'll make tea and food for when they're sick, the people I'll tell 'I love you', the people I want around me and who I feel most alive around.

I'm generalizing, of course. Not everyone, aro or allo, feels the same intensity of, or desire for, platonic relationships, and there's an emerging community of 'aplatonic' people who don't experience a platonic attraction to others. There's very little research into aplatonic people thus far, and as such there's little information available, and the community itself is still debating on the term's definition. So, for now, I will simply say this: no one's worth as a person is dependent upon their ability to form friendships nor their inclination to do so. No aromantic experiences are the same. While I am discussing, here, the experiences of those who do place a great deal of value upon friendships, this is by no means universal.

For those of us who *do* have a drive towards close friendships, platonic feelings are a powerful thing – and this is true whether you're allo or aro. I've felt the same burst of delight on seeing a message from a particular friend light up on my phone as (I assume) alloromantics feel on seeing one from their partner; I've yearned for friends when separated from them. When I was thirteen, I believed for a time that I had a crush on a male classmate; later, I realized I'd just had an intense desire to be his friend. I wanted to spend time with him and talk about dragons and horses and the other things we both loved. It wasn't romantic. I never once imagined kissing him or holding his hand or going on dates with him, and if he had ever expressed feelings for me, I would have told him I didn't feel the same. But it was still a craving for closeness.

When, in later years, the two of us were moved to different classes and rarely had the chance to speak anymore, I felt the loss. Because friendships have ample opportunity for heartbreak, just as romances do. The end of a friendship can be devastating, and you can pine to be a closer friend to someone just as you might to be romantically involved with them. As Theo puts it on a post they made on their Tumblr blog:

> romance does not have a monopoly on love, you know this, that's step one. step two is that romance does not have a monopoly on yearning, on heartbreak. it's easy to think yourself immune, that you've been dealt a hand that'll let you dodge those arrows, but do you know how many ways there are to break a heart? how many ways there are to fall, even if not in love? your heart is just as strong as anyone's, so be kind to it.
>
> don't get me wrong, i love being aro and i love that i'm aro. the good news is that you don't actually miss out on anything. the bad news is that you don't actually miss out on anything.[6]

In other words: aros don't miss out on closeness and intimacy just because we don't experience romantic feelings. But neither do we miss out on both the triumphs and the tragedies that come with human relationships.

This post became what Theo laughingly refers to as 'a bit of a therapy post'. If you scroll through the notes left on the post by other Tumblr users, you'll see dozens of people describing their own platonic heartbreaks, their own experiences of unrequited desire for friendship or better familial relationships. And not only do aromantics experience our own platonic yearnings and heartbreaks, but many of those I spoke to said that they sometimes feel their friendship breakups and longings often seem more intense than those of their allo peers. Take these comments, for instance, posted on the aro forum 'Aropocalypse':

> Brotzman_t: My aro-ness really affects my friendships. As a kid and even into college, I would always be the one who had the hardest time grieving friends who moved away [...] I will get instantly and strongly attached to certain people within days of meeting them for the first time. The best way that I can describe it is that I just *care* so hard about them, for some reason that even I can't always figure out. It's just an instant, undefinable spark. I suppose it's like a platonic version of 'love at first sight.' The problem is, since the average person is alloromantic, they rarely grow to care about me quite as much as I care about them – and even if they do, it's never as quickly as I do.
>
> Rabbitastic: I have realized that my standards for what makes a person a friend are much higher than my non-aro friends' standards. They have admitted to stuff such as having work 'friends' who they actively avoid outside of work or friends who they do not trust. I can't imagine those sorts of conditions in my friendships at all.
>
> Roboticanary: I place a high value on relying on friends, as in if someone was worried about a something, or someone was dealing with a difficult event in their life I have no expectation of having a partner to comfort me, so I see that as something that a friend just does. I would jump up

> at two in the morning and travel to the other side of the country to be with a friend in need. I would drop my plans and take care of a friend's child if I knew they were stuck for options.[7]

Perhaps the defining feature of these comments is a level of intense commitment. Because aros have no anticipation of a romantic partner, we often tend to place a level of devotion and a desire for sustained closeness beyond that of most alloromantic friendships. This is not to say that aros inherently form 'better' friendships. But many of us are inclined to give them a more prominent place in our minds and to commit more emotional energy to them – if just because we know that we *can*, because there is no romantic partner to put above them.

As a result, living as an aromantic in a world where friendship is assumed to take second place to romance can be incredibly isolating. I am certain that this assumption is a factor in our current loneliness epidemic. The very language we use in our day-to-day lives encourages us to view our friendships as lesser, to pay less attention to them than we do to romantic partners, and to place all the weight of our emotional vulnerabilities and needs, all our hopes for happiness, upon romance. We say 'just friends', qualifying friendship as somehow *only*. You can have a thriving, loving circle of close friends, and still be asked if you've 'met someone yet'. Romance novels are a tradition; the closest thing we have to a 'friendship novel' is the buddy comedy. It saddens me that such friendship-centric stories seem only to exist in the comedy genre, while romance stories are so much broader and often go so much deeper into the emotions involved. Why are friendship-driven tales limited to light entertainment, as if they're inherently shallower? Could we not have a story that feels like a platonic *Titanic?* A platonic *One Day?*

When your romantic partner is supposed to be your source of everything, the dominant wellspring of intimacy and connection in your life – how can we not be lonely? We focus everything on a single person, at the expense of giving more time and emotional energy to our friendships, and appreciating the unique things that each friend gives you that your partner might not.

Recently, many of my older brother's friends got married, and my parents warned him to make sure he kept meeting up with them regularly, 'or this might be the last time you see a lot of them'. It was experience talking, I found, when I asked them. They tend to see their truly close friends only once every few months. 'Once you and your friends get married,' my dad said, 'people move away and settle in different places. Your priorities shift, and all your time is spent looking after your family, providing for them. It's not like when you were all single, and you lived close by, or even together, and saw each other every day.'

'Do you ever miss that time?' I asked.

'Yes,' he said. He didn't even hesitate. 'And… yes, I do get lonely.'

What about his parents? Did they have close friends? He paused to think, then said, 'Yes. My father had one.'

This is clearly a generational habit. We learn from watching our parents that it's normal not to have many friends later in life. Of course, having a spouse and children does require a heavy time commitment, so it's understandable that those who do couple up have less time on their hands for platonic meetups. But we should be careful to maintain platonic bonds as much as we can – because as much as romantic relationships provide companionship, they can also create isolation.

Coupledom and marriage are often described as a kind of social glue, something that binds an individual to the community. But much more often, they end up creating insularity. It's all too common that once people form a committed, long-term relationship, they start to feel like they don't really need any more social connections. 'When couples have children,' writes DePaulo, 'they often settle into the comfort and privacy of their own home. They might slip out now and then for a baseball game or a pizza, but like the cliché says, their home is their castle. [...] they practice what I see as intensive nuclearity. They act as a tight, self-contained unit.'[8]

In 2015, a study in the *Journal of Social and Personal Relationships* set out to compare whether singledom isolated people from their communities or integrated them. The researchers asked people who were married, who had previously been married or who were never married how often they interacted with their close relationships outside of a spouse. Had they socialized with their neighbours and friends at least several times a month? Had they seen their parents or siblings at least once a week in the last year? Had they given or received help from parents, siblings, neighbours, friends or co-workers – any 'advice, encouragement, and moral or emotional support; help with shopping, errands, or transportation; help with housework, yard work, car repairs, or other work around the house; or help with childcare'?[9]

The results were unequivocal: those who were married socialized least with family, friends and neighbours, and they gave and received the least help. This remained true even when the researchers controlled for factors such as age, financial resources and parenthood – meaning that it's not just the time-consuming business of child-rearing that influences married people to see their community less. The researchers suggested that their results might be tied to Western individualism; to how much we prize being independent and self-reliant. 'Americans,' they state, 'believe couples should be able to make it on their own – both practically and emotionally, and spouses are expected to rely on each other for their day-to-day needs and act as each other's soul mates and confidants. [. . .] such disengagement would be far less common in those 'traditional' societies, where extended kinship is the primary source of support and marriage is primarily a linkage forged between groups rather than between two individuals who marry.'[10]

And this kind of retreat into the family unit is not a temporary thing, a symptom of the honeymoon infatuation. Studies carried out over a six-year period found that married people were still less likely to be in contact with their families, friends and neighbours at the end of that period as when they had first married.[11]

Sociologists call this *dyadic withdrawal:* the retreating of the married couple into the 'dyad', the two, at a distance from the other relationships in their lives. What does this look like? Perhaps something like the dozens of threads I found on 'ask' pages, such as Reddit, Quora and agony aunt-esque columns: 'Why do friends dump their best friends after they get married?' 'Why do married people seem to totally ditch their single friends after the wedding?' 'Does anybody feel left behind by their married friends?' In *Psychology Today*, Bella DePaulo published a letter from a single person whose longest, closest friend, someone the writer used to see and talk to every single day, had suddenly withdrawn after her marriage. 'Weeks would pass between phone calls. I couldn't call her, because she was always busy when I did, so I'd wait for her to call... and wait, and wait.'[12]

Dyadic withdrawal can affect everyone whose friends suddenly pull away to focus on their spouse; the writers of so many of those internet threads seemed stunned, bewildered, feeling that their friends' sudden step back had been completely unexpected. Others had dreaded this for years, and were now watching their fears play out. And that dread is particularly pronounced for aspec people, for whom friendships are often so crucial. I saw the same questions asked again and again by my survey respondents and interviewees: what if all their friends coupled up and left them behind? What would they do once everyone they loved had moved on to 'more important' relationships?

The message that dyadic withdrawal sends to aromantic people is beyond alienating. When coupled friends suddenly draw away, they unconsciously send us a message. *Friendships*, they tell us, *these bonds that are at the core of your life, that nourish and fulfil you – they're a secondary form of love. Now I have a source of greater, more real love, I no longer need you.*

And when we try to protest, we rarely meet with much understanding. A common theme on all those online threads was people telling the askers *this is just what happens. People's priorities are different once they marry. They want to focus on their spouse now.* The woman who wrote to Bella DePaulo stated that when she'd told an acquaintance of how heartbroken she was by her friend's withdrawal, that acquaintance 'wondered why I was so upset', and decided that she must secretly be in love with her friend. The message of such a statement is loud and clear: it's not normal to be so distressed at the loss of a friendship. The only way the writer could be so upset was for her to have romantic feelings.

All of this tells aromantics, *you don't love as fully as the rest of the world does. There is a depth of feeling that you are incapable of, and the love that you want to give is not equal to everyone else's. No one will ever see a connection with you as being as important as a romance. When others find romance, they will leave you behind. And you just have to accept that.*

*

Even if amatonormativity could somehow be erased, there are still a multitude of practical obstacles in the way of having stable, intimate friendship groups. Many of my friends live hours away, and I most often see them through online calls. A handful are friends I made online and who, with a few wonderful exceptions, I've never had a chance to meet in 'real life'. None of my close friends live within a walkable distance.

Even when our friends are close at hand, intimacy can remain at arm's length. Western society draws a hard line between friendship and romance, with particular activities or levels of physical touch that tend to get sorted into a romantic activity category or a platonic one. Sex, for the most part, is considered something that happens between romantic partners. So is living together permanently, making a big gesture to show your love, going to a party together. Raising a child together is something romantic partners do; going out with someone you don't know well with the hope of getting to know them is a date, and dates are romantic.

The total demarcation between romance and sex is, in many cases, a Western phenomenon. Ethiopian writer Mihret Sibhat writes powerfully of how commonplace physical contact was in her formative years in Ethiopia, both between and across genders. The lines between romance and friendship were often blurry and fluid: she knew of women married to men who, at the same time, had romantic relationships with women. 'Men are for family,' a saying went, 'women are for love.' Sibhat writes of how 'passionate same-sex friendships, even those that occasionally slipped into sex – had not been considered homosexual activities that required a rigid identity'.[13]

But then came increased Western influence, and with it, the vilification of homosexuality. Sibhat noticed people touching each other less, a gulf appearing between platonic and romantic where it had not existed before. 'The shades of platonic intimacy that filled the space between friendship and more permanent sexual relationships are vanishing. The edge of romance is now a cliff.'

Something similar is happening in Lesotho. Historically, the Basotho (the people of Lesotho) have had the concept of *motso-alle:* women who share intimacy both physical and emotional, often alongside having a husband. In her autobiography, *Singing Away the Hunger: The Autobiography of an African Woman*, Mpho 'M'atsepo Nthunya writes of her *motsoalle* in a chapter called 'When a Woman Loves a Woman':

> When I was living in the mountains I got a special friend [...] I passed her house when I was going to church every month. One day she saw me and said [...] 'Today I want to talk to you. I want you to be my motsoalle.' This is a name we have in Sesotho for a very special friend. She says, 'I love you.'
>
> It's like when a man chooses you for a wife, except when a man chooses, it's because he wants to share the blankets with you. The woman chooses you in the same way, but she doesn't want to share the blankets. She wants love only. When a woman loves another woman, you see, she can love with a whole heart.
>
> I saw how she was looking at me, and I said, '*Ke hante,* it's fine with me.' So she kissed me, and from that day she was my motsoalle.[14]

The lines between friendship, sex and romance were not the same as in the Western conception. When K. Limakatso Kendall, to whom Nthunya dictated her autobiography, asked about women in Lesotho who 'share the blankets with each other: 'M'e Mpho found that uproariously funny. "It's *impossible* for two women to share the blankets," she said. "You can't have sex unless somebody has a *koai* [penis]."'[15] Kendall discovered that many Basotho women engaged in intimacy that was not considered 'sex', although an outsider would have viewed it in that way. This intimacy between women was entirely socially acceptable, often taking place alongside heterosexual marriage and considered completely compatible with it.

Motsoalle were a traditional part of pre-colonial Basotho life, but, with time, the pressures of Western, Christian society promoted the heterosexual, monogamous marriage more and more, and *motsoalle* began to disappear. Nthunya was writing in 1997, by which time the ways she'd grown up with were already vanishing:

> In the old days friendship was very beautiful – men friends and women friends. Friendship was as important as marriage. Now this custom is gone; everything is changing. People now don't love like they did long ago. Today the young girls only want men friends; they don't know how to choose women friends.[16]

Indian writer Samir Chopra speaks of a similar phenomenon when he moved from India to the USA. In India, 'physical contact was relatively unproblematic,' he writes. 'I put my arms around my male friends' shoulders, did not rigorously negotiate inter-personal physical space, and demonstrated affection and companionship through a variety of physical gestures.' But other Indian immigrants warned him he could not do the same in the USA. 'America seemed – from a distance – to be suffering a national crisis of masculine insecurity [...] men were not physically demonstrative in their claims of friendship; they did not hug their male friends; they did not put arms around male friends.'[17] If they did, Chopra says, you would be called a 'fag' or a 'homo'.

Western judgements about how much physical affection is acceptable between friends are not universal truths, or just the way humans always behave. They are specific to locations and time periods; they are born from insecurity, homophobia and the writing of Western ideals over those of other cultures.

Chopra's experience also speaks to how gendered these judgements about 'acceptable' platonic intimacy are. Certain types of touch might be considered platonic when between women (or people perceived as women) but are pronounced romantic should they occur between a man and a woman, or two men. Cuddling, playing with someone's hair, holding hands, touching or kissing foreheads – even between women, some might feel these touches cross a line.

You can go on holiday with a friend who is (perceived as) the same gender as you, unless those around you know or perceive you to be gay or bi. But do that as a man and woman, and you'll likely have people assuming that you're together. 'Men only get to show each other affection when it's laddish,' says Jan. 'You can slap each other on the back, you can be in a sports huddle, but you can't have a long, tender hug. I know a friend who had a [male] friend sleeping over at his for a few days, and he said, "I hope people don't think I'm gay."' Author Adam 'Smiley' Poswolsky echoes this sentiment in his book *Friendship in the Age of Loneliness: An Optimist's Guide to Connection*, talking about his frustration with 'awkward hugs – you know, the kind where two men are afraid of demonstrating how much they actually love each other [...] I drink beer, you drink beer, too? I like sports, you like sports too, right? I'm not gonna get too close because people might think we're lovers, and I'm still afraid of being called "gay".'[18]

Especially in the USA and UK, men are deprived of gentle physical affection and discouraged from giving it at a young age. As Mark Greene, author of *Remaking Manhood*, writes in a powerful article, many parents 'step back from physical contact with boys when their sons approach puberty'.[19] Boys then grow up in a culture of internalized homophobia where physical affection between men, any association with the traits typically associated with femininity – such as talking in depth about feelings, or being soft and nurturing – is labelled as 'gay' and unmanly. They are presented with role models in the media and popular culture who tend not to show gentle physical affection towards anyone but (usually female) sexual partners or family members. 'All opportunity for potential physical touch is abruptly handed over to young boys' female peers,' Greene writes. 'The vast universe of platonic human touch is suddenly reduced to the exclusive domain of one person and is blended into the sexual.' The message to men is clear: 'Find a girlfriend or give up human contact [...] American men are never taught to do gentle non-sexual touch.'[20]

When men are discouraged from intimacy, both physical and emotional, they can struggle to form deep and intimate friendships. Of course, men have friendships, but when philosophers Larry May and Robert A. Strikwerda asked their male peers about their friendships, they found that most of them had friendships based in comradeship (such as sports teams and other social groups that create a sense of belonging and team identity).

These involved shared activities and 'parallel play', where men performed the same activity together – drinking in a bar, for example, while commenting on sports – without engaging on a more emotional level.[21] 'Such companionship is enjoyable, [but] if *all* of one's friendships display such a lack of intimacy, then one's life will be impoverished [...] if men are open to intimacy only with female friends or partners, they cut themselves off from deeply rewarding relationships with other men, as well as help perpetuate a debilitating gender pattern in which women do the emotional work for men.' A key component of emotional intimacy is self-disclosure: revealing personal information about yourself, your life and your feelings to another. But, as May and Strikwerda point out, 'in order to be able to engage in self-disclosure, persons must be able to gain access to the feelings they are trying to disclose to friends'.[22] How can you reveal your feelings if you've never been taught to recognize and interpret them, and if you've always been told that being openly emotional disqualifies you from being a real man? And if this kind of disclosure is off limits to you, how can you form any emotional intimacy, and get the physical intimacy that might come with it?

Considering this, it should be no wonder that people go to Bug, and its fellow sex workers, just to be held. Just to have a shoulder to cry into. Just to have the nurturing physical touch that men, in particular, find hard to source elsewhere. People feel starved of closeness. It makes sense that they seek out human touch, human connection. (No two humans need the exact same things, of course. Plenty of people don't need much or any physical contact, whether because of neurodivergence, trauma or personal preference.)

We are in an age of loneliness. We have fewer people to be vulnerable and affectionate with, and we are farther from them.

We have fewer people with whom we share gentle touch. So, it's time to start considering how to keep our friends closer.

*

It may seem counterintuitive when we're talking about friendship – but first, let's take a closer look at dating.

Dating is, without question, a romantic thing. It's something people do to figure out if there's a 'spark' between them, to see if they might be compatible in a long-term romantic relationship. Endless columns, podcasts, videos, classes, seminars and books exist to tell prospective partners how to handle themselves on a date; how to appear attractive, what to say, how to flirt, how to assess the other person's body language. How to spot the signs that someone will be a bad partner; how to gauge whether the 'vibe' is right for a kiss at the end.

Before I figured out the whole 'aroace' thing, this last one always bewildered me. I remember how, every week, my mother and I read the blind date column in the Saturday paper, eager to see if this week's couple had liked each other or not – but I was always a little confused by the whole process. How was anyone supposed to know that they wanted to kiss a person, let alone pursue a relationship, after one date? Never having experienced attraction, I had no idea that it was a bodily sensation, and so assumed that it was just a synonym for 'falling in love'. No wonder I didn't think one date was enough.

Of course, I eventually had this epiphany – and realized that attraction is exactly what people are hoping for on a first date. They're looking for the 'spark', the chemistry, a romantic and sexual pull. If it's not there (from what I understand), people are unlikely to arrange a second date. To go back to those blind date columns: I've lost count of the number I read where participants finished up by saying some variation of 'we had a great time, but there wasn't a spark'. Some would say that they'd love to meet again, 'but only as friends'. They would praise their date as a wonderful person, 'but romance wasn't in the air'. They didn't kiss, they'd say, because 'it wasn't the vibe'.

For many people, this formula works just fine. But for a sizeable portion of the aspec community, this approach – the format of meeting someone, seeing if there's a spark, and if there isn't trying someone else – does not work. More than that; it can't work.

A few years ago, Isaac (he/they) went looking for a partner via a dating app. To his surprise, he met with a lot of responses very quickly. 'It was insane,' he laughs. 'I don't think I'd really expected anyone to be interested in me.' But when it came to Isaac's turn to respond to his unexpected slew of suitors, he realized he had a problem. Namely: he's demiromantic.

Asexual and aromantic identities are, like so much of human experience, a spectrum. At one pole, there are allo people. At the other, fully ace or aro people like myself. And between these poles are a multitude who don't feel entirely like one or the other. Some are demisexual and/or demiromantic ('demi'), like Isaac, meaning that they need to form a strong emotional bond with someone before sexual and/or romantic attraction can occur. Others experience attraction very rarely, very weakly, or only towards a certain person or handful of people. These people might identify as 'grey-asexual' or 'grey-aromantic', so called because their experiences of attraction fall into a grey area between being fully allo and being fully aro or ace.

Greys and demis are not simply being picky. A grey-aro or demiromantic person may grow up not understanding their peers' sudden flurry to date, bewildered by the priority that society places on romance. A grey-ace or demisexual person will not be attracted to strangers, may struggle to understand the elusive term 'hot', and may be labelled a prude for their disinterest in sex. In these ways, their experiences align with mine, even though they can feel attraction and I cannot. And yes, many people choose not to have sex or to commit to a romantic relationship until they are emotionally close to their partner, but that isn't the same as Isaac's experience of *lacking a form of attraction altogether* until he's formed such a bond.

One model that many aspecs find useful is the distinction between *primary* and *secondary* attraction. Primary attraction is an attraction based on what's available to you instantly at your first look at a person: their appearance, their smile, their smell, their build. Secondary attraction is an attraction based on information that isn't instantly available, such as a person's personality, interests, opinions, and what their company is like. Different people will need different amounts of time to get to know a person well enough for secondary attraction to occur.

To be clear, no one is suggesting that secondary attraction is a better or purer form of attraction. It's just a useful distinction: an allo person will experience both primary and secondary attraction. An aroace person will experience neither. A demi person won't experience primary attraction, but *will* experience secondary attraction.

Consider this scenario: you've been chatting to a new acquaintance with whom you've been getting along well. They ask for your number, suggesting that they're interested in dating you. For most allo people, you'll already know whether you want to give them a yes or no. You can make the decision based on the presence (or lack) of primary attraction. If you're demi, however, an honest answer would likely be, 'Can we be friends – maybe for months, maybe for years – until I know whether I could be attracted to you?' It's only the information that isn't immediately on hand that will allow a demi person to know if secondary attraction will come along.

But that is not how dating works. As Isaac considered how to respond and who to respond to, he realized that his potential dates would all be looking for chemistry – not just the interpersonal chemistry of friends, but romantic chemistry – on a first date. If Isaac responded to any of the unexpected multitude of potential dates, he'd have to admit that, while he was interested in getting to know them and having a relationship, he was not yet attracted to them, and might not be for months, at least – if he ended up romantically attracted to them at all.

He couldn't see many of his unexpected slew of suitors being open to such a thing. Most allo people would be unlikely to want to pursue dating for that long without knowing if it was 'going somewhere'. So Isaac deleted the app.

In the end, he did find a partner. His current boyfriend began as one of Isaac's friends, already sharing time and interests with each other, and their feelings grew naturally out of that. And Isaac's story hints at a problem with our formula for dating: it's so focused on looking for a 'spark' early on that potential relationships – romantic and platonic – can be discarded or overlooked because the chemistry isn't present.

Should we really be expecting 'chemistry' to come along so fast? It's obviously useless for demis, as well as for plenty of ace people. But there's evidence that even for a majority of allo people, most relationships don't arise from an early-onset spark. Most romances in fact begin, as Isaac's did, between people who already know each other.

'There is more than one pathway to romance,' writes Danu Anthony Stinson in a 2022 study on relationship initiation. Most studies on how relationships begin, Stinson points out, 'overwhelmingly focus on romance that sparks between strangers and largely overlook romance that develops between friends. This limited focus might be justified if friends-first initiation was rare or undesirable, but our research reveals the opposite.'[23]

In fact, Stinson found that whatever movies lead us to expect, most of us don't form 'dating initiation' relationships. As many as three-quarters of couples begin with 'friends-first' initiation, where the participants were already friends before romantic feelings began to bloom. Moreover, when surveyed, most said that they *preferred* such a start to a relationship. When asked what the best way to meet a partner was, almost 48 per cent said: 'a friendship turning romantic'. Some of the next most common options included varieties of situation in which people might already know each other, such as having mutual friends, being at the same school or university, attending the same religious group or sharing a workplace. Only one respondent out of 1,897 said that online dating services were the way they preferred to meet a partner, and there were only four votes for bars or social clubs.

And regardless of what cynics might say about heterosexual men and women being unable to form friendships without sex getting in the way, 70 per cent of friends-first couples really were platonic first; the friendship didn't begin because one partner wanted to get into the other's bed. And the study indicated that friends-first partners do take a long time getting to know each other – an average of just under twenty-two months before things turn romantic.

Stop and consider that for a moment. A majority of romantic relationships occur out of existing friendships. Most people *prefer* this approach. The average time for such a friendship to change shape into a romance is almost two years.

And yet we expect people to decide whether they're attracted to a person on the *very first date?*

There are plenty of reasons to give more air and attention to friends-first relationship initiation. For a start, as Stinson points out, 'if people assume that men and women cannot be platonic friends because sexual attraction inevitably gets in the way, and if researchers assume that everyone desires and prioritizes romantic relationships over friendships and singlehood [...] it may be difficult to conceive of the possibility that men and women might maintain a platonic friendship for months or even years.'[24] But men and women clearly do have truly platonic friendships, even if they do eventually turn romantic. Stinson also points out that gendered expectations tend to fall away between partners who are friends first. 'First dates involving (presumably heterosexual) women and men typically follow gender-role prescriptions,' Stinson writes (we can assume she is referring to things such as men 'making the first move' and paying for the bill, and women feeling pressured not to appear too up for sex or too prudish, and so on). 'Expectations for first dates are more egalitarian during friends-first initiation,' Stinson continues, 'which may alter the power structure of developing relationships.'[25] Good.

And let's reconsider that one phrase: 'if researchers assume that everyone desires and prioritizes romantic relationships over friendship and singlehood'. It's amatonormativity showing its face again. Relationship studies have assumed that friends-first initiation isn't as common as dating-first, and focused their efforts on it, because they assume that people will choose romance over friendship. And this helps erase the reality of friendships between women and men.

Of course, that leaves the 30 per cent of friends-first couples who became friends because one of them had an attraction to the other. Sometimes, things turned romantic after that person expressed their feelings, but this often isn't the case. Plenty of people have unreciprocated feelings for a friend and, if turned down, deal with it maturely and respectfully. There are, however, those who'll cling to another concept that's strengthened by amatonormativity: the 'friendzone'.

The term 'friendzone' implies more than just unrequited love. Someone – although the term is most often applied to men – has been 'friendzoned' if a woman (and it is usually a woman) sees them as 'just a friend' when the man had a romantic and sexual interest.

As plenty of criticism has already pointed out, the problem with the 'friendzone', as distinct from normal unrequited love, is that the term has connotations of blame, or at least responsibility, for the lack of a romantic relationship. 'I had feelings for her, but she didn't feel the same way' is not a statement that places blame on anyone. 'She put me in the friendzone' implies that she has *done something* to you, relegated you to an 'inferior' level of relationship – one from which you don't return. 'I could have had a relationship with her,' the sentiment is, 'if she hadn't friendzoned me.' The lack of a relationship is based on the woman arbitrarily deciding to put the man in the friendzone, rather than any judgement she has made about their compatibility or her preferences.

In the way the term 'friendzone' quickly became used, it vilified women who didn't return someone's romantic feelings, implying that the man had *earned* a right to romance by being nice to her – even if he had been nice to her purely in the hope of having a relationship. He was wronged when the object of his affections placed him in friend purgatory.

Make no mistake, it's a misogynistic culture and mindset that causes someone to look at a woman who has rejected them and see her as having *wronged* them. It is misogynistic to look at a rejection and, rather than seeing it for the individual, personal thing it is, to declare that all women are incomprehensible beings who make arbitrary judgements. And the friendzone feels like the modern version of archaic structures that viewed women as the providers of sex to men – as *obliged* to provide sex to men.

And, as well as reducing women to caricatures and sexual objects, the friendzone reinforces that boundary between friendship and romance. It places friendship solidly on a lower tier than a romantic and sexual relationship, the second-best relationship for runners-up and also-rans.

Misogyny and allonormativity are inseparable. They feed into each other. We tell people that having a romantic and sexual partner is the only correct life state. And so people build all their hopes upon having a sexual and romantic partner, because how can they be happy without one? Combined with the pressure put on men to be sexual in order to be a 'real' man, a rejection can feel like it undermines their male identity *and* takes away their chances of happiness and self-validation in a single blow. And some lash out. They accuse women of friendzoning them; in the worst cases, they turn to incel spaces for comfort, for anything that will tell them it's not their fault that this has happened to them. Blaming all women is easier.

This is how we get 'nice guy syndrome'. This term refers to men who perform nice or friendly acts for a woman with the motivation of being able to have sex or a relationship with her. It's about giving in order to get. It is manipulative and transactional: 'I was nice to you, so you should give me what I want: a relationship.'

While I condemn this behaviour, I can see the weight of amatonormativity behind it. How often do we tell stories where a man who is good and helpful does *not* get the girl as a part of his happy ending? It's rare to see stories where a good man is rejected, and is able to live a content life anyway, because romance was not essential to his joy.

'Nice guys' believe that acting this way will enable them to purchase love, and love is what will make them happy. Their sense of self-worth becomes outsourced to the object of their affection. Should they be rejected, their chance at happiness is lost.

This is an intimidating knot to unravel. So many factors feed into these behaviours, from gendered social pressures on men, to misogyny, to the online 'manosphere' of incel culture. But one place to start is to break down that societal message that having a romantic and sexual partner will complete you. We tell people that your partner is the source of your happiness and, as a consequence, people are left to fixate on the prospect of romance. They neglect other opportunities for relationships, and lose out on building other strong bonds that could make them happy.

One human can never be your source of worth and happiness. It's unfair to expect such a thing of them – and it's unfair to you, too. Because as long as you are convinced you will only find those things in another person, you cannot find them in yourself.

*

We need to build up our platonic relationships. We need to decrease our dependency on a single romantic bond. So, what if we went about trying to create friendships with the same outlook we bring to looking for romantic partners, investing a similar level of time and emotion, with the aim of long-term commitment to the relationship.

Dating does not have to be inherently romantic. What if it were seen as a way to get to know someone in any capacity, as a potential partner *or* a potential friend? Imagine if you could meet people with an understanding that romance would be an enjoyable bonus should it happen, but for now you'll have other priorities: hanging out in cafés, playing board games and introducing each other to your social circles. The benefits could be myriad. In this scenario, you don't have to decide within hours if you're attracted to a stranger. You're encouraged to try out new activities and visit new places. If romantic feelings eventually arrive, you get to form the friendship-first romance that many prefer, often with more mutual understanding and perhaps even a better gender balance than you'd get in dating-first romances. But if they don't, you've made a friend.

What better way to combat today's loneliness epidemic?

I'm not alone in thinking that it might be helpful to blur the boundary between romantic dating and platonic 'hanging out'. 'Smiley' Poswolsky encourages people to approach potential friends the same way you might a romantic partner: 'always go on a second date'. Take more time to get to know a person rather than writing them off based on a single interaction. To examine how people might build more meaningful connections, Poswolsky contacted Dr Marisa Franco, a psychologist and friendship expert, who advised signing up to a regular activity or commitment with a potential new friend. 'This practice reflects a psychological principle known as the *mere-exposure* effect, which reveals that the more we see someone, the more we like them. This is why Dr Franco recommends signing up for ongoing activities like a book club, improv group, language class [...] more than going out to a bar or a one-off event. The repeated interactions you have with other attendees at those gatherings can lead to fruitful friendships.'[26]

Which is a very good point, and one that can apply to both friendships and dating. If you're not the kind of person who can be certain that you have a 'vibe' with someone over the course of one date – whether because you're demi, another aspec identity, or simply prefer friends-first initiation when it arises – then maybe the usual formula for single-event dates isn't right for you. It might be better to join a regular club together.

To be clear: trying to go directly to lovers is not a bad thing. It's great that we have an existing structure for those for whom this approach works. The problem is that it doesn't work for far, far more people than we tend to assume.

In fact, the expectation of sexual chemistry on a first date, and sex itself shortly thereafter, can be downright dangerous. The inherent risks of dating a stranger for anyone, but especially for women, queer people and people of colour, is only exacerbated when aspec identity is thrown into the mix as well. Juliet (she/her) knows this too well. 'So many men have threatened me with sexual assault as a means to cure me,' she says. 'On dates, I'd try to be open about the fact that I'd never even kissed anyone, and would not be kissing them on a first date – trying to set expectations and define boundaries – and it absolutely changed a man's expression when he looked at me. It was horrific. I could pinpoint the moment I stopped being a person and became a potential conquest.' And if she persisted in saying no, 'they called me a cold bitch who was wasting their time.'

For Juliet, dating has come to feel pointless. 'The general expectations of society make it impossible to get to know someone over a long period of time without them hounding you for sex. I literally have no idea how to meet people who are interested in getting to know someone for the sake of *getting to know them*, without sex as an immediate end goal.'

*

While technology can help people share some hobbies or activities remotely, in most cases, it can't replace one-on-one, face-to-face bonding – you can't have your own little side conversations as you might in a real-world meeting. If you want to go to the same club or class with someone, you need to live close enough to meet. Which brings us back to the issue of proximity.

In his book, Poswolsky points to research by Jeffrey A. Hall, a scholar of communications studies, that suggests it takes about fifty hours of shared time 'to go from acquaintance to casual friend, around ninety hours to become a true friend, and more than two hundred hours to be close friends and feel an emotional connection with someone'.[27] How can we carve out that much time to spend with someone when they live hours away from us?

Distance is not always a barrier to friendship. I've forged more than one close online friendship with people I haven't seen face to face more than once or even at all; I met friends during the pandemic years who I spoke to remotely long before we met in the 'real' world. But distance can contribute to a sense of loneliness. Even though I know my friends love me from counties or even continents away, it can be hard for that love to feel real when I don't get to have these people as a regular presence in my life.

Reading Stinson's study, a few of her results stood out to me. Stinson found that students and younger people were more likely to form friends-first relationships. I would guess that this has to do with the fact that students are *constantly around each other.* For many students, the problems of forming friendships and close relationships that I discussed earlier are diminished: you're usually within a walkable distance of each other, and you're often sharing many of the same communal spaces – kitchens, common rooms, student union bars and cafeterias, libraries. Of *course* more friends-first relationships begin among students. It's easier for students to find and make friends when a lot of people of the same age are together, living in a semi-communal manner – even helpfully sorted into groups of people who share interests by the different courses they study and the different societies they join.

So if this is the period of life we reminisce about the most, isn't it time to start looking at how we could incorporate a similar way of living into our adult lives?

It was with this in mind that I went to visit Marmalade Lane.

This small development on the outskirts of Cambridge in the UK is a story of happy accidents. Developers had walked away from the plot of land where it now stands, and the city council, who owned the plot, funded the development of a new co-housing initiative. Co-housing seeks to create communities more fluid, and more connected, than the traditional model of multiple separate households, each containing a self-contained family unit. Families or individuals have their own private home, but there are also shared facilities, such as communal gyms, kitchens and allotments. In the case of Marmalade Lane, the residents formed a new co-housing group and were involved in the planning of the community, ensuring that it was 'built according to the needs of residents rather than the profits of house builders'.[28]

The first thing that struck me when I arrived was the pedestrianized main street. There's a small car park at the entrance, but no vehicle access into the community itself. The street is thick with planters. As I waited for my guide to arrive, a child of about seven emerged, scooting on a toy car – completely unaccompanied. Why shouldn't he be? There were no cars around. By the time I left, a half-dozen kids had convened in the street, playing completely independent of oversight – because they *could*. Here, there was no need to go through the bureaucracy of adult arrangements for playdates: they could simply gather in a safe environment and wander.

The lack of cars, my guides told me, is critical. The architecture of the lane is centred around creating 'incidental connections'. Rather than existing in a self-contained unit, walled off from your neighbours, you can meet them as you go to the communal bins or laundry, as you work on the shared allotment (not the usual model, where a single household gets a little plot of land; it's one big garden for the entire community). There's a small gym, a workshop with a pottery wheel and woodworking tools; a small shop run by community members, lounges and playrooms, a study area and even a sauna. While some facilities, such as the gym, are communal, every house has its own kitchen and washing machine in addition to the shared ones; residents can enjoy as much privacy as they want, and join the communal spaces when they want. The architectural choices build in 'liminal space': areas that aren't quite public and aren't quite private. My guides pointed out the open back porch areas behind a row of flats that opened up onto the route to the communal compost bins and chicken pens. It's all built to facilitate people simply *running into each other*. And there are group activities: two communal meals a week, which residents can sign up for; parties; meetings to discuss the management of the community.

'The whole reason I became interested in co-housing,' one of my guides told me, 'was to avoid social isolation. My husband and I were in our terraced house in London, wondering, what happens when we're older? When we can't take care of ourselves? When one of us is gone, who's going to take care of the person who's left? Now, there's a community on their doorstep.

Marmalade Lane has, through its design, solved many of the problems I've discussed in this chapter. Rather than needing to pay to sit down with a friend, there are sitting rooms and a common area and green spaces everywhere. Rather than needing to travel and fork out money to share activities with anyone, you can stroll over to the gym (which is for everyone, no expensive membership required) or the workshop. For those with children, there are resources for kids less than a minute way, with that open play street, a climbing frame and trampoline, and indoor play areas: all of which the kids can roam by themselves without their parents having to supervise them 24/7. It's not some magical community with all lines between families knocked down – as my guides told me, it's not as if other families look after other people's kids as if they were their own – but it *is* an environment that eases dozens of small, everyday pressures.

Marmalade Lane is not the only place of its kind. In the UK, there's New Ground in London, a co-housing group of twenty-six women over fifty, based off the Dutch model of 'living groups as an alternative to expensive nursing homes and care institutions. [...] not only would it be cheaper, it would allow older people to mutually support each other and stay healthier, happier and more active'.[29] Each resident has 'health buddies' who check in on them frequently. When one resident broke her shoulder, 'my daughter and granddaughter came to visit, but they didn't have to keep coming round to make sure I was fed and watered. I had people to do my shopping and pop round for a glass of wine.' Or there's Cannock Mill in Essex, a co-housing group built to be environmentally friendly and to tackle loneliness. The residents run a car club – five cars for fourteen people – share their bikes, hold regular communal meals and have a social hub at the heart of the community.

Co-housing isn't the only form of communal and semi-communal living. Since 2019, 'Smiley' Poswolsky has lived in a co-living house with eleven housemates. Because of the communal areas, Poswolsky says, he and his friends constantly run into each other, with more people joining conversations and gatherings. 'The spaces in between being alone are filled with deep moments of connection.'[30]

But while there are myriad forms of communal living across the globe, it is still uncommon. There are only 302 homes in ten co-housing builds in the UK. Marmalade Lane was only built because the housing crisis of 2008 caused a developer to walk away from the site; otherwise, it would have been yet another housing estate making profit. And that's the problem: building green space and common houses isn't profitable for developers. What's more, buying into co-housing can be prohibitively expensive. While Marmalade Lane is cheaper than many of the surrounding estates, at the time of writing, it's still £195,000 for a single person's apartment to £530,000 for a five-bedroom home. In 2022, a house in Cannock Mill cost £689,000, and a flat was £271,000. It's a daunting prospect for a young person who might want to move into such a place, and it makes co-housing much less accessible for anyone who isn't white, middle-class and able-bodied.

This is probably why the most common form of communal living is the houseshare. For many younger people, those unable to work due to age or disability and those working minimum-wage jobs, a houseshare – where tenants live together, usually all contributing to pay rent to a landlord – can be the only option. While younger people do still make up the bulk of houseshares, the flat-sharing site SpareRoom has seen major increases in those seeking shared accommodation in every age group, with the largest increase in those aged 55–64: a 239 per cent increase between 2011 and 2022.[31] Some initiatives exist to match eligible people, including across the generations:

Homeshare UK, for instance, matches older people with younger tenants, usually with the older providing the living space, the younger providing some home assistance, and both providing companionship.[32] The problem with houseshares is that, both on the tenants' end and the landlord's, they exist for financial reasons: many of those living in them would like to live solo but can't afford it, and the landlords run houseshares intended to cram in the maximum number of people. They're far less likely to have common areas, sitting rooms, spacious kitchens, and all the spaces that places like Marmalade Lane build in to increase social connection.

While there are many factors at play in why our way of living is so individualized and self-contained, with the profit of developers perhaps foremost, I do think amatonormativity has a hand in it too. It's easy for us to receive the message that having a romantic partner will fulfil all your social needs and protect you from loneliness; that you don't need anything more than them and perhaps your children. And this can make us ready to accept the idea that the default way to live is in a home structured around romance and the nuclear family, walled off from even your immediate neighbours. Again: there's nothing wrong with this in itself, nor with anyone who finds that a perfectly healthy and happy way to live. Co-housing and communal living is not for everyone. But nuclear households should be *one option of many*, not the only one. And at the same time, communal living should be an *option*, not something people are forced into because solo living is too prohibitively expensive.

We need to put pressure on local councils and governments to create more co-housing builds; we need to make property developers see that this kind of construction will be in demand. We're a social species, and at heart, I doubt we were meant to live in individual homes, seeing our neighbours and friends only in snatches. They say it takes a village to raise a child. So why should it not take a village to maintain an adult, too?

*

October 2017. It's my first day at university. I've arrived earlier than almost everyone else; the corridors are empty, my bag unpacked. I've made a pledge with myself that I will be out and open about my identity here, and as I wait for the other new students to arrive, there's a thrill in imagining having friends who have never assumed me to be allo; people who know exactly who I am and welcome it.

Voices outside. I pull my door open to find a small crowd in the corridor, fellow freshers introducing themselves. One of them turns to me with a bright smile. 'Hey! I'm Aryehi, and I'm right here' – she waves at the door opposite mine – 'so I guess we're neighbours!'

We get talking. Within minutes, she's asked me the question that's the key to my heart: 'what genres of fiction are you into?' We're both English students, so we plunge into talking about books, TV shows, everything. We cook together, share lecture notes, cry into each other's shoulders. For the rest of our time at uni, we make sure we're never more than a door away from each other.

This year – seven years since I opened my door and saw my future favourite human being smile at me for the first time – I read a book that told a story so close to this experience, so familiar to me, that it felt like coming home. That book was *Loveless* by Alice Oseman, who's best known for her *Heartstopper* series of graphic novels. Oseman's protagonist, Georgia, is a first-year university student who has always loved romance, fanfiction and the whole concept of love. As the term goes on, however, it becomes clear to her that she is aromantic and asexual. At first, she's stricken, as she has always wanted the trappings of romance – the companionship, the big declarations, the overwhelming love.

But with time, Georgia realizes that none of those things have to be limited to romance, and her revelation helps her allo friends understand this too. Her lonely roommate, who has struggled to find the connection she's looking for in her sexual or romantic partners, finds in Georgia the life partner she's been craving. The two push their beds together and sleep side by side. Georgia makes a grand, public proposal of 'college marriage' to another friend and, by the end of the novel, Georgia's friend group is moving into a house together.

Oseman's novel is a wonderful, warming depiction of what aromantic visibility can do. Georgia's realization that she's aromantic is instrumental in helping not only her but her allo friends realize how integral their platonic love is to their lives, how much they want to prioritize each other in a way none of them have ever assumed they can do. All of them were living with the amatonormative assumption that you don't choose a platonic relationship as your life partner. Georgia, just by being an aroace person living her life, helps them question their assumptions and realize what they're really looking for: love and connection, in all its forms.

I had the chance to ask Oseman about loneliness; about how *Loveless* defies the idea that being aroace means being alone. 'One of the most freeing things anyone has said to me is this: being in a romantic relationship doesn't guarantee you won't be lonely,' Oseman told me. 'Even if you get married, have kids and grandkids, circumstances can occur that will still result in you being totally alone, or even dying alone. Being aroace doesn't cause loneliness. Anyone can be lonely, or end up alone, no matter their sexuality.'

What's different for aspec people, they said, is that we have to 'look outside the traditional structures of heteronormativity and amatonormativity to find those relationships, and maybe that's a little more challenging than if you were a straight person going down the marriage-and-babies route, but they absolutely can be found.'

What Oseman said brought my thoughts right back to where I began: with Bug's offhand comment about people hiring it just so they could be held. I think people do assume that having a romantic partner is a shield against loneliness; and in the absence of a romantic partner, or a happy relationship, people can fix upon the idea of sexual intimacy as a way to fill that void – even if, once they get there, they find that all they want to do with a sex worker is cuddle – or they fixate on the prospect of having a relationship. So often, in the media and in popular culture and the way we talk about people's lives, the narrative is that getting the right romantic partner will lead to happiness. No more loneliness, no more being alone.

But Oseman is right. There are a thousand ways to be lonely when you have a romantic partner, whether because the relationship is unhappy or because you've focused on your partner so other relationships have fallen by the wayside. Aroace people are no more uniquely predisposed towards loneliness than anyone else. But we are more disposed to opening up our concepts of family and love.

Oseman's novel was so comforting to me in part because I had lived it. Unlike Georgia, I'd gone to uni with the advantage of already knowing I was aroace, but I followed a similar path to hers. Just like Georgia, I 'college married' my best friend. (This is a tradition in many UK universities, where people 'adopt' new students to mentor and help adjust to university life, and are considered 'college married'.) Aryehi and I began to refer to each other, jokingly, as 'wives'. We shared many of our highest and lowest moments. When she was buried in work, I cooked and brought food to her door. We became each other's people.

A few years ago, on a video call in the depths of the pandemic years, I told her about those old worries I'd had since I first realized I was aro. Most other people, I said, could be fairly sure that they'd find someone to be their life partner, someone to be close to, someone to share their feelings and bills and troubles and home. 'And I won't have that,' I said.

'What are you talking about?' she said, staring at me. 'When we can afford it, and I move back to the UK, we can move in together!'

I never set out to find a life partner. But I now have someone I can (and do) invite to family events, someone I have brought in among my relatives as part of the family. And I learned that I could do this by talking to my fellow aros, by learning about QPPs and amatonormativity, about how I wasn't limited to only doing certain things and not doing others because our relationship is platonic, not romantic. Love is so much bigger than that.

Knowing Aryehi – loving her – and knowing the countless possibilities in aro relationships, has taught me just how wrong I was at seventeen, convinced that romance and singledom were my only options. I can live with a friend, prioritize her in my life, and hopefully someday be committed to her to the point that I can share my finances, home, fears and food with her. And at the same time, I will have a web of other friends who share interests with me that she doesn't, who share aspects of my identity that she doesn't – and she will have the same.

Romance does not prevent loneliness. It is not a quick fix for a larger problem: the structure of our society that shuts down other opportunities for human connection, where the weight of amatonormativity tells us we need to prioritize just one human bond over all others. What will fight loneliness is not romance, but all of us widening our horizons, and putting in the emotional work to maintain a larger web of relationships. It won't be easy, because the framework to support this kind of expanded love is far less widespread than that which supports romance. But it is possible. We can build it ourselves.

I will gladly live without romance. But I will never live without love.

8

The Body

An Aspec Perspective on Body Politics

When the novel *Lady Chatterley's Lover* was finally released in the UK in 1960, full and unexpurgated, it was met with immediate furore. Scandalized critics derided its explicit sex scenes, its portrayals of female lust, its profane language and its depiction of a cross-class romance. The publishers, Penguin Books, were accused of obscenity and brought to trial. The prosecution tore into the book's portrayal of sexuality, accusing the plot of being nothing but an excuse to cram pages with sex scenes.

Penguin Books prevailed. The jury returned a verdict of 'not guilty', and *Lady Chatterley's Lover* was permitted onto bookshop shelves. But there is one part of the book's sexual politics that went little remarked on at the trial, and that few have paid much attention to since. It concerns neither Lady Chatterley (Connie) nor her lover, but her husband, Sir Clifford Chatterley: a paraplegic man who, because of his war injuries, cannot have sex with his wife. Connie brims with sexual frustration and aches to be touched; it is this that leads her into the arms of the gamekeeper, Oliver. The world around Sir Clifford sneers at him. Connie's father calls him 'a lily-livered hound with never a fuck in him', and Connie comes to despise him for shackling her; while married to him, she can never publicly embrace her new love. 'He was not in touch with anybody,' she thinks. 'Maybe there was nothing to get at ultimately.'[1] And the narration joins in, portraying him as vacant, not quite real; self-pitying and simmering with bitterness. Eventually, Connie abandons him, and Clifford is resigned to the care of a nurse who despises him and thinks him worth less than 'the merest tramp'.[2]

I've talked a lot in this book about one of the core assumptions of compulsory sexuality: that a normal human is sexually (and romantically) active and, therefore, to be ace or aro is to be abnormal. Now, though, I want to look at the other side of that coin: the assumption that, if you are, for whatever reason, perceived as abnormal, you must therefore be sexless. A body that is not perceived as normal – because of disability, fatness, skin conditions, visible scars and so on – can end up labelled not only as unappealing sexually, but as lacking sexual capacity and even sexual feeling.

As the author, D. H. Lawrence, sees it, when Clifford loses his able-bodied status, his physical 'normality', he loses his sexuality too. The book's sympathies lie entirely with Connie, with how she has been deprived of sex and physical affection – and ascribes the fault for her loneliness to her husband and his disability. As the disabled critic Louis Battye says, Lawrence wrote from a perspective that prized 'the physical, the sensual', and this 'deeply prejudiced him against the physically abnormal [...] Sex is good, a feeble broken body an insult to the dark gods. When Sir Clifford's body was smashed, he automatically ceased to be a man.'[3]

Lady Chatterley's Lover is almost a century old now, and yet we have not moved on from the assumption that it made: disabled people do not have sex lives or sexual desires. Take what happened in 2022, when the lingerie brand Victoria's Secret launched the lingerie line Love Cloud with a diverse cast of models, including Puerto Rican model Sofía Jirau. On her Instagram, Jirau announced, 'I am the first Victoria's Secret model with Down's syndrome!', calling the opportunity a 'dream come true' that she had worked towards for years.[4]

Much of the reaction was positive. Unfortunately, a vocal minority reeled at the idea of a woman with Down's syndrome modelling underwear, especially the famously 'sexy' lingerie of Victoria's Secret. Jirau was twenty-four; she is an entrepreneur with her own brand of clothing and accessories, Alavett; she has been modelling since she made her debut in 2020 at New York Fashion Week. And still, commenters protested that she was clearly not capable of making decisions for herself; that it was 'practically paedophilia' to present a model with Down's syndrome. Victoria's Secret, they claimed, was wrong for 'sexualizing' a disabled person; that they were exploiting her.[5]

These commenters were echoing the same kinds of sentiments that D. H. Lawrence poured into *Lady Chatterley's Lover:* disabled people are non-sexual beings. The 'paedophilia' comments reduced Jirau to a childlike, and therefore non-sexual, state. The cries of 'exploitation!' betrayed the commenters' beliefs that Jirau had to be shielded from anything marginally involving sex; because of course she didn't have any sexual feelings herself. She would not, *could* not, choose such a thing for herself. But she did.

When I mentioned this story to Afana, who is disabled, she recognized the sentiment immediately. 'The minute you see someone in crutches, or in a chair, or using any sort of assistive technology, they get turned into a child,' she says. 'There's an assumption that that person doesn't have any sort of sexual existence, and that it's bad to be attracted to a disabled person. Just because you can't do jumping jacks, you're unable to consent.'

Of course, this is untrue. Plenty of disabled people are allo, and have sexual and romantic lives. 'We are sexual beings,' writes disabled journalist Hannah Shewan Stevens, in response to the backlash to Jirau's inclusion in Love Cloud, 'regardless of how uncomfortable it makes non-disabled people [...] we have sensuality, sexual interest, kinks, turn-offs, and thrive in sexual situations – as long as we are equipped to do so.'[6]

Part of the problem is that both able-bodied people and disabled people themselves are not primed to see disabled people as romantic or sexual. Emily, a full-time wheelchair user, told me that she has been desexualized for as long as she can remember. 'I was never asked out by anyone,' she says. 'Growing up, I was barely ever included in conversations about love and never expected to fall in love,' she says. The kinds of conversations that (allo) teenagers have about crushes and dating, one of the supposed milestones of someone's maturation into a sexual adult – Emily was not given a space to join in.

And think about how disabled people are shown – and not shown – in the media. Kids' books and young adult media that show disabled people falling in love, navigating dating and sex are vanishingly rare. Even when disabled characters do make it into the media in a romantic context, the way they are treated is telling. In Suzanne Collins's *The Hunger Games* trilogy (2008–2010), the protagonist's love interest Peeta loses a leg at the end of the first book, using a prosthetic for the rest of the series. But the film adaptation (2012) erases this detail entirely, making Peeta completely able-bodied. Why? Would a prosthetic leg have detracted from his status as an attractive love interest? Was the disability not considered an important part of the character? In James Cameron's science-fiction film *Avatar* (2009), the main character is paraplegic and ends up abandoning his disabled human body to live in a synthetic alien body with his romantic partner. He must escape disability to find romantic love, and to be happy. In the film *Me Before You* (2016), a quadriplegic man falls in love with his carer, and pursues assisted dying because he feels that he is being a burden upon her, leaving his money to her so that she can fulfil her dreams. The film's focus is on the tragedy of an able-bodied person loving someone disabled, and the conclusion it reaches is that they are both better off once he's dead.

None of this encourages anyone to understand that disabled people can, and do, have romantic and sexual existences that are happy and healthy.

Of course, the media is not the only thing that gives us our ideas about the world. Real life should inform us too. Unfortunately, the reality is that all too often real life does not provide disabled people with the support framework they need to find and maintain relationships. When sociologist and bioethicist Tom Shakespeare carried out a study into disabled people's romance and sex lives, one of his interviewees stated that part of his problem with having relationships was nothing to do with his disability itself, and everything to do with the cuts made to the social service support he should have been getting for it. 'How can you possibly have a sex life if you can't even be clean and washed and feel sexy?' he asked. 'It's not going to be "do you want support to go out and flirt with someone", it's going to be, "we'll give you support if you need to have an injection, 'cos you can't do it yourself".'[7]

Without proper social support, disabled people's social worlds get shut down. And so people continue to see them as non-sexual, non-romantic. Abnormal.

For disabled aspecs, this can make identifying with aromanticism or asexuality that much harder. Emily, for instance, credits her exclusion from romantic discussions and education as 'why it took me so long to realize I'm aro'. If you're excluded from the romantic world, you have nothing to compare yourself to.

And belonging to a desexualized group as an aspec person can be deeply invalidating. 'There's always this fear,' Emily says, 'that I'm repressing my attraction because no one is interested in me and getting into a relationship would be really hard for me.' Her words were echoed by several more of my disabled interviewees (and my neurodivergent interviewees, too, as I discussed in Chapter 2). How do you know you're really aspec? What if you're just internalizing what the world says about you? Are you giving in to abled people, letting them make you into the sexless, loveless creature they see you as? (Answer: no. You're just aspec.)

Getting accepted as *really aspec* by the people around you is still trickier. Sasha (it/they) is blind, and says that their 'least favourite' response to coming out is when people say, 'you're blind, so you can't see how attractive people are', as if their disability alone would disqualify them from attraction. 'I've had a lot of sighted people tell me that I'm not actually aroace, I'm just blind and don't appreciate how "hot" people are because of it.' Similarly, Sonja (she/her) is visually impaired. 'My vision loss makes people think of me as more innocent and naïve, and also as less desirable,' she says. 'Who would want to date someone who's basically blind?'

There's that infantilization again: disabled people existing in the heads of some abled people as helpless children, in a state of permanent pre-pubescence.

Disabled aspecs can end up in a kind of Catch-22 situation. As Angela Chen succinctly puts it in *Ace*, 'the disabled community has spent a long time fighting the idea that disabled people are, or should be, asexual. The ace community has struggled for as long as it has existed to prove that asexuality has nothing to do with disability. If you're aspec *and* disabled, then your very existence "complicates both these political agendas".'[8] Small wonder that some disabled aspecs, like Sasha, fear that they are somehow invalidating their own community. 'I sometimes have the – probably irrational – fear that coming out as aroace is going to somehow perpetuate one of these stereotypes somehow,' they say. They appear to contribute to the idea that a blind person cannot do anything by themself – including having a romance or sex life. They have no attraction, and therefore, they are exactly what some abled people seem to want disabled people to be.

*

What makes a body morally good?

Nothing. A body is value-neutral, just as sex is value-neutral. And yet our society has a predisposition to view certain bodies as better than others. Certain bodies will see their owners being judged, instinctively, as simply *not as good* as others. And very often, that metric – the scale by which a body is judged as good or not – is conventional attractiveness.

This is a big claim, so let's start at the beginning. Let's talk about fatness.

If a body is perceived, by broad societal standards, as being undesirable, then that body's owner gets desexualized. It happens to disabled people, and it happens to fat people. Fat teenage girls have fewer dating opportunities than their thin peers, and are less likely to engage in sexual activity.[9] And because so many thin people don't see fat bodies as desirable, they don't portray them as such. We've had Disney princesses of colour and a Disney princess who wore glasses, but we haven't had a fat Disney princess. I enjoy video games, and I've been playing them for over a decade; I have played *one* (the multiplayer game *Star Wars: The Old Republic*) that allowed players to create a fat avatar for their hero. Even then, this body type was only available to men, while the equivalent female body type was really just a thin person with curves in all the right places – suggesting, once again, that a lack of conventionally accepted attractiveness, and by extension fatness, is more acceptable in men than women. These examples feel especially egregious to me because game avatars are often a kind of self-insert, the player's reflection in this other setting. And yet anyone who isn't skinny just doesn't get to create a character who looks like them being the hero.

It's even more glaring in the romance genre. One study of fat characters in romantic fiction found that they were far, far less likely to be the love interest, and on the rare occasions that they did have romantic relationships, it was with love interests 'who had already been judged by others as clearly flawed and/or who were also the butt of jokes'.[10] Even when a piece of the media sets out to portray a fat person in a positive light, or as desirable, blunders are common. There's a scene in the 2008 spy comedy *Get Smart* where the protagonist, Maxwell Smart, asks a fat woman to dance. She turns out to be an amazing dancer, and the two wow the entire room. Actress Lindsay Hollister enjoyed the role, calling it 'fun and positive' – and it is. The audience is clearly meant to side with the fat woman over the thin women sneering in the background, and celebrate her confidence.

But there's a problem with the framing of the scene. Max asks the woman to dance not because he wants to, but because he needs to get the attention of his fellow agent, who's ignoring him so she can dance with someone else. The scene is framed so that we can't see who he's asking to dance at first, and then the crowd moves aside so we see the punchline: the woman in question is fat! The idea of a thin man asking a fat woman to dance is still a joke. He only does it because he has an ulterior motive.

All of this – the smaller likelihood of seeing fat people in romantic relationships in your formative years, the lack of any media portraying fat people as desirable or even *feeling desire*, leads to an assumption that fat people must have no desire at all. One 2012 study asked college students to rate a hypothetical person's level of sexual desire; a fat man's level of desire was judged to be virtually identical to a thin man's, but when asked to rate fat women, the students' opinions shifted. A fat woman was assumed to be not just less sexually attractive than a thin woman, but less sexually experienced and less interested in sex. She was judged as having less agency in sex, and as being less warm or responsive as a sexual partner.[11]

When fat women *are* portrayed as serious romantic leads or in sexual situations – or simply live their lives as fat women in relationships – the backlash can be venomous. Influencer Alicia Mccarvell has posted on her Instagram a collage of the hate comments she receives for being a fat woman in a relationship with a thin man: 'he is unhappy and pretending'; 'yea he's def cheating'; 'bruh that's just disrespectful loose [sic] some weight for your man'.[12] Online vitriol against media that portray fat women in romantic and sexual plotlines is rife, such as actress Gabourey Sidibe's 2015 sex scene in the drama series *Empire* being mocked as 'yuck' and as the show having 'gone too far'.[13] More recently, the Netflix show *Bridgerton* featured a fat character, Penelope Featherington, as the romantic lead opposite a thin man, and once again people just couldn't stomach it. Writing for *The Spectator*, Zoe Strimpel declared, in a now rather notorious article, that 'the only physical attribute that works against universal erotic capital in almost any context is fat':

> [Actress Nicola Coughlan] is not hot, and there is no escaping it, as I was reminded recently when she graced *Harper's Bazaar*'s cover in a fabulous outfit that still did not change her not-hotness. Coughlan is an actress of great value, and might be adored, but she is simply not plausible as the friend who would catch the handsome rich aristocrat Colin Bridgerton's eye in that way. She's not shapely – which can work as sexy even in Hollywood; she's fat. There's nothing wrong with fat – it's hardly a moral shortcoming – but a zest for equality and diversity (and in this case good acting) just isn't enough to make a fat girl who wins the prince remotely plausible.[14]

Let's unpack the implications of this poisonous little rant. Strimpel doesn't find Coughlan hot; so why does that make it 'not plausible' that any thin, attractive man might? Why didn't Strimpel also complain about all the decades of media in which fat men have thin female love interests – Homer and Marge Simpson, Peter and Lois Griffin in *Family Guy*, Tony and Carmela in *The Sopranos* and many more?

Perhaps a fat woman receives such judgements in comparison with her male peers because in her supposed unattractiveness, she has *failed*. 'If the feminine ideal is that of the delicate, fragile, innocent, selfless, undesiring, mild-mannered, and easily-controlled woman, then a fat woman, by virtue of her fatness, cannot be feminine,' writes essayist Paisley MacLeod. 'Fatness is perceived as grotesque, large, dense, heavy, gluttonous, sinful, selfish, lazy, rude, and uncontrollable. For a woman to be fat is for her to fail in her gender performance.'[15] And if she is not feminine, how can she be appealing as a sexual partner? Why would she be having sex at all?

These assumptions have consequences. MacLeod notes experiences of fat people receiving less birth control information than their thin peers, and struggling to come forward after sexual assault because they anticipate a humiliating, dehumanizing struggle to convince the law that anyone would *want* to rape them. And it is true; fat women are less likely to be believed when they come forward.[16]

Blogger Aubrey Gordon, who writes as 'Your Fat Friend', echoes these experiences, writing about men who told her they fantasized about assaulting her. When Gordon told one to stop, he told her that he thought she'd 'be grateful'; others told her she should be flattered by the attention. A fat woman, they seemed to think, should be glad to have anyone lusting for her, even in a violent form. Any sexual attention fat women receive is treated as a windfall worthy of congratulations, an erroneous impossibility, or an out-and-out lie. Fat women are expected to be grateful for any expressions that could be mistaken for want, including assault and harassment,' she writes. 'After all, who would want to rape us? We should be grateful.'[17]

What's more, not only might fat people receive less information on contraception, but some emergency contraceptive measures, such as the 'morning-after' pill, are less effective on larger bodies. This leaves fat women with fewer recourses in the case of unintentional pregnancy, especially in the aftermath of the Roe vs Wade ruling being overturned in the USA. This is not common knowledge, even among fat people; the US Food and Drug Administration has not changed packaging labels to inform users of this issue (although this has taken place in Europe), and the limits of the 'Plan B' pill remain unknown to many. 'Discovering plan B doesn't work when you're overweight explains why I'm laying on a playmat watching sesame street with my 9m old,' writes one Twitter user, in response to a discussion of the issue.[18]

And I cannot help but wonder if this is influenced by the deep-buried societal assumption that fat people are not having sex, or *should* not have it. If emergency contraception didn't work for another, less stigmatized societal group, would there be more of a public awareness campaign? Do some people, even subconsciously, think that this lack of health information is acceptable because it could discourage fat people from having sex? Is it not considered a priority, because fat people have 'done this to themselves' and on some twisted level, deserve the consequences? (Perhaps not; US leadership in recent years has not seemed like a fan of emergency contraception for anyone. All the same, I wonder.)

Fatphobia and racism often go hand in hand. Body mass index (BMI), the usual metric of measuring if a person is, supposedly, overweight, was entirely based on what the researchers assumed to be a 'normal' body: a white, male body. As a result, 'Black and minoritised bodies whose composition differs in terms of muscle-to-fat ratio are inaccurately recorded and inappropriately treated when stacked against the white norm of the BMI.'[19] Asian people, for instance, tend to have more body fat than white people at the same BMI, and Black people slightly less.[20] This can lead to people of colour being inaccurately classed as 'healthy' or 'unhealthy' based on BMI alone, and this has an impact. In the USA, BMI is often used to calculate life insurance rates; this alone has a ring of fatphobia, and the harm is only compounded when a person of colour risks being charged more for the same care because of an inaccurate measuring system. Inaccuracies in the BMI can also result in people of colour finding their health conditions being overlooked altogether, chalked up to their high BMI.

Structural racism can also mean that fatness is more common in communities of colour; chronic stress, which they may suffer from experiencing structural and active racism, can lead to weight gain. BIPOC people are also more likely to live in deprived areas with budget stores that sell ultra-processed foods, and such foods are often cheaper and thus more accessible to poorer communities.[21] And fatness is yet another tool used to desexualize certain people of colour: consider the 'mammy' caricature. 'Mammy' is the maternal Black woman as presented in works like *Gone with the Wind* and *The Help*, an idealized caregiver content to be subservient to white people and their children. And she is fat; likely because this diminishes any conception of her as a sexual figure. She cannot be a sexual figure, because her duty is to be a safe, nurturing carer for white children.

For fat aspecs, all of this can form yet another obstacle on the road to self-recognition. Erin (he/they/she/it), for example, felt for a time that fatness somehow disqualified them from being ace. 'When I was younger, I had a brief period of feeling like identifying as ace would just be making excuses for no one finding me attractive because I'm on the larger side.' Zefir (they/them), told me that they 'kept asking myself if I might be just "unfuckable" and pretending to not be attracted to people in retaliation. People act like having sex with someone who looks like me is the ultimate punishment, or a gross fetish, so it was initially hard to draw the line between me internalizing that and genuinely lacking sexual attraction to others.'

Even once a fat aspec person has settled into their identity, they can still find themselves craving the validation of feeling that others can be, and are, attracted to them. Because it is good to be desirable. It is good to be attractive. Mira (she/her) is active in kink and fetish communities; she both reads and writes about fatness. And yet, she says, 'I don't actually believe that anyone could find my body attractive. There's a disconnect in my head, that fat bodies are normal and people can love and lust for them, just not me. Not mine. Because I'm a bad person for being fat. It's exhausting.'

Look closely at Mira's words. *I'm a bad person for being fat.* Fatness is not just undesirable; it makes you *bad.*

I have heard thin people speak of fat people with a kind of scorn and disdain with which they would never speak of other stigmatized groups. And when I ask why just *seeing* a fat person prompts them to adopt such tones, there are an array of justifications. Fat people, they say, clearly cannot be bothered to eat less or to eat healthily. But, as I discussed a moment ago, social inequality is a huge factor behind fatness; if we're going to speak of anyone with scorn, shouldn't it be the companies who make and market ultra-processed foods? Or governments who don't do more to provide for disadvantaged or deprived communities?

'They should take care of themselves better,' people respond. 'They should diet and exercise more.' But the efficacy of dieting is widely questioned, and there are those who can exercise all they like and still find their body holding onto weight. According to a Harvard study, genes can contribute to fatness, 'by affecting appetite, satiety (the sense of fullness), metabolism, food cravings, body-fat distribution, and the tendency to use eating as a way to cope with stress.' How much genetics have an impact on weight varies between people: 'for some people, genes account for just 25% of the predisposition to be overweight, while for others the genetic influence is as high as 70% to 80%.'[22] For this latter group, losing weight can be difficult or impossible 'even if you increase your physical activity and stick to a low-calorie diet for many months'. And in just about every case of dieting, weight loss is very rarely permanent.

Physical health is not a sign of moral goodness. We are not living in some moral novel where people get sick as some kind of karmic punishment for their wrongdoings. Physical health can be the consequence of a thousand social and biological factors, but it is not a reflection of our souls.

I can't help wondering if all these justifications are just socially acceptable covers for the thing that people don't want to admit. Ultimately, I think a lot of thin people view fat people as blameable and bad because they are not conventionally attractive. Because they are (supposedly) undesirable. Because these thin people have internalized the equation of beauty with goodness; physical perfection with moral worth; because they have assumed that attractiveness brings good internal qualities with it.

How many fatphobic people are willing to look long and hard at the cold seed behind those other justifications: *you are not attractive to me, and therefore, I do not consider you good?* Or to consider the dark logic behind that sentiment: *it is being sexually attractive that gives you moral worth*?

*

On the school bus one day, a boy lurched down the aisle toward Cyn (she/they), who had been staring out of the window, hoping people would leave her alone. 'Hey, Cyn,' he said, grinning. 'Do you want to go out with me?'

Cyn knew immediately that it was just that old bully tactic of pretending to be interested in them, only to reveal it all to be a joke. And Cyn, who was aroace, also knew that they were immune to it. 'No.'

The boy's friends hooted with laughter. He flushed. 'Whatever. I only asked you as a joke. No one wants your fat ass anyway.'

As he stumbled away, Cyn knew that it shouldn't have hurt as much as it did. The idea of not being attractive to the boy should not be painful when she knew that she had no interest in being attractive to anyone. 'I didn't want to be dateable,' they say, 'but I knew that on their scale, being dateable and being pretty was what made me valuable.' Even now, years later, when Cyn is proud and free in their asexuality, the thought will still resurface. *No one wants you anyway.*

Cyn is right. While it's still frowned upon for anyone, especially a woman, to present themselves too sexually or be 'too' sexually active, this paradox remains: to *not* be sexual, for whatever reason, deprives you of value. (I wonder if part of this paradox comes from a sense that, while women should be sexually *available* to others' interest, so as not to 'deprive' them of sex, they should not have too much desire of their own, or they could be tempted into infidelity, or be confident enough with their sexual desires to reject people they don't want.)

Sexual desirability does give people worth in the eyes of others. In fact, it gives more than that. Psychologists have found that conventionally attractive people are considered to be more trustworthy.[23] They're judged as kinder, intelligent and more socially competent.[24] They even receive better grades and better outcomes in mock trials.[25,26] Overall, they receive better educations, go on to better-paying jobs and make more money, probably through a combination of the improved self-concept that comes with attractiveness and its perks, and the favourable treatment of others.[27] And people seem generally more willing to be helpful and considerate to conventionally attractive people: one study placed a fake college application in an airport terminal, and monitored whether people who found it would mail it to its supposed owner. When they placed the picture of an attractive person on the application, people were more likely to mail it back, even when the rest of the document remained the same.

This study formed the basis for a fascinating short story by Ted Chiang: *Liking What You See: A Documentary.* Chiang posits a world in the near future where scientists have found a way to deactivate the part of the brain that perceives attractiveness. This mental alteration, known as calliagnosia ('calli'), can be switched off and on with a quick trip to a doctor. For some, calli is a way to ensure that they don't judge others based on looks, or to eliminate their own insecurities about their appearance. Chiang's protagonist, Tamera, is unconvinced. She went to a school where calli was a requirement, to stop children bullying each other based on appearances. Tamera is eager to switch off her calli now she's going to university, so that she can see faces as they really are, and she's fascinated by what she discovers. Observing one good-looking boy, she realizes that, because he's attractive, 'it was easy to imagine that he was a nice guy'. She knows it's illogical, but she can't shake it.[28]

What Tamera experiences here is called the *halo effect.* The halo effect occurs when a single positive attribute about someone – such as attractiveness – causes others to credit them with other good attributes: for example, a good-looking person also being perceived as kind, confident and other positive characteristics.[29,30] This bias in favour of attractiveness is reinforced every day through the messages we receive from popular culture. The media tells us that beauty is good and 'ugliness' – i.e., any body perceived to be somehow abnormal – is morally bad. It gives us villains with facial scars, such as the Joker, or Blofeld from *James Bond.* It gives us villains with physical disabilities:

Darth Vader, Captain Hook, Richard III. It gives us fat villains: Jabba the Hutt, Ursula from *The Little Mermaid,* the Dursleys in *Harry Potter*.

Even the body positivity movement, which aims to ensure that everyone can have a positive view of their body, can fall into the trap of fixating on attractiveness. Telling us that sex and romance are what makes a body good. 'Fat positivity is centred around how we're *still attractive enough* for other people,' says Alex (they/them). 'How sexy guys with tummies are. How cute fat girls look in lingerie. People saying, "you'll find someone who's into you!" It's always about sex.' Alex is certainly right that a lot of body-positive posts on platforms like Instagram are often about appearance – which still entwines self-worth with looks. While it is certainly a good thing that we are pushing back against the notion that only a certain type of body can be attractive, we cannot allow our own feelings towards our body to be ruled by how it appears to others. As Alex says, 'Why can't I have value and deserve respect as an individual, without having to rely on how other people perceive me?'

This is even more important for aspecs. 'The way the body positivity movement has morphed from *all bodies are unique* into *all bodies are attractive* really bothers me as an ace person,' says Erin. 'Being told that the only way to love my fat body is to accept that other people want to have sex with it is revolting.'

Some body-positivity activists call for celebrating what your body can do, rather than how it looks, but this too has its pitfalls. 'Progressive thinking has moved on, a little, from judging women's appearances, but we're still very happy to judge abilities,' writes disabled journalist Lucy Webster. 'Every time women are encouraged by a pastel-coloured Instagram post to love their bodies for what they can do instead of how they look, I want to scream. The truth is, some bodies can't do very much at all. And some bodies are sites of life-altering pain and illness. But [...] these bodies are no less worthy of care and respect.'[31]

The impact of these messages can have a very real impact on people's physical health, as well as their mental wellbeing. 'I'm on medications that help me function,' Afana told me, 'but they also cause me to gain weight. I'm not going to lose that weight while I'm on that medication. People tell me to consider going off these medications, because they're causing me to gain weight. And I'm like, *why? They're helping me!*' Her medical providers seem more concerned by her weight gain than the health problems that make it hard for her to function without her treatment; they go so far as to suggest taking her necessary treatments away so that she can have a normative body.

Another pitfall of the *all bodies are attractive* sentiment is that there will always be a societal standard for what is attractive. And that standard is, far too often, the standard of white people. This isn't even limited to the West; colourism or 'light-skinned privilege' is a pervasive phenomenon in many, many countries worldwide, where people of colour who are closer to the white beauty standard are socially preferred. This often involves having paler skin, but can also include having straight hair, light eyes and small noses.

This goes beyond just valuing certain traits. Afana vividly remembered what happened when the burkini – a swimsuit often worn by Muslim women that covers the whole body except for the face, hands and feet – was banned in many French towns and cities. When French police found women wearing burkinis at the beach, they would issue tickets, and demand that the women remove the offending garments.[32] 'I remember watching a video where the police forced a woman in a burkini to take off all her clothes right there in front of them on the beach,' Afana says. 'I felt so violated just watching. Someone tried to hold up a blanket to give her some dignity, but everybody else was just watching as this woman was stripped against her will and acting as if it was a good thing.'

The French government's justification was that the burkini was incompatible with 'good morals and secularism'. But Afana also found white students in the UK trying to justify these incidents. 'They were saying, this is protecting women from pressure, and encouraging body positivity, and women being able to show their bodies,' she recalls. 'But these women were being stripped in the name of bodily autonomy and female empowerment. Where's the autonomy in that? Where's the freedom in that? All that happened was that, by policing what women wore, these women couldn't go to the beach or feel safe at all. This is what happens when a body liberation movement becomes a sexual liberation movement.' And, crucially, a sexual liberation as judged by white people.

So *all bodies are attractive* is not the answer. Bodies, by themselves, are value-neutral. All bodies are *human* – and all human beings have a right to dignity, respect and kindness. And so our bodies, bodies that are part of the sum of who we are, bodies that we spend our lives in, have a right to be treated with care and dignity as well.

*

Incidents like the French persecution of the burkini have a ripple effect far outside the borders of the countries where they take place. The UK has no such bans on clothing, but Islamophobic attacks do occur, such as the 2022 case of a man who tried to tear off a woman's hijab on a London train.[33] Comments such as that made by former Prime Minister Boris Johnson, claiming that burka-wearing women looked like post-boxes, only inflame matters and give a sense of justification to such attacks. And while this climate persists, Afana cannot present her body in the way that would make her feel most comfortable.

'If I weren't worried about being hate-crimed, I would wear a burka,' she says. 'It's seen in the West as a very oppressive thing, but it's not like that at all. It's a personal choice, a fashion choice. They can be fancy or casual, but they're always comfortable. My mum used to wear it when she was feeling too lazy to dress up in fancy clothes, and just throw it on over her tracksuit and shirt.'

For her, being able to dress this way would be a huge improvement. Because Afana, like many of the aspecs I spoke to, identifies with something that Canton Winer told me that he had noted among many of his own ace interviewees: 'a deep ambivalence toward not *their* body specifically, but *having* a body. There was a discomfort with embodiment. Several people said something to the effect of "I wish I could be a shapeless blob".' And I found the same, from the person who responded to my survey to tell me that their gender identity was best described as 'a vague shape floating in the immeasurable abyss' to those who told me that they wished they could just 'not be perceived'. And this speaks to a fundamental truth: the simple act of having a body is always judged, and always judged by standards of attractiveness. And this can make owning a body a complicated tangle for aspec people.

'So much of the experience of being an embodied person,' Winer told me, as we discussed this running theme through the ace community, 'is that you have to make your body appealing sexually to others.' When other people's judgements of our bodies are so often fixated on how attractive we are to them, then just having a body exposes you to something that a lot of asexual people find irrelevant or uncomfortable. Because you can control how you present your body, but you *cannot* control how other people will react to it. You cannot affect what they find attractive or how they might attach a moral judgement to how attractive they find you.

And that makes your body an enemy. Owning and living in a body becomes an uncomfortable, unpredictable thing. And this is only amplified when, for whatever reason, your body comes with others' negative judgements always attached.

'I feel like I'm not attached to my body,' Afana told me as we talked. 'I don't exist in my body very much, because if you spend your entire life with people constantly judging your body, you don't *want* to exist in it. If I'm out in public, just existing, doing whatever – I'm aware that people are looking at me and judging me.'

I mentioned to Afana the sensation of ace disembodiment that I had discussed with Canton Winer, and she agreed immediately. 'That's definitely it. Everyone around you is evaluating something about your body that you can't see. It's like always having an extra tab open in your brain. One tab is just running me. And in the other one, I have to consider all the hangups that I don't have, as an ace person, but everyone else does. Always wondering, *how is this person perceiving me? How is that person perceiving me?*'

If she could only wear a burka, she says, she could finally close one of those tabs down. 'They can't judge you if there's nothing to see! It's comfortable, and it's controlling what other people see of your body. But if I did, people would worry about me being repressed, or they'd say, *this isn't appropriate, we need people to be able to see your face.*'

And this is not right. Afana's body is her own, and she should be in control of how much people see of it.

We all live in a human body. This is not always easy. Our bodies let us down; they get sick, they develop pains and illnesses that can provide minor inconveniences or alter lives. They need constant feeding and copious amounts of water and rest. Life in a human body is *a lot*. We don't need to make it so much harder on ourselves, constantly, by continuing to reinforce a culture where everything that your body is, does and looks like is analysed through the lens of attractiveness. One way we can make the experience of living in a body that little bit easier for everyone, allo or aspec, disabled or abled, fat or skinny, is to refuse the message of compulsory sexuality that pushes us to analyse our own bodies, and others' through the lens of how desirable they are.

So often, our bodies – especially women's bodies, or those assigned female – are expected to be available to other people's attraction and consumption. We change our bodies for others' expectations and preferences. But being aroace has been instrumental in helping me divorce my attitude to my body from my external appearance. It has helped me stop seeing my body through other's eyes, and consider my own preferences for it. And it has helped me stop seeing other bodies through that lens as well.

We are all prone to making judgements about others' bodies. I've heard people tut at dyed hair, tattoos, alternative fashions such as goth and punk aesthetics, certain hairstyles, and much, much more. There are plenty of things that we might not like the look of. But here's the question we need to get used to asking ourselves: *what does it matter?* These are not our bodies. They belong to others, to people who deserve to live in them happily and comfortably.

If there is something you dislike in another person's appearance – tattoos, hair dye, fatness, body hair, piercings, anything – and your response to it is to judge that person negatively, I want you to stop and consider this: where does your dislike come from? Is it because you don't find that person attractive? You are entitled not to find a particular aspect of a person attractive, of course. But bear in mind: your lack of attraction to them is ultimately irrelevant. It should not influence your judgement of them. Being desirable does not give someone worth. Being attractive to you does not make someone a good person, because the halo effect is a mental fallacy.

Another person's body is *not meant for you.* It is meant for them.

So here is yet another reason to refuse amatonormativity and compulsory sexuality: by doing so, we can develop a healthier relationship with both our bodies and others. Noora (she/they) told me that, 'one positive aspect of my life that I attribute partly to my asexuality is my relaxed attitude toward my body. I've never considered myself particularly beautiful, just kind of average. I'm a bit on the short side due to a genetic illness affecting my bone structure, and I wouldn't mind losing 10–20kg or so. But I've never been super concerned about how I look and how my body is inadequate, other than being frustrated when my legs hurt or don't function right.'

For Noora, asexuality helps her look at her body with clear eyes. 'My body isn't for anyone's consumption. It is meant for me to enjoy my life in, and dressing up and looking nice when I feel like it is something I do for my own sake. Of course, this isn't something that's unique to ace people, but sometimes listening to people worry about being ugly and unattractive, and craving a romantic and sexual connection to validate their self-image… makes me feel like there's a difference there.'

Noora's final statement, in particular, stuck with me. It made me think about all the young adult books I read as a teen where a 'plain' female protagonist stopped being self-conscious about her looks because a man told her that she was beautiful. A romantic or sexual relationship is, all too often, considered the vindication of someone who isn't conventionally attractive. But sex is value-neutral, and that means that sex appeal does not create value either. When we challenge amatonormativity and compulsory sexuality, then attractiveness and desirability are no longer benchmarks that we need to reach to be seen as worthy or deserving of respect. The respect should be inherent – and the worth already is.

Calliagnosia does not exist. But perhaps if we push ourselves to see sex and attractiveness as the value-neutral things they are, we can create something close to it. We would still see beauty, but it would have less power to affect our judgements. What would happen to society then?

For a start, all those aspects of pretty privilege seen in education, the legal system and the workplace would no longer exist; we would no longer falsely judge someone as a better or worse student, more or less trustworthy, or more or less capable at their jobs because of their physical appearance. Relationships might well be easier: there would be less pressure to consider whether someone is 'out of your league' if there are no leagues at all. Looks would still influence people's attraction to someone, of course, but there'd be no more judgement from others or yourself about who your looks *entitle* you to date.

Men would not receive the same level of pressure to be sexual, nor women the same level of shaming for *being* sexual. We might stop seeing anything associated with sex as somehow dirty: kink, sex toys, sex workers. If so many people didn't see sex workers as somehow morally corrupt, we might be able to look at them for what they are: people doing a job. That would take us closer to providing them the same worker's rights as everyone else. And for asexuals, a lack of attraction and/or interest in sex would no longer carry a kind of reverse halo effect, leading people to believe that, without sexual attraction, we must be cold and unfeeling.

We could be more content with our own bodies, and more appreciative of others' as their own. Bodies judged as outside the norm of conventional attractiveness would no longer be labelled *bad.* And lest this seem like an improbable fantasy, I've spoken to many who've already taken steps towards it. Plenty of my interviewees started out full of shame about their bodies, a shame that clouded their ability to look clearly at their own sexuality and desires (and lack thereof). And they have taken steps towards seeing that shame as externally imposed, placed there by others' arbitrary and subjective judgements.

Zefir who once worried about being 'unfuckable', has channelled their growing confidence with both their asexual identity and their body into art. 'I portray fat AFAB people in loving sexual relationships, even though it's not something I am personally interested in,' they say. They have gone from judgement about their own body and sexuality to portraying fat bodies as something to be celebrated and embraced. In bold lines and warm colours, they show bodies as being worthy of love and respect not because of whether anyone is attracted to them but because they belong to *people.*

It's taken time, but Zefir is getting there. And perhaps we can all do the same.

9

Legitimate

Asexuality, Aromanticism and Institutionalized Discrimination

Not long after my mother came to understand my aroace identity, she showed me something that troubled us both. It was a fat book with a glossy green cover: the *Employment Law Handbook*, the book that compiles every law related to work in the UK, from laws on health and safety to those on whistleblowing and unfair dismissal. My mum, a former employment lawyer, knew well what its pages contained – and, in one case, what they *didn't* contain.

The page she pointed me to is the one that details 'protected characteristics' – any aspect of a person that causes them to have legal protection from discrimination. One of them is 'sexual orientation', defined as the following:

> Sexual orientation means a person's sexual orientation towards –
>
> (a) persons of the same sex,
>
> (b) persons of the opposite sex, or
>
> (c) persons of either sex.[1]

There's nothing for *no persons of any sex*,' my mum said. 'It doesn't account for asexual people.'

I read the lines again. 'And there's no catch-all "don't discriminate against any sexual orientation" law?'

'No. If you're not in the exact wording of the Equality Act, you're stuffed.'

I sighed. 'I'm not surprised,' I told her, 'but it doesn't feel great.'

Later, I looked up the Equality Act to figure out exactly what this meant for me. The answer: quite a lot. According to the gov.uk website, legal protection from discrimination covers the following:

- direct discrimination – treating someone with a protected characteristic less favourably than others
- indirect discrimination – putting rules or arrangements in place that apply to everyone, but that put someone with a protected characteristic at an unfair disadvantage
- harassment – unwanted behaviour linked to a protected characteristic that violates someone's dignity or creates an offensive environment for them
- victimization – treating someone unfairly because they've complained about discrimination or harassment.[2]

Remember: asexuality and aromanticism *are not protected characteristics.* Which means we are not, legally speaking, protected from any of these things. If I came out as aroace at work and my colleagues began to insult or belittle me for it, I would not have any legal protection from it, because their behaviour would not be 'linked to a protected characteristic'. If my boss had known I was aroace when hiring me, and for some reason decided to pay me less because of this, and I was able to prove it – I would still not have any legal protection, because it would not count as 'treating someone with a protected characteristic less favourably than others'.

This is often a surprise to allo people. When I wrote about this very issue in a nonfiction creative writing class, one of my classmates left a comment on my piece: 'This can't be right? Surely there's an anti-discrimination law that protects against this kind of thing.' But that's exactly the point: *there isn't.* The excerpt from the Equality Act I quoted, defining sexual orientation, *is* the anti-discrimination law. Aces and aros would have to be included in the Act for discrimination against us to be illegal. And we simply aren't.

Outside the UK, the same is true: aspecs are largely left out of anti-discrimination laws. In the USA, only a single state, New York, prohibits anti-asexual discrimination under its Sexual Orientation Non-Discrimination Act (SONDA). SONDA covers 'heterosexuality, homosexuality, bisexuality, or asexuality', and protects these orientations from discrimination in matters involving 'an individual's civil rights', as well as in employment, education, housing, credit, and public spaces.[3] This is wonderful. What's not wonderful is that *one state out of fifty* has included asexuality in its laws, and none at all have included aromanticism.

Much of the legal discrimination against aspecs follows this pattern. It's rare that lawmakers have deliberately singled us out; far more often, the lack of awareness of our existence means that no one accounted for us. We are excluded from protections, barred from certain benefits and left without rights that allos take for granted – often by complete, ignorant accident.

Not all legislators have made this mistake. The German General Act on Equal Treatment 2006 simply prohibits discrimination against people on the grounds of 'sexual identity', with the Federal Anti-Discrimination Agency clarifying that 'the term sexual identity refers to lesbian, gay, bisexual, heterosexual and also to asexual or pansexual persons'.[4] *Any* sexuality is covered by the words 'sexual identity', asexuality included – although this does still leave out aromantic people, focusing on *sexual* rather than *romantic* orientation. Personally, I think this is the best way to write such legislation: rather than making a list of protected identities, which will always run the risk of leaving something out, simply state that *any* discrimination on the grounds of sexual and/or romantic orientation is illegal. I particularly like the German route of using *identity* rather than *orientation*; this leaves fewer loopholes for people to claim that aces or aros are not covered thanks to having a 'lack of orientation', and also avoids defining queer identity in the language of attraction.

*

In 2023, a Stonewall investigation headed by aroace activist Yasmin Benoit set out to investigate what this lack of legal protection means for the lived experiences of ace people in the UK. The report focused on asexuals, although much of what it discussed is also relevant to aros, as I will discuss later. Still, I hope there will be an equivalent aromantic report in the future.

As I discussed in Chapter 2, the report found that far fewer aces were 'out' at work in comparison with the LGBTQIA+ community as a whole. This should not be surprising to anyone. Coming out for many aspecs involves insensitive, personal questions that one would normally never ask of someone with any other sexual orientation: 'Do you masturbate?' 'Have you had therapy for that?' 'Do you not have sex with your partner? You do? How often?' (These are all things my interviewees reported having been said to them.) I have had casual acquaintances who knew my orientation and made fun of me by trying to find innuendo in anything I said and by trying to trick me into saying sexual things. They found this hilarious; I found it both upsetting and disturbing. This wasn't, fortunately, in a work environment, but I've often wondered what someone would do if they ever encountered something similar in a place of work. Trying to get official support would involve having to explain your orientation to your boss, who might not have heard of asexuality. If they did not act, you could maybe escalate to the HR department – if your company was big enough to have one – where you would have to explain it all over again to strangers. And then, you'd have to face the fact that if you chose not to act, you would have *nothing*. You couldn't bring a claim against your employers, because legally speaking, you would not have experienced discrimination. And if you can't endanger your company by bringing a legal claim against them, what *would* motivate an HR department or line manager to step in?

This is a hypothetical case – but it is not hyperbole. The 2023 *Ace in the UK Report* stated that 'being open about being asexual [at work] almost inevitably led to inappropriate curiosity for participants', often with a 'persistent, bullying nature' to the comments. And even when the questions were truly well intentioned, this still forced asexual people to step up and invest the time and emotional energy to educate their colleagues while on the clock. This should really not be our responsibility, but that of diversity and inclusion training by employers. (And, ideally, it should be covered far earlier by sex education in schools – but for adults, it is already too late for that.)

The *Ace in the UK Report* was unequivocal about what needs to be done: the Equality Act must be amended to include asexual people (I would add that aromantic people should, ideally, be added too). 'This,' the report states, 'would act as a catalyst for driving toward ace inclusion in the workplace by legitimising ace identities as real and worthy of protection from harassment and discrimination. It would also provide a backstop for challenges when ace people do experience harassment and discrimination at work.'[5] In the meantime, the report recommends, diversity inclusion programmes should include education on aspec folks. I would add that more needs to be done to push these programmes in the workplace; training on queer identities, aces and aros included, could be a mandatory part of new employees' introduction to a job. It wouldn't have to be very much: just a small overview of the fact that these identities exist and provide resources in case people want to learn more.

What of the USA? In 2020, the US House passed the Equality Act, which would add sexual orientation to anti-discrimination laws for the USA. Unfortunately, this act is currently stuck in the Senate, which means it has yet to pass into law. And it again defines 'sexual orientation' as 'homosexuality, heterosexuality, or bisexuality'.[6] Even if it passes the Senate – which I hope it will – it will do nothing for aspecs.

Getting these laws amended and passed would be an enormous step forward, and not just because it would protect us in the courts and workplace. While asexual and aromantic identities are unprotected by law, nobody *needs* to be aware of us or to see our orientations as valid. And so, when they encounter us, they have little motivation to take us seriously – which can have dire consequences when our health is on the line.

*

Back in Chapter 3, I told the story of Anne, an aspec person who left a cervical smear exam bleeding heavily because of the nurse's ignorance about asexuality. The nurse believed, wrongly, that a married person must be sexually active (despite Anne having informed her, both on her form and verbally, that she was asexual, and despite her trying to explain what this meant). Anne's experience is both shocking and part of a larger pattern of medical ignorance and assumptions leading to poor healthcare outcomes for aspec people.

Some of the biggest barriers to care are in the field of mental health. According to the *Ace in the UK Report*, mental health professionals were found to assume a patient's asexuality had caused their mental health problems, causing them to focus on 'fixing' their orientation rather than on their real issues – effectively, conversion therapy, although the practitioners probably didn't realize that was what they were doing. Asexuality was assumed to be a 'trauma response' rather than a true orientation. Practitioners advised their patients to take medication to increase their libido.[7]

Even where asexuality should have been completely irrelevant to patients' treatment, medical professionals often *made* it relevant. One ace patient seeking treatment for pelvic pain was told by her doctor that she had 'complex psychological issues around sex' because of her asexuality. He 'refused to send her to a gynaecologist and would not allow her to have a referral at all unless she agreed to see a psychosexual therapist' – something the patient knew was unnecessary but went through with, since it was the only way to access the care she did need. The delay in accessing treatment led to her pelvic pain worsening, and she now 'has extensive muscular damage to her pelvis because of the extra year waiting for treatment'.[8]

Afana, from Chapters 2, 4 and 8, told me about how being ace has made seeking treatment for her disabilities harder. There are a thousand pitfalls that come from simply being without a partner; health providers, she says, are often hesitant to offer any kind of intensive treatment if you don't have someone to pick you up from the hospital, preferably a spouse. They may even recommend less aggressive treatments because of it. And then there's what Afana calls her 'wiggly diagnosis'. She almost certainly has endometriosis, but her health providers have not yet been able to give her a solid answer. Why? Because when she was seeking diagnosis, she was told that the doctors couldn't carry out a gynaecological exam, because she was a virgin.

'Are you intending to have kids?' the gynaecologist asked.

'No,' Afana said.

'Are you married? Is your husband intending to have kids?'

'I'm not married, and I don't have a husband.'

'Okay, then. Once you're married, come back, and we can do a full exam and see if this is endometriosis.'

Afana, being aroace, has no intention of getting married or having penetrative sex. 'So I'm just going to spend the rest of my life with this wiggly diagnosis,' she says, 'and no actions I can take to treat the cause of a lot of my pain. I'm just sort of stuck. I actually sat down and thought, once, should I go and hire someone to get it done with, just so I can get that gynoscopy?'

Did they give her a medical reason, I asked, for why being a virgin meant she couldn't get the treatment she needed?

'They said it was a case of not being used to penetration,' she told me. 'But quite frankly, with the amount of pain I'm in, I'd rather just deal with it then and there. And I've had a cervical smear test, and with the way it occurred, I don't think I qualify as a virgin anymore, the way that woman went at it to get the smear! So… what's their criteria? If I need to have had sex to get this exam, does it have to be with a living thing? Can I go to Love Honey [a UK sex toy shop] and see what happens?'

Afana's experience is not an outlier; the consequences of doctors' lack of knowledge about asexuality are often most serious in the fields of gynaecology and reproductive health. One couple in the *Ace in the UK Report*, an asexual man and woman, were both experiencing fertility problems that led them to seek access to fertility treatment. They were told that they did not meet the requirements, because obtaining IVF in the UK requires a person to have had 'regular sexual intercourse' for the past year. The couple had been doing regular home insemination, but this was not considered 'regular intercourse'. Unless the two of them were diagnosed with a 'psychosexual problem', they were told, they would have to have unsuccessful physical sex to qualify.

This might seem reasonable to some people, until you look more closely at the guidelines for this kind of care. In the UK, fertility treatment usually begins with IUI (intrauterine insemination), progressing to IVF (in vitro fertilization) if three or four rounds of IUI are unsuccessful. According to the website for the UK's National Health Service: 'you may be offered IUI if you're unable to have vaginal sex – for example, because of a physical disability or psychosexual problem', or if 'you have a condition that means you need specific help to conceive. For example, if one of you has HIV and it's not safe to have unprotected sex', or if 'you're in a same-sex relationship and have not become pregnant after up to 6 cycles of IUI using donor sperm from a licensed fertility unit'.[9]

Think about what this means. A same-sex couple can try six rounds of home insemination using donor sperm, and qualify for professionally assisted IUI if it fails. But that asexual couple with known fertility problems did the exact same thing, and yet they were *not* eligible. We would not tell a lesbian couple who wanted to get pregnant that one of them should just suck it up and have sex with a man. Why are we telling asexual couples in the same situation to do exactly that?

These guidelines could very easily be amended to account for asexuals. They haven't been, because no one has thought to do so. If you or your partner is a sex-repulsed asexual, for whom having sex would be an uncomfortable and even distressing experience, and home insemination has not been effective – why should you not qualify as needing 'specific help to conceive'? If having sex would be negative for your mental health, or your partner's, why shouldn't that count as a reason for being 'unable to have vaginal sex'? We should not have to accept our identities being pathologized as 'psychosexual conditions' in order to access care.

All the more reason, then, to make asexuality and aromanticism protected characteristics, and to include them under the UK's proposed ban on conversion therapy (the text of which, thus far, does not include us). This is especially necessary considering how the medical system is very much stacked against us. As discussed in Chapter 3, the *Diagnostic and Statistical Manual of Mental Disorders*, or DSM-5, included a 'persistent lack of sexual desire' as hypoactive sexual desire disorder, or HSDD. Thanks to the campaigning of asexual activists, an exception was added, stating that, 'if a lifelong lack of sexual desire is better explained by one's self-identification as "asexual," then a diagnosis should not be made'.[10] This is good, but the asexual exception is not a perfect solution. Using the exception requires either the health practitioner or the patient to already know that asexuality exists – and, as we have discussed, knowledge of asexuality is not widespread in the healthcare profession.

If the practitioner is not informed about asexuality, it's easy to see how a patient's lack of knowledge might lead to them getting wrongly diagnosed with HSDD. Imagine a person who has never experienced sexual attraction and who, thanks to compulsory sexuality, feels like there is something wrong with them. Maybe their partner is frustrated with their lack of interest in sex. Maybe they've internalized the idea that only cruel, inhuman people, or those with some kind of disorder, aren't interested in sex.

As an experiment, I tried googling variations of what I thought such a person might search for: 'why don't I want sex?'; 'no sexual desire'; 'no libido'; 'I don't want sex what's wrong with me'; and the like. Whether my search results included information about asexuality seemed to be entirely down to luck. Most search results led me to medical resources for addressing low libido, suggesting the problem might be due to fatigue, exhaustion or certain types of medication, and pointing me to relationship counselling. When I googled 'no desire for sex', one of the first results was a WebMD page entitled 'HSDD and libido loss'. Since plenty of people don't make a distinction between libido and sexual attraction, someone could well mistake their asexuality for 'low libido'. According to the advice on this page, 'symptoms of desire disorder may include: low libido, no sexual fantasies or sexual thoughts, avoiding sex or genital contact with your partner [and] distress at the thought of having sex'.[11]

I'm sure you can see the problem here: these things might indeed be caused by HSDD, but they are also common in asexuals. To its credit, the website adds that 'if your lack of interest in sex doesn't concern you or your partner, then it's not a disorder'. But why that 'or your partner'? Why on earth should a *partner's opinion* determine whether someone has a disorder or not?

What's more, our hypothetical asexual person might well be distressed by their disinterest because of the social forces upon them – because they believe that being sexual is the norm, and there's something wrong with them for lacking attraction. And even if they aren't distressed, their partner might be. Remember Jules, whose partner coerced them into sex repeatedly; remember the weight of compulsory sexuality and amatonormativity, and how they can combine to make a person feel, in the words of one of my interviewees, 'confusion and shame'. An asexual person could very easily seek treatment for HSDD, a condition that they do not have, because they do not know enough about asexuality to 'self-identify as asexual' and trigger the exception clause.

I was startled, during my experiment, how the slightest changes in my search terms might lead me either to a wealth of asexuality education resources, or to lists of HSDD symptoms. One small change we could make, then, is for medical practitioners to include asexuality resources in any resources discussing absent libido, lack of desire and the like, so that patients know it is a possibility. And rather than asexuality being an 'exception' to diagnosis with HSDD, medical practitioners should be encouraged to check whether *anyone* pursuing HSDD treatment might be asexual, and assist them in the way they would be expected to assist someone of any other sexual identity.

Right now, the DSM-5 states that one of the diagnostic criteria for HSDD is that 'the sexual dysfunction is not better explained by a non-sexual mental disorder or as a consequence of severe relationship distress (e.g., partner violence) or other significant stressors and is not attributable to the effects of a substance/medication or another medical condition'.[12] I would propose an additional criterion, along the lines of, 'the apparent dysfunction would not be better explained by the individual being asexual, i.e. the sexual orientation of having little or no attraction to others', ideally with additional information about what exactly asexuality is and how it is distinct from HSDD.

The 'asexual exception' is also US-only. Elsewhere, for instance, practitioners tend to use the International Classification of Diseases (ICD), which is maintained by the World Health Organization. And the ICD has not been amended in the way the DSM was. In any country that uses the ICD, the persistent lack of sexual desire is, therefore, still a mental disorder.

Is it any surprise that so many asexuals get sent for psychosexual counselling?

In the ICD, lack or loss of sexual desire is listed as 'frigidity' (how very Victorian) and 'hypoactive sexual desire disorder'. 'Sexual aversion and lack of sexual enjoyment' is classified as 'sexual anhedonia', in which: 'either the prospect of sexual interaction produces sufficient fear or anxiety that sexual activity is avoided (sexual aversion) or sexual responses occur normally and orgasm is experienced but there is a lack of appropriate pleasure'.[13] At the very least, this could be amended to include, 'and the patient is not asexual (naturally experiencing little to no sexual attraction to others)'. Anything that would require a healthcare practitioner to consider the possibility of asexuality and to discuss it with their patient before making a HSDD diagnosis.

The *Ace in the UK Report* concludes its section on healthcare by recommending that asexuality be removed as a disorder from the ICD, as well as ensuring that all demographic monitoring forms include asexuality as an option so that healthcare outcomes for aces can be monitored, and 'that healthcare professionals and healthcare students should undertake training about asexuality'.[14] Perhaps then we will be able to be open about our identities with our doctors and therapists without being sent home bleeding from the wrong speculum or packed off to psychosexual counselling.

And if your response is to say, *just don't tell your doctors*, I would remind you that in some forms of treatment, discussing asexuality (or aromanticism) might be very relevant to your care. Someone seeking mental healthcare, for instance, might very well need to talk about their orientation, if part of their problem is the social pressures of living as aspec in an allo world. But more importantly: we shouldn't need to conceal parts of ourselves to access healthcare. We should not have to *lie* to access healthcare. (It is worth mentioning, here, that for aspec people of colour, as well as aspec women and those perceived as women, this is just one more brick on the pile of bias they face in medicine. No one needs more.)

A straight, cisgender, allo person does not need to fear that if they're open about having an opposite-sex partner, or if they mention that they're sexually active, their health providers will flurry to send them off to counselling or bungle their treatment because of a lack of awareness of what being straight means. Aspec people deserve the same.

*

Our healthcare and legal systems promote something strange: a hierarchy of sex acts. Specifically, the consideration of penis-in-vagina sex as somehow the most legitimate or 'complete' form of sex, with everything else ranked below. It's a belief with ancient precedent. In many Western, culturally Christian cultures, sex was seen as a necessary evil for the sake of procreation, and thus non-procreative sex was by nature sinful. Even when opinions began to shift in the seventeenth century, to viewing sex as a pleasure ordained for married couples, it was believed that sperm was a 'vital fluid' and that too much ejaculation could ruin a man's health. Thus, ejaculation was not to be wasted on acts that couldn't contribute to procreation.

This was by no means a universal assumption. Indeed, outside of the Christian West, ideas about sexuality and gender, and thus about what sex acts were acceptable, were (and often still are) far more fluid. As just a handful of examples, there are the *motsoalle* of Lesotho (see Chapter 7, although, as mentioned, physical intimacy between women was not considered sex). The Langi, Iteso and Karamojong peoples of modern-day Uganda and Kenya have always had the *mudoko dako*: 'effeminate males [who] were treated as women and could marry men'.[15] Across the Atlantic, the Indigenous peoples of what is now the USA had a vast array of gender and sexuality identities across various tribes and cultures: to take just one, the Navajo have six distinct gender categories, including lesbians and gay men as separate genders, as well as genders for masculine women and feminine men. (This is another reason why we should be hesitant to declare gender identity and sexual/romantic identity to be completely different things: in some cultural gender frameworks, they are not.)

It was Western colonization that overwrote these cultures' understandings of sex and gender with a Christian one. And so beliefs about what sex acts were and were not permissible were enforced upon cultures that had formerly embraced non-procreative and non-heteronormative sex. This is part of the appalling legacy of colonialism: the queerphobia that exists in many post-colonial countries is something that Western people brought there, and left behind.

Many of these countries are now pushing to reclaim their traditional understandings of sex and gender. And those of us in the West should remain aware of the imprint these historical beliefs left in our own society. Most people no longer believe that sperm is a vital fluid or that non-procreative sex is immoral, and yet our laws still echo those outdated values.

In the UK, it is possible for a marriage to be declared legally 'voidable'. This is not the same as a 'void' marriage – one that was never legally viable, such as a marriage to a minor. A voidable marriage is, in the words of one lawyers' website, 'flawed in its validity'.[16] A voidable marriage is significant because it can be ended via annulment, not just divorce – in other words, in the eyes of the law, the marriage never took place.

One factor that can render a marriage voidable is if it is unconsummated, legally defined as 'you have not had sexual intercourse with the person you married since the wedding (does not apply for same sex couples)'.[17] This obviously renders any marriage between asexuals (and anyone else, for that matter) who choose not to have sex as 'flawed in its validity' – or even, in the words of another family lawyers' website, 'defective'.[18,19] Aside from how chilling it is to realize that a completely happy relationship between two aces might be considered legally defective, there's something curious here. When I first read this description, I thought, *hold on.* Why does it not apply to same-sex couples?

Because, according to the law, same-sex couples aren't having 'complete' sex. A legal precedent set in 1845 says that legally speaking, a marriage requires 'ordinary and complete' sexual intercourse rather than 'partial and imperfect' sex.[20] And yes, legally, 'ordinary and complete' still refers to penetrative sex, specifically penis-in-vagina. This means that same-sex couples cannot apply for divorce on the grounds of non-consummation; they must wait a year and apply on the grounds of 'unreasonable behaviour'. It also means, bizarrely, that a couple could be having oral sex all day long and still have a 'voidable' marriage, as long as they've never had penis-in-vagina intercourse. All because of a law from *1845*.

This strange prioritizing of penis-in-vagina sex even extends to the definition of adultery, which is still defined – and was clarified by the Marriage (Same Sex Couples) Act 2013 – as cases of penis-in-vagina sex. 'Only conduct between the respondent and a person of the opposite sex', the law states, 'may constitute adultery.'[21] Which means a spouse having extramarital sex with someone of the same sex doesn't count as adultery – even if it is a same-sex marriage – and neither does extramarital oral sex between anybody.

These kinds of cases might seem too esoteric to be important. After all, if an ace couple have fallen out to such an extent that one of them is prepared to use their lack of legal consummation to annul the marriage, what does it matter that their marriage is legally voidable? It matters, though, because it is another dehumanizing indignity lumped on aspecs. Bear in mind: an asexual person in the UK has, according to the law and the ICD, a mental disorder, and doesn't have any legal protection from discrimination. On top of that, if they are married and they don't have sex, their marriage is also 'flawed in its validity'. The 2019 Ace Community Survey found that 41.8 per cent of respondents had a mental health issue, and the Trevor Project's 2022 survey on queer mental health found that a significant proportion of aces suffered from anxiety and depression: 74 per cent and 58 per cent respectively.[22,23] (This was average for the queer community as a whole: the mean average for anxiety was about 73 per cent and about 60 per cent for depression.) This is, unfortunately, one shocking and sad result of facing such fundamental disrespect against our health, our bodies, our rights and even our relationships.

But, as well as mental health and societal implications, this obsession with sex as the validator of a relationship has another brutal, real-world consequence. A crackdown on sham marriages in the UK led to some telling behaviour from the police: 'Dawn raids [were] carried out to check if couples were sharing a bed. In one case, a couple were told their relationship could not be genuine because they were wearing pyjamas in bed.' Another couple 'were taken into separate rooms and asked about their sex lives, including details about sexual positions and contraception'.[24] In these officers' minds, sex was the make-or-break for the genuine nature of a relationship. As I discussed in Chapter 1, a marriage to someone from another country of origin can be classed as a sham marriage if sex has not occurred. Yet another legal framework that does not support asexual couples who aren't having sex.

Researching these laws put me in mind of the case of Ewan Forbes, a transgender man who, in 1968, risked losing his inheritance and his marriage. A family member challenged Forbes's right to inherit on the grounds that he was assigned female at birth. If judged by the court to be female, Forbes's marriage would have been labelled a same-sex marriage, which was currently illegal, and he would have been guilty of perjury for having married at all. In the trial, Forbes's wife Isabella was asked to testify, and asked if she was able to achieve 'complete satisfaction' through sex with her husband.[25] Apparently, this was crucial evidence of her husband's maleness and their marriage's validity.

That was 1968. I am writing in 2024, and for some reason, we are still using 'ordinary and complete', penis-in-vagina intercourse as the litmus test for whether a relationship is 'real'.

*

Last year, my brother moved to Canada for his work. His girlfriend moved with him, and my brother's employer paid for her to fly out with him. I was happy for them both, but I was also struck by the fact that if I had been in my brother's position, I doubted an employer would have paid for, say, a best friend, or a queerplatonic partner, to fly to another country with me (unless I were to pretend the QPP were a romantic partner). The same is true, in many countries, for those who want to get visas to live or work there: in Brazil, for instance, you have to be legally married to a Brazilian citizen to get a marriage visa; in Japan, you need a spouse visa to work in the same country as your partner, which means you have to be married. It's one of the many ways that amatonormativity is institutionalized – written into our laws, and into the ways in which companies and organizations are run, from employment to housing to filing taxes – leaving those who live outside of a single, monogamous, romantic relationship to miss out on benefits and end up disadvantaged.

Marriage is a protected characteristic. Being single is not. And one of the many faces of amatonormativity is how singlism – the discrimination against single people – is normalized in our society, even though being single is increasingly common. In *Singled Out*, Bella DePaulo points out just how many benefits are granted to married couples that singles lack, and how odd the world would look to everyone if the positions were reversed:

- When you tell people you are married, they tilt their heads and say things like 'Aaaawww' or 'Don't worry, honey, your turn to divorce will come.'
- When you browse the bookstores, you see shelves bursting with titles such as *If I'm So Wonderful, Why Am I Still*

Married, and *How to Ditch Your Husband After Age 35 Using What I Learned at Harvard Business School.*

- Every time you get married, you feel obligated to give expensive presents to single people.
- When you travel with your spouse, you each have to pay more than when you travel alone.
- At work, the single people just assume that you can cover the holidays and all the other inconvenient assignments; they figure that, as a married person, you don't have anything better to do.
- Single employees can add another adult to their healthcare plan; you can't.
- When your single co-workers die, they can leave their Social Security benefits to the person who is most important to them; you are not allowed to leave yours to anyone – they just go back into the system.
- Candidates for public office boast about how much they value single people. Some even propose spending more than a billion dollars in federal funding to convince people to stay single, or to get divorced if they already made the mistake of marrying.[26]

DePaulo makes some good points here. A survey carried out in 2006 found that: '34% of single workers were expected to work more at weekends, 29% had to work longer hours, and 27% had to attend more out-of-hours social functions than their colleagues in relationships. One in five said they had been expected to travel more for work than their colleagues in formal relationships.'[27]

And being single is expensive. In previous chapters, I've discussed some of the practical challenges faced by those who don't want to partner up, from having a harder time buying a house to something as day-to-day as supermarket meals being sized for two. In the USA, another huge price tag is attached to singledom: the fact that you can't file your taxes jointly, which is cheaper than filing singly. I will be honest: as neither an American nor an accountant, I'm not entirely certain how this process works. Thankfully, studies have been performed by people who do, including one in 2013 by Lisa Arnold and Christina Campbell. The study compared how much two hypothetical married women, one earning $40,000 a year and the other $80,000, might make in comparison with two unmarried women with identical salaries.

Arnold and Campbell took into account the benefits of joint tax filing with spouses, as well as the various social security benefits that the married women could enjoy. (For example, a married person in the USA can make an Individual Retirement Account (IRA) and put two people on it, while 'a single person can't put away that money in support of someone else'.) They added up the money that the hypothetical single women lost as a result of not getting certain social security benefits, as well as all the extra tax they had to pay thanks to not having a husband to file taxes with. Ultimately, by retirement, the lower-earning unmarried woman missed out on $484,368 that she might have been able to save if she'd been married. The higher-earning unmarried woman lost $1,022,096 that a married woman would have been entitled to. 'More than a million dollars,' Arnold and Campbell write, 'just for being single.'[28]

Given this, and the fact that single people don't have anyone to combine their finances with (unless they have a platonic life partner, QPP or similar), home ownership is even farther out of their reach than it is for most people right now. So naturally, most of them need to turn to renting – but here, too, the system is not in their favour. For a start, landlords tend to see couples as more stable renters; with two incomes to support them, they're less likely to move out. In the UK, homeowners are two-thirds more likely to rent to a couple over single tenants. And there are legal incentives for doing so: if more than two unrelated people want to rent together, the landlord needs to have a Household Multiple Occupancy licence. This is not the case for couples, who count as a single 'family' for this purpose. If a property is 'occupied by persons who comprise no more than two families', a landlord doesn't need this licence. The upshot? A landlord is better off renting to two couples than to four single friends, despite the same number of people occupying the address, since they don't have to register and pay for an extra licence. Not great news for polycules (a unit of polyamorous partners), intimate tribes or any group of more than two friends who want to rent together. This is another example of amatonormativity becoming compulsory: if two single people want the best chance at getting a place to rent, they have to pretend to be romantic. Because there are tangible repercussions for failing to do so.

I would understand the sentiment expressed by some landlords that a dual-income couple is a safer bet than a single person – if it were true that, in cases when a single person, or two unrelated friends, have as good an income as a couple, landlords were no more likely to choose married people. But they *are*. An experiment performed by Bella DePaulo and her colleagues presented subjects – actual landlords, and university students asked to imagine they were landlords – with a list of potential tenants. Some were married, some single, some cohabiting couples, and some cohabiting platonic friends. Participants were then asked: who would you prefer to rent to?

In every iteration of the experiment, even when there was 'no substantial differences between applicants', the married couple were chosen most often (with 61–80 per cent of participants choosing them) and the cohabiting friends least often (8–15 per cent).[29] Married people were also chosen consistently over single people, even though the same participants were shown to view single women, though not men, as positively as married people and no more likely to be delinquent tenants. In fact, 'the married couple was even preferred over alternatives who were not perceived as significantly more delinquent or more likely to leave the rental property sooner'.[30]

When asked for their rationale behind renting to the married people, 'they rarely mentioned perceptions of delinquency or how long they expected the applicants to stay in the house. Instead, participants often explicitly stated that the applicants' marital status influenced their choice.' The tenants' relationship status alone was made 'a basis for their decisions'. Finally, the study found that participants were unlikely to view a landlord's decision to prefer renting to married people – even in a scenario where the single person was described as a model tenant and willing to pay more than a couple – as a form of discrimination. 'Participants,' the study concludes, 'rated discrimination against singles as more legitimate than discrimination against virtually all of the other groups.'[31]

And all of this barely scrapes the surface of the levels of privilege and support given to couples, especially married couples, that are not received by anyone who defies the amatonormative framework. As Brake discusses in *Minimizing Marriage*, spouses have a guaranteed position as next of kin in case of emergency.

They can benefit from each other's insurance – such as health, disability and life insurance – and from each other's pensions. They have rights to each other's property on marriage and can expect recompense in divorce; they have hospital and prison visitation rights. They have the right to inherit from their spouse if their spouse dies intestate, and they have authority over the disposal of the spouse's body. They're entitled to bereavement leave; they can sue for a spouse's wrongful death. In the USA, according to Brake, they may qualify for Medicaid, housing assistance loans, food stamps, military commissary benefits, spousal immunity from testifying, entitlement to burial with one's spouse in a veterans' cemetery and so on. The list just keeps going.[32]

Which prompts the question: how is this not discrimination?

Discrimination is treating someone less favourably because of some quality that they possess. And we seem entirely comfortable treating single people less favourably. As DePaulo puts it, 'for eighty-six dollars, I can book a round-trip fare' for a shuttle trip to the Los Angeles airport. But a couple can book it for just fifty-eight dollars each. 'The owners of the shuttle service don't really care about my marital status. They just want more people to sign up for their rides. They think they are pursuing a wise business practice. I think they are practicing discrimination.' And they are – just not legally, because being single is not protected under US law.[33]

This isn't right. As DePaulo says, if companies really want to encourage more people to use their service, then they shouldn't be allowed to discriminate based on an inherent quality like singledom; rather, they should give discounts to people who use their services often.

But we persist on giving benefit after benefit to married couples. And if this is the case – if society is not even ready to face up to the fact that it discriminates against singles every day – then why is our definition of marriage still so narrow? Why are these benefits still given only to two people who have a romantic and sexual relationship?

Take polyamorous people. Since, legally, polyamorous partners can't marry, polycules have had to have 'commitment ceremonies' instead – which means they don't have the legal backing of monogamous marriages. Despite these partnerships being consensual, loving relationships, they miss out on all the benefits I have just described – and that's on top of the general anti-polyamory prejudice that poly people face all the time. If a landlord prefers to rent to married couples over single people or cohabiting friends, how much less likely are they to rent to a polycule? Polyamory is not a protected characteristic, so there's nothing to prevent a landlord from refusing to rent to a polycule purely on the grounds of their relationship type.

The consequences of this kind of discrimination are very real. In 1998, a child in Tennessee was removed from her three parents – her mother and her mother's two partners, all of whom were in an open, consensual relationship – and placed with her grandparents on the grounds that 'polyamory could endanger the morals or health' of the girl.[34] But looking at this decision in the wider context of how, practically, children are often raised by more than two parents, the foundation of this decision falls apart. And no, I'm not even talking about poly parents, co-parents, or queerplatonic units – I'm talking about stepparents. I know plenty of people whose biological parents divorced, and who were raised by one biological parent and a stepparent, with the other biological parent also having a major role in their upbringing. This happens *all the time.* Three people are, unquestionably, being involved in the upbringing of these children, and most people don't clutch their pearls over how this surely endangers the 'morals and health' of anyone involved.

I know that blended families like this are not always idyllic; ill feeling can exist between any of the parents involved, and swapping back and forth between their parents' homes can be hard for a child. But generally, we all agree that these difficulties are worth it to allow a child to be raised by all of the parents whom they love, and who love them in return. So, if we support families of three or more parents in this context, even when they present difficulties, why do we deny the right for children to be brought up by multiple parents who *all live together in a loving, happy, stable relationship?*

For generations, marriage has been used as a tool by which to contain and control people's (mostly women's) sexuality. I hope that we have now grown beyond that. I hope we now see marriage as a declaration of commitment between people who love each other and want to be recognized by the law and society as a unit, for as long as love lasts. And if this is the case, there is no reason for us to keep limiting our definition of marriage to romantic love alone, nor for us to prescribe that such a commitment can exist between only two people. Platonic love is love, and can be just as binding and devoted as romantic love. There is no reason to force the enormous reserves of love and potential for devotion that exist within the human heart to one partner alone. If we are going to keep piling all these social benefits onto marriage, then at least make them accessible to forms of love outside the romantic and outside the monogamous.

I have spent much of this book arguing for a shift in societal mindsets. Now, though, I want to push for something more tangible: true changes in legislation. Amatonormativity shaped the laws we have, and while these laws exist – providing financial, legal and social benefits for romantic couples at the expense of anyone who lives outside that description – they continue to reinforce that amatonormativity. Being asexual, aromantic, single and polyamorous all need to be included in our anti-discrimination legislation. No company or service should be allowed to charge single people more than they charge couples. Marriage between more than two people needs to be legalized. A lack of sexual intercourse must no longer be grounds for a marriage to be voidable, and while we're at it, we need to either change the definition of 'consummation' so that it is no longer limited to penis-in-vagina sex, or stop seeing consummation as legally relevant altogether. Asexuality, aromanticism and polyamory need to be covered by bans on conversion therapies. And all of this needs to be reinforced with training on ace and aro identities in workplaces and medical care.

Which brings us to the next question: how can we make this happen?

10

Invisible No More

What's Next?

Eight years after I first tried to come out to my brother, I decided it was time for a second attempt.

It felt bizarre to me, and a little irritating, that I was more nervous now than I had been at seventeen. Perhaps it was because I was more certain of my identity now than I had been then, and a rejection of it would hurt more. Perhaps it was that being disbelieved as an adult – someone who my family should trust to be able to come to my own conclusions – would feel even more diminishing than being disbelieved as a child. But I was also armed with the knowledge that being disbelieved by allo people was not the end of the world after all.

He was lying on the sofa with a book, and I approached him and told him I wanted to talk to him about something. This time, I didn't dance around the point. 'So... I wanted you to know: I'm asexual.' (I decided to leave out the whole aromantic and agender parts for now; until I knew how he'd respond, I wanted to keep it simple. Besides, I was already working on this book by then, and knew he'd find out soon enough.)

He closed his book. He waited for me to finish explaining – nervously, because it's still easier for me to write a book for thousands of people I've never met than to talk about my identity to those who've known me longest – what this all meant. When I was done, he told me that he was glad I'd told him, and that it didn't change anything about our relationship. I admitted that my nerves were mostly to do with what he'd said at nineteen. He didn't remember it, so I reminded him of the conversation – and he laughed sheepishly. 'Yeah. That does sound like the kind of thing I'd have said back then. I think I've grown out of judging other people for how they live their lives now.'

As I walked away, I felt a strange, calm sense of closure. This felt like the end of a story I'd started at seventeen, when he'd been the first person I'd tried to come out to, and it hadn't worked. There had been no closure then. I had it now.

Of course, like I said in Chapter 2, coming out is neither the end of any story, nor the defining part of queer existence. Living my best aspec life is about far more than how the allo people around me see me. The real victory of this moment was knowing that if my brother hadn't believed me, I would have been hurt and angry – but I would also have been fine. I would have said my piece anyway, told him to do some research, and carried on with my life without letting it crush me the way it did when I was a teenager. I walked away knowing that I was far, far ahead of where I once was.

The same is true of the aspec community.

Strangely, I often feel that the aspec movement is in a similar position to myself. It's even roughly the same age as me. I was born in 1998; the first internet resources and forums for asexuality were created in 2000. Like me, this community is starting to assert its existence, and, like me, the community still has a long way to go, while still being far ahead of where we were. One of the reasons I was so frustrated and unhappy at seventeen was the dread of this being how things would always be: never being respected as an authority on my own mind and body, and never being taken seriously. I was terrified that emerging into the adult world would change nothing, and I would still hear the same thing from all sides. *This is impossible*, or, *this isn't important.*

I was wrong.

Since the aspec movement began, there have been a number of legal decisions made around the world that have opened doors for us. Many of them involved situations that did not specifically involve aspec people at all, or if they did, the aspec identities of those in question were not the key issue. All the same, the decisions made in these cases supported the rights of non-normative relationships and households: a hopeful sign that we are learning to move past our obsessions with the nuclear family and amatonormative relationships and welcome in expanded forms of love.

*

In 2022, a case came before the Swedish supreme court. It involved two women who had lived together as platonic partners, sharing a joint household and joint finances. Tragically, in 2018, one of them died – and so began a legal battle between her family and her partner.

The deceased woman had named her partner as the beneficiary of her life insurance compensation. Her parents, however, believed that they were the ones entitled to that compensation. Her parents didn't dispute that she had lived with her partner on a long-term and committed basis – but, they argued, the partner couldn't be considered as having the same entitlement to the compensation as a spouse would have, because she had been their daughter's friend, not a romantic partner, and the two had not been having sex.

They had legal grounds for arguing this. Swedish law at the time stated that '*couple relationship* means that the persons must live together in a relationship that normally includes sexual cohabitation'. The Swedish Supreme Court, however, chose to rule in favour of the surviving partner, stating that to do otherwise would be to suggest that the law dictated how individual cohabiting people should conduct their relationships. That, they said, was neither the aim nor the spirit of the law. Rather, 'the idea is to express that the persons should be in such an emotional relationship with each other that sexual intercourse is usually included in similar relationships. Even a relationship without sexual cohabitation can constitute a couple within the meaning of the law, and this applies regardless of the reason why no sexual cohabitation occurs. What is decisive is instead that the relationship should be characterized by such a close community in personal terms that normally occurs between married couples.'[1]

The crucial thing, the court declared, was that there should be a 'special affinity and trust between the persons and a willingness to share life together similar to what usually exists between those who choose to marry each other', and these women clearly fit that description. Thus, they were a couple in the sense of the Cohabitation Act, and the surviving woman was therefore entitled to the insurance compensation, just as her partner had wished.

There was so much more at stake in this case than *did the surviving woman deserve some money or not.* The insurance compensation was just a vessel for a larger conversation about the level of respect that the Swedish government was willing to show to the woman's relationship with her platonic partner. The real issue was about a woman going through a terrible bereavement and then having people step in and say, *no, this doesn't matter as much as you say it does. Her love for you was not as important or binding as a romantic relationship, and we don't think her wish to support you after her death should be respected, because your relationship was not what we think a relationship should look like.* It's about the invalidation of the deceased's love, and the survivor's grief.

For a court to step in and say *no* – to say that a non-normative relationship is no different from a romantic one in terms of how much love and commitment exists between those involved – is a tectonic shift from the status quo.

It doesn't matter whether the Swedish women were asexual, aromantic or not. What matters is that they were life partners, and that the court honoured that decision. This is a great leap forward from Nancy Inferrera only being allowed to stay with Mildred Sanford because she was her 'carer' (see Chapter 3). One thing that haunts me about Inferrera's case, even though it ended happily for those involved, is that they never received any official acknowledgement of the fact that their relationship was one of family; that they were equivalent to a normative relationship.

But times are changing.

*

It's not often that you get to praise the Church of England for its attitude to queer people. Same-sex couples are still not allowed to get married in UK churches; priests with same-sex partners are still supposed to be celibate. But in 2023, they released guidance for priests on blessing same-sex couples… and for blessing what they called 'covenanted friendships': platonic relationships between individuals who wished to have some official recognition for their bond.[2]

Over in the USA, the legal position of non-normative families is dependent upon what state they happen to live in. Some states have nothing. But some states have passed legislation that's a boon for non-normative families, such as allowing children to have three or more legal parents. Specifically, California, Delaware, Maine, Vermont, Washington state and Connecticut all have laws that allow courts to recognize more than two people to be legal parents to a child.[3] In other states, no such legislation exists, but court rulings on individual cases have allowed specific families to have three or more legal parents, which at least provides a hopeful precedent to guide any similar cases in the future. One, for example, was motivated by the case of a child who would have been placed in foster care when her mothers were no longer able to care for her. Her donor father campaigned to be allowed to be legally recognized as a parent so that she could pass to his care.[4]

There's been a backlash, of course. When California was initially considering such legislation in 2012, conservative groups said that it would allow children to have 'six, eight, even a dozen parents'.[5] What these critics did not seem to realize is that multi-parent recognition was nothing new. The earliest known cases of a court allowing more than two parents to be legally registered to a child had nothing to do with donor parents or polyamorous parents. It occurred in cases where a child's biological father and their mother's current partner wanted to be equally acknowledged as parents, such as in the case of women who ended one relationship and then formed a new one, or had affairs outside marriage. These new rulings just expanded and confirmed the protocol for something that was already happening.

Besides, if six parents all commit to loving and raising a child, what exactly is the problem there?

Many would immediately argue that this introduces more points of failure. If 50 per cent of marriages end in divorce, how much more friction could there be with more than two parents?

But I am not convinced by this. If we say that people shouldn't be allowed to raise children because there's a possibility that the relationship will turn sour, then monogamous couples should not be allowed to be parents either. Again: 50 per cent of marriages end in divorce! Does this mean marriage is so unstable an institution that monogamous married people can't raise children?

What's more, as I have discussed before (Chapter 6), monogamous relationships pile an incredible level of responsibility and focus onto one single person and relationship. Surely this pressure can only be lessened when there's no one single load-bearing relationship; when love and emotional needs are spread across a larger network? I'm not saying polyamory is for everyone; it isn't. But I do not believe a polycule is inherently any more or less stable than a monogamous couple.

A few rare places are starting to explicitly account for poly people in their laws. The city of Somerville in Massachusetts has a domestic partnership ordinance that gives polycules 'the rights held by spouses in marriage'. The ordinance had been initially intended upon its creation in 2020 to apply only to partnerships of two people, but was amended when a city councillor realized that it would be exclusionary to polyamorous people. And crucially, the ordinance does not define domestic partners as romantic. Somerville residents can now register as domestic partnerships without needing to be a romantic couple, which means that platonic and queerplatonic partners can now share health insurance benefits, for example.[6]

Perhaps the most impressive legal change is what happened in Cuba in 2022. So far, I have largely discussed small-scale progress, affecting a single city or only establishing a legal precedent that might later be struck down. But when Cuba held a referendum to amend their Family Code in their Constitution, it passed with

66.88 per cent of the country voting in favour. The amendments made same-sex marriage legal, and widened the definition of a family structure, emphasizing that structures beyond the nuclear family exist and need protection.

The official newspaper of the Cuban Communist Party declared that 'guaranteeing the same rights to all families is essential to securing social justice', and that 'different family structures, based on a relationship of affection, are created among relatives [...] a family is not based on its structure or the number of members. A family is a social structure that recognizes itself as such and takes on the duties and responsibilities it entails.'[7] (It was a strange experience to read something I agreed with so strongly on a news website that contained links to articles with titles such as 'Why We Don't Need More than One Party', but this is a useful reminder. Both groundbreaking advances in social justice *and* severe violations of human rights can occur in the same place simultaneously, and on any side of the political spectrum.)

Again, this does not seem to be a decision that had aspec people in mind. But anything that challenges amatonormativity is a benefit to aspecs. The more we open our doors to relationships outside the romantic, monogamous, sexual norm, the easier it becomes for aspecs to exist with our queerplatonic partners, our intimate tribes, and all our other forms of non-normative relationships. And, of course, the more we banish the belief that a single, sexual, monogamous relationship is normal and necessary for humans, the less stigma will persist around not being sexually active, or around being single, whether by circumstance or by choice.

These are some of the big, landmark victories, but we should not ignore the small victories either. A thousand small changes are making our identities ever more visible and providing them with more social support and respect. Some of the less conventional dating apps, like Feeld, provide options for users to declare whether they're looking for monogamy or polyamory, for open relationships, for emotional intimacy or something casual, and even for celibate relationships. (I would, of course, like these apps to take the step of adding queerplatonic relationships to the options they offer.) Many apps, including more mainstream ones like OkCupid, now allow people to select aspec identities on their profiles. On a recent trip on the London Underground, I was pleasantly surprised to see an advert for the dating site Hinge that mentioned demisexuality.[8] Small steps, yes, and the cynical part of my brain muttered something about companies only mentioning our existence so they could use us for marketing – but I still wondered if that ad might have done some very real good. I wondered if anyone saw it, googled demisexuality while waiting for their train, and ended up learning something. I wonder if people see asexuality on people's OkCupid profiles and decide to do some research. Any time aspec identities are put into the public eye is a chance for us to become less invisible. Companies using queer identities to make money is uncomfortable and ethically murky, but it does give me this encouraging thought: at least the companies know what side of history they need to be on. At least queer allyship is where the money is. At least it sends a message to those who sneer at queer folks that society is not on their side.

Of course, visibility alone is not enough.

I opened this chapter with accounts of our victories, because it is important to know that such victories *are* possible. In fact, they are already happening. When we live in the reality of being an ignored orientation – when doctors send us for psychosexual therapy, when we put up with insensitive comments at work because we have no legal recourse, when we see new LGBTQIA+ rights bills proposed that do not cover or even acknowledge us at all – it is easy to get dispirited. We can end up feeling like I did aged seventeen: that the weight we need to shift is too much. But it can be moved, a little at a time. Which is why I'm dedicating the rest of this chapter to listing some of the practical steps that you can take, whether you're aspec yourself or an allo ally, to make tangible differences in the legal and social treatment of aspecs.

Small steps. Let's get walking.

1. Let's amend our legislation

We have to make this non-negotiable. We need discrimination protection, because every human being deserves it. We need to be a protected characteristic, and the legal equivalent thereof, *everywhere* we possibly can. On a practical level, being legally protected will arm us in doctors' offices, at gynaecologists and in the workplace. On a wider, social level, laws are a reflection of what a society will and will not tolerate. We need it to be clear that our society will not tolerate sending aspec people to conversion therapy, denying us fertility treatment, refusing to give us the same legal rights as romantic couples, or any of the other instances of discrimination I have covered in this book.

So, what can we do, as individuals, to get the laws of our countries changed?

First, we need to remember that the likelihood of our laws changing will be down to what government is in power. So – and yes, I know we're all tired of hearing this – vote, if you are old enough and permitted to do so. And secondly, write to your representatives. For US citizens hoping that the Equality Act will be passed, the website inclusiveea.org has a sample letter which you can send to your representatives, arguing for ace and aro (and pansexual) people to be included, as they currently are not.[9] For UK citizens, we need to amend the Equality Act, *and* we need all LGBTQIA+ identities to be covered under the proposed ban on conversion therapy. I have yet to see any corresponding sample letters that we can send to our MPs, so I've created my own. (Crucially, transgender people are also not covered under the current proposed ban, so I strongly recommend using the sample letters available from trans rights charities, such as Mermaids, to campaign for their right to be included in the ban as well.)

Dear [MP name],

I am one of your constituents, and I am writing to ask you to confirm your support for the ban on conversion therapy. It is well past time this outdated practice was made illegal in UK law, and your support of this bill means/would mean a great deal to me as one of your constituents and a member of/ally of the LGBTQIA+ community.

However, I am concerned that the proposed Act does not provide protection to all of the LGBTQIA+ community. The current ban protects only gay, lesbian and bisexual people, which excludes asexual, aromantic, transgender and gender-diverse people. You may not be aware that conversion therapy against asexuals is the most common form of conversion therapy in the UK. The National LGBT Survey (2018) found that asexual people are 10 per cent more likely to be offered or to undergo conversion therapy than people of other orientations. It is a huge oversight to forgo banning conversion therapy against the group it now targets more than any other queer identity.

If you are unfamiliar with asexuality, aromanticism and the discrimination these identities face within the UK, I strongly advise you to read the 'Ace in the UK Report' from Stonewall, which lays out the shocking levels of prejudice present in our society and the ill-treatment that people of these orientations face every day. Asexuality and aromanticism are still not covered by the 2010 Equality Act, meaning that discrimination against these identities remains legal in UK law.

I am [an asexual/aromantic person/an ally to asexual and aromantic people] and I am very concerned about the potential for [myself/my loved ones] to remain unprotected by this proposed ban. I ask that you push for the conversion therapy ban to include all LGBTQIA+ identities, so that we can begin working for true legal protections and rights for all of our citizens.

Please act to ensure that these inhumane practices are outlawed in the UK so that all LGBTQIA+ people have the same protections as everyone.

Thank you,

[Your name here]

There's no movement in Parliament on the table (yet) to include asexuality and aromanticism in the Equality Act. We need to create one. Again, write to your MPs, write to the Minister for Women and Equalities, and start the push for getting the wording of the Act changed.

Dear [MP name]

I am one of your constituents, and I want to call on you to protect the rights of the LGBTQIA+ community in the UK. You may not be aware that several LGBTQIA+ identities are not yet included in the 2010 Equality Act. Asexuality and aromanticism are not protected characteristics under the law, and this means that discrimination against [us/people of these identities] is entirely legal.

If you are unfamiliar with asexuality, aromanticism and the discrimination these identities face within the UK, I strongly advise you to read the 'Ace in the UK Report' from Stonewall, which lays out the shocking levels of prejudice present in our society and the ill-treatment that people of these orientations face every day. Conversion therapy against asexuals is the most common form of conversion therapy in the UK. The National LGBT Survey (2018) found that asexual people are 10 per cent more likely to be offered or to undergo conversion therapy than people of other orientations – and yet [we/they] have no legal protection from this. This is both an oversight and an injustice.

I ask that you do all within your power to push for an amendment to the Equality Act so that asexuality and aromanticism are included as protected characteristics. As [an asexual/aromantic person/an ally to asexual and aromantic people], I do not want to live in a country where [I/my loved ones] go without one of the most basic rights and protections that everyone else can take for granted.

Thank you,

[Your name here]

Send these letters. Send them twice. Send them so often that your representatives will be sick of seeing your name.

For those in the rest of the world, look at the wording of any anti-discrimination laws, and make sure you know whether aces and/or aros are protected. Canada, Germany and Finland have legislation that covers all sexual orientations. If you live in a country like Sweden or New Zealand that specifies that 'sexual orientation' only applies to certain listed identities, alter the above letter and send it to them. (Indeed, it would be a good idea for some kind of official initiative – perhaps from AVEN, AUREA, or Stonewall – to document the exact legal state of aces and aros worldwide, determining which countries have laws that already protect us and which do not. This would be a long and arduous undertaking, but I think it would be worth it.)

We need to push for discrimination protections. We need to do this en masse, until lawmakers realize that we are here, and we are not going anywhere, and we demand the rights and protections that we should get for simply being human.

2. Challenge others' language, and change your own

Our language and our thoughts form a self-reinforcing circle. What we say reflects what we think. Just look at the words coined in any year, and you'll see what concepts were on people's minds, what ideas they had to make words for. *Disco* and *space walk* in 1963. *Search engine* and *hate crime* in 1984. *Arab Spring* and *deadname* in 2010.[10]

And what we say affects what we think as well. Since I started making an effort to stamp out my inclination to use gendered language towards anyone whose gender I don't know, and instead making a deliberate choice to always say 'they', I've found myself much less likely to assume gender in general – not calling reckless drivers 'he', for instance. And this isn't just me: a study on how language influences social opinions towards gender in Sweden found the same pattern. People who described a genderless cartoon figure with the Swedish gender-neutral pronoun *hen* were less likely to assign 'cognitive salience' to men – for example, if asked to complete a sentence about a person running for office, they were more likely to assign the person a female or gender-neutral name than to assume such a person would be a man.[11]

So, if small changes in language can affect how we think, what happens when we constantly reinforce compulsory sexuality and amatonormativity with our words? When we use language such as 'just friends', as if friendship is an *only*, or use virgin as an insult, when we say 'I wonder why X doesn't have a partner yet?' or 'you need to get laid' or 'they're going to die alone', we reinforce patterns in our brain. We drive it home to ourselves that anyone who diverges from allonormativity is lacking.

But because changing our language can also change our minds, the simple act of watching our words, and holding those around us accountable for theirs, is a small but truly impactful way we can make a society more welcoming to aspecs. If you hear someone using these phrases, or anything else that suggests that sex and romance are the norm or the default, that lacking them is unnatural or uncool, then – if it is safe to do so – challenge them. A touching example of this in action occurred on Twitter in 2020 when an anonymous user of the site asked the actor Rahul Kohli – very politely – that he not use virginity as an insult, as it was hurtful to aces. 'It's just as harmful as calling someone a slut and contributes to rape culture,' they said. Kohli responded, 'I never considered how using that word as an insult could harm/upset people from that community. My deepest apologies, and thank you for bringing this to my attention [...] I hope by spreading this, others will be aware too.'

As often happens when people in the public eye speak up for any marginalized group, there was a backlash, with another Twitter user responding, 'Jesus Christ... getting to the point where the term virgin is a slur.' Kohli smacked this down. 'You don't have to change a thing about the way you live your life innit. Me? I want to be better, I want those who follow/support me to know that I see and support them. I'm more than willing to make changes and educate myself if it makes others feel heard and safe.' He added, 'Happy Asexual Awareness Week.'[12]

This story is not only heartwarming and heartening, it's an example of how we can bring about these shifts in language. If you see someone in the public eye who uses amatonormative or aphobic language, and it's safe to do so, then reach out to them as that anonymous Twitter user did. Include links to resources such as AVEN or the website asexualityarchive.com so that they can educate themselves if they wish to. We need a global discussion about asexuality and aromanticism – so let's start some conversations.

Be aware, of course, that if you do this online, there may be public backlash. Please protect yourself against internet hate, since we all know how harmful and targeted it can be. It may be worthwhile to send such messages anonymously if possible, or ask that the people you contact conceal your usernames, as Rahul Kohli did with the ace person who reached out to him.

This doesn't have to happen between individuals; companies, businesses and corporations can be targeted too. In 2016, the fashion company American Apparel released a tote bag in its Pride collection. It showed a list of identity labels, the first letter of each one forming the acrostic 'LGBTQA'. They were Lesbian, Gay, Bisexual, Transgender, Queer – and *Ally.* The ace, aro and agender communities – and our allies – took to Twitter and Instagram to challenge American Apparel on their erasure of aspec and agender identities: 'Allies do not need representation. Asexuals do.' 'The LGBTQ+ community LOVES their allies, but the A in LGBTQIA stands for asexual.' 'Invalidating ace/aro/agender folks by claiming the A they've fought hard to make visible is the exact opposite of allyship.'

On this occasion, the call-out was only somewhat successful. American Apparel apologized, but they also made the feeble excuse that, 'there are so many identities to recognize [...] we believe in the power of allies to speak up'. They continued to sell the tote bag without amendment to its design. Still, this incident did one very good thing for aspecs (and agender people): it got people talking. Online news sites reported on the incident, discussing American Apparel's misstep and including screenshots of the tweets people had sent to the company demanding that they change the design.[13] Although American Apparel sidestepped responsibility, the community and our allies rallying to make it clear that their actions were unacceptable demanded that people recognize us. It was a refusal to be made invisible.

Something similar happened in 2024, when the dating site Bumble released an advertising campaign that was both sexist and steeped in compulsory sexuality. The ads were targeted at those frustrated by getting nowhere in dating: 'You know full well a vow of celibacy is not the answer,' one read, and 'Thou shalt not give up on dating and become a nun'. Once again, not having sex is 'giving up', something undesirable. Keep having sex, the ads seemed to say; keep dating. Don't do the uncool thing, don't become an uncool person. Oh, and keep giving us money, too.

The justified criticism of the ads came quickly. Many women who used Bumble pointed out that the reason they had given up on dating was because of uncomfortable interactions with men on the platform: 'Stop trying to shame women into coming back to the apps,' one said, and another, 'Bumble put millions of dollars into an ad campaign basically blaming women for not fucking men […] so now a dating site for women is gaslighting them into fucking for revenue?'[14]

As I trawled the internet, looking at the responses to the controversy, I found one that stuck with me. As usual, a Reddit user was complaining that the backlash was caused by people 'being triggered by everything'. Another user replied, 'I wouldn't say it was triggering, but as somebody who doesn't prioritize sex, it does make me question if I should be using the app. If Bumble encourages a mindset that the people using it are better off because they are having sex, do I belong there if I don't want sex that much? I'm not offended, but it does make me wonder if the "temperature" of the app is ultimately inappropriate for me.'

Which, I think, goes to show: people can be aphobic without thinking about aspec people at all. (In fact, it's often because they *aren't* thinking about aspec people at all.) To that Reddit user – who might well have been aspec, or might just be someone who doesn't prioritize sex in their relationships – the adverts seemed to be saying *you don't belong here.* And it further reinforces that when you fight against this sentiment, when you push back against amatonormativity, you're pushing against other things as well. This ad campaign was as steeped in sexism as it was in allonormativity: the idea that sex is cool and that celibacy is 'giving up' was being used to encourage women to use their app. Which makes it still more crucial to challenge this kind of language, because destabilizing allonormativity can destabilize these other axes of oppression.

Bumble listened to the criticism. The ads were removed, the advertising space was given to the National Domestic Violence Hotline, and the company openly apologized, stating, 'We made a mistake.'[15] They even apologized directly to the asexual community, 'for whom celibacy can have a particular meaning and importance'. This is not entirely accurate – plenty of aces are sexually active, and even those who aren't might not consider themselves celibate; personally, I feel that 'celibate' describes abstaining from sex, and I, quite honestly, have nothing to abstain from. But, however belated and, to many, performative, the apology did at least happen. Bumble acknowledged that its behaviour was unacceptable rather than making excuses. Sometimes, as happened with American Apparel, speaking out doesn't cause those who misstepped to change their behaviour. But sometimes it does.

Of course, challenging these things does not only need to happen on public and online forums. It can, and should, happen between individuals as well. If you can do so safely, then challenge the language of those around you. Point out the problems of virgin-shaming and the 'dying alone' rhetoric. Point out to them that ace and aro people exist, and that this kind of language both erases us and demeans us.

Back when the COVID vaccine was introduced, no amount of public health campaigns and news reports were as influential in persuading people to get the vaccine than just the experience of seeing the people around them take it, and having friends and family members talk to them one on one. The opinions of loved ones can be more powerful than any government act, and it's often at the most personal level that change begins.

3. Tell your story in any way you can

We owe our movement to each other.

It was aspec people who first established the online forums where we first developed a community. It was aspec people, not academics or psychologists, who coined the idea of the Split Attraction Model, who invented the terms for sex stances, who came up with language for queerplatonic partnerships. I asked everyone who took my initial survey how they first realized they were aspec, and so, so many people told me that it began with other aspec people talking about their lives, both in person and online. For me, it began with some unknown aspec person who made a joke and shared it online. Something that small, and the result is this book. (In fact, I have encountered another ace person who realized their identity because of the *exact same joke.*)

We have built our own momentum; now let's maintain it. Here are just a few ideas for what you can do:

- Write. Whether you're aspec or allo, including aspec characters in your works and doing so with love and respect can go a long way. While you may not be lucky enough to be in charge of a show as impactful as something like *BoJack Horseman*, don't discount what small-scale creations can do. For many of those who responded to my survey, it wasn't mainstream media, but fan content such as fanfiction that caused their lightbulb moment.
- If fiction isn't your area, you could instead write nonfiction articles about aspec life and experiences. Online platforms such as Wordpress and Medium are one option for sharing these: the latter allows you to submit works to publications, and there are a few publications centred around aspec

writing. If you have a local newspaper, or a university newspaper, submit pieces to them. If you're adept in web video, and confident speaking to thousands of people on the internet (I salute you), you can make videos to talk about the asexual and aromantic experience.

- If you're confident with public speaking, contact your current or former schools, universities and the like, and ask if you can give a presentation to students on aspec identities.
- Contact your workplace HR department and suggest that they provide official guidance on being inclusive of aspec people. For example, my workplace recently brought out a guidance document on how to be inclusive of trans people, neurodivergent people and disabled people, advising staff and managers on what language to use. Such guidance could very easily be updated to include avoiding amatonormative language too.
- If your workplace or place of education has a diversity or inclusion group, join if you can, and give feedback on how to make the situation better for aspec people.

4. Join campaigns – and make sure all queer campaigns are aspec inclusive

Queer rights charities are already pushing for better recognition and rights for aspec folks. If you are able to, volunteering or working for a queer rights charity is one way to push for change, as you get a direct line of communication to those working for queer rights. If this isn't an option for you, then you can contact your local queer charities and encourage them to direct resources towards aspec rights – remember, conversion therapy levels are higher among aspec people than among any other sexual orientation identity, and any worthwhile queer group should find that as troubling as aspecs ourselves do. Demand that these groups carry out research similar to the *Ace in the UK Report*, assessing the situation and needs of aspec folks, so that they can plan actionable steps for better inclusion.

If you are part of a Pride group of any sort, make sure your space is safe and welcoming to aces. You can do this by scheduling events for ace and aro people, by making sure that aspec people are included in your discussions, and even by simply putting up posters that make it clear your doors are open to the aspec community. Speak to the leaders of your Pride groups and encourage them to take these steps. Make sure that any aspec person who walks through your doors knows they are welcome.

5. Live with joy

I know: this is the sappiest thing I have said in this book. I know it seems a shallow, wishy-washy statement, in the fact of the often-harsh realities I have unpacked for the last ten chapters. And I know it can be hard. Mental health conditions are more common in our community than in any other sexual orientation group. All of us experience minority trauma, and for many of us, other factors, from race to neurodivergence to disability to gender – only amplify that.

But we cannot allow ourselves to be defined by that pain. We cannot allow the James Somertons of the world to declare that we are not truly queer until we have suffered. We must acknowledge our pain, yes – and there are situations in which we must make it known and then leverage it. Legislators are unlikely to pass laws unless they have proof that tangible harm is being done by their inaction. This is exhausting and exposing. For many of us, pointing out the very real harm done by aphobia, compulsory sexuality and amatonormativity is a mortifying process that forces us to relive some of the most traumatic and invalidating moments of our lives, offering them up to strangers to prove that our hurt is real, that we deserve equal rights, *please.*

The process of gaining true rights and recognition is going to be long and hard, and will require a lot of emotional labour from us all. This is unfair. It is unfair that when we are the ones most hurt and most *tired* by the assumptions of others, we are the ones who have to do the work to change things, and to make others change. We are allowed to be frustrated. We should all take a moment to scream.

And when we can, we should also take a moment to celebrate. Our joy is important, not despite that pain, but because of it.

Joy in our identities is what helps us focus not on what we lack – every right and every kind of social respect that allos take for granted – but on what we *do* have. It is what helps us remember that we are more than the ignored, invisible orientation: we are people, and we are a community. Like queer people across the ages, we have found ways to embrace and rejoice in who we are. We have made our subcultures, we have found and built our own families and relationships, and we are living the most vibrant of lives.

For all the stories I read of isolation and erasure, there were also stories of happiness and love and confidence. There were people, hundreds of people, who discussed how enriching being aspec was to their existence.

Kai (she/they), for example, finds that being aroace is a boon to their art. 'Someone once said to me that aspecs make the best romance writers, because we constantly have to analyse interactions and dynamics to determine what make a well-developed relationship,' Kai says. 'I believe that's true. I'm a creative. A storyteller. Whether it be through illustrations or writing or song, I have a story to tell. And not to toot my own horn, but I like to think that I'm a very strong writer. Every piece of feedback I've gotten has always been positive and always mentions how the chemistry [in my stories] feels so real and natural. Being aroace helps me in my passions, and I don't think I would be the creative I am today without being aroace. I wouldn't trade my identity and the experiences that come with it for anything else!'

To many aspecs with no interest in sex or romance, being free from the emotional complexities of dating is not an absence; it's a delight. 'I love being free of the sense of dependence many people seem to have on romance,' says Imogen (she/her). 'Not just on their partner, but on needing a relationship to be satisfied, needing sex to be satisfied, always looking when single, and always expected to be looking. I'm not saying it's bad to be allo, of course, but there are definitely a number of challenges that allo people face that I have simply avoided. And I love the outlook on life it's given me: it has helped me step away from caring about my appearance, as well as others'. It's helped me value and realize the possibility of lifestyles totally varied from the typical nuclear one. It's helped me to appreciate so many things and just see the world from a totally different perspective compared to everyone else. I genuinely, truly think of it as like a superpower.'

And I agree. Moving through life with an aroace filter has made me see so many things I would have missed if I had been allo. Without being aroace, would I ever have noticed the level of undue weight that society puts upon romance? Would I ever have given thought to relationship types outside the norm? Would I have learned so young to stop judging my own appearance? Would I feel so strongly about the need for intentional communities and non-nuclear families? I don't know that I would. And that seems like a sad fate.

Many aces and aros told me that their friendships are stronger because of their identity, and this, too, I can relate to. A friend who recently went through some complicated relationships told me how much he values my friendship, because with me, he always knows where we stand, and he always knows I'll have uncomplicated, complete friendship to give to him. And in turn, I have learned to try my hardest to give my friendships the weight they deserve. Acknowledging my friendships as the most important bond in my life made me realize that I could, and should, take the time to visit them, and tell them how much I love them, and make plans for my future that include them.

So often, aspec people are defined by what we are not. We are described in terms of lack: lack of attraction, lack of romance. We are 'regular' people but with one piece missing. The aspec community has been declaring for years that we have nothing missing, and this is true, but I'd like to add something more: we have something *more.* We have aromanticism and asexuality. We have the distinct filter on life that these experiences give us. We truly have a gift for seeing through arbitrary assumptions about sex and romance and relationships. The aroace youtuber JaidenAnimations discusses in her coming-out video how she feels that 'aroace is one of the coolest or most confident orientations out there. Not needing a single gram of romantic or intimate validation from anyone is so cool. All you need is yourself to be happy, maybe friends and family too… and birds.'[16] And I think she's right.

In a 2015 study, researchers asked US adults who cheered them up when they were sad, who they turned to when they were anxious or angry, and who they wanted to tell when there was something they were really happy about. The people who named the same person repeatedly were the least satisfied with their lives; those who turned to different people for different emotional needs were more satisfied overall.[17] And I believe that aspecs have a gift for this. By our nature, many of us are not driven to find a single person on whom to source all of our emotional and social comforts. Even if we do seek a single life partner, we are more likely to question the structure of romance that says one person should be our source of *everything*. We appreciate the value of our friendships; we cultivate networks.

I fully believe that aromantics and asexuals are social connectors. As a young teen, I saw my identities as orientations that isolated me; cutting me off from other people by the huge *something* they had that I lacked. I could not have been more wrong. My aroace identity makes me look outwards: towards the various friendships I want to carry with me all my life. We invest in our platonic bonds. We explore and create new forms of intimacy. We do not accept a single script; we pick apart the lines, write new directions and, if necessary, throw out the whole thing altogether.

If you are allo, then first of all, I want to thank you for reading this far, and for caring about the aspec people in your life and world enough to try to understand our perspective. I now want to encourage you to take up that perspective yourself now and again. Think hard about what you want from your life and relationships. It may be the normative nuclear, sexual, monogamous romantic relationship – but it may not be. Love is not one-size-fits-all, and it is frankly bizarre that we think it should be, especially when so many cultures across history have shaped the family and relationship in different ways, and still do.

If you are sexually active, look again at your sex life, and make sure nothing you do is done purely because it feels expected. Think of the aces I spoke to who found ways to balance disparities of sexual needs: holding their partners as they masturbate, exploring kink and BDSM. Break down the hierarchy of sex acts that says that penetrative sex is king and everything else is on a lower rung of a ladder, and think about what *you* and any partner or partners you have enjoy most. Consider what sex means to you and what it gives to you.

If you are in a romantic relationship, ask yourself how many of your emotional, social and practical needs you and your partner(s) source in each other. Are there other significant relationships in your life that could also share some of your focus? Do you invest the level of time and energy into your friendships that you want to? Are your living arrangements, sleeping arrangements, and other practical matters of your relationship what you want and prefer, or just what you have always assumed to be normal?

Of course, your answer to these questions may be that your life and your relationships are pretty normative, and you're completely fine with that. That's okay. In fact, it's wonderful; everyone is fortunate to find a formula that works for them. Normative relationships are not bad. They are just not the only option. And I think there's a lot to gain from stopping to wonder, *how would an aspec person approach this? Is there anything I'm doing because compulsory sexuality and amatonormativity make it out to be normal? Is it what I actually want?*

And for my fellow aces and aros, I want you to know this: you are indispensable. You are an essential part of this world and of human life. We have so much to offer. Our identities do not hurt;

erasure hurts. Lack of awareness hurts. Prejudice hurts; being left without legal rights hurts; stereotypes about your sex life and romantic nature hurt. But we are so much more than what other people put upon us.

Our pain is very real – but so is the fact of our happiness. In the moments when the enormity of everything we still have to accomplish starts to overwhelm me, that is what I focus on. I remember people like Kai, the aroace storyteller whose aroace identity gives their stories a new truth and strength. I think of people like Ace and Petra, forming non-normative families and living their best and brightest lives. I think of the changes we *have* brought about: getting asexuality removed from the DSM-5, getting multiple US states to recognize aspec awareness events, and every legal ruling that has broken down the hierarchy of the normative relationship.

I think of how young our movement is. I mentioned earlier that I am about the same age as the ace movement: most people who are older than me have not heard of aspec identities, but the majority of those younger than me have. We are living in a world where the younger, internet-literate, often queer-friendly youth are being introduced to our identities at a young age, whether online, through word of mouth, through the influence of shows such as *Heartstopper*, or simply by having aspec friends. I want to believe – I *choose* to believe, because it keeps me moving forward – that each generation will be more aware, more open, than the last.

I think of how, in the short couple of decades that the aspec movement has existed, we have exploded in size, visibility and power. We have gone from being unspoken of, invisible, to having a flourishing community both on and offline. We have caught the interest of scholars and academics such as Canton Winer and

Bella DePaulo who are realizing just how much ground there is to cover in studying our identities, and how much our experiences might add to the literature and science of relationships and identity. I have no doubt that this wealth of representation will grow, and grow more diverse as it does, to encompass the range of experiences from aspec people of all identity variations and all genders, as well as doing more to include people of colour, disabled and neurodivergent people, and ultimately a broader depiction of aspec experiences than white, able-bodied men.

We absolutely should dream of a world a hundred years from now where our identities are unquestioned. We must, aspec and allo alike, pull together to make this vision a reality. But we must also not forget that aspec joy and aspec flourishing is not a distant ship on the horizon. It is not a pipe dream, a far-off thing we will not see in our lifetimes. It is already here. Where it isn't, we must create it.

Aspec joy is our reality. And our future has to be now.

Endnotes

Chapter 1

1. Plato, *The Symposium*, ed. by Christopher Gill, revised edition (Penguin Classics, 2003), p.24.
2. Bella DePaulo, *Singled Out: How Singles Are Stereotyped, Stigmatized, and Ignored, and Still Live Happily Ever After* (Griffin, 2007), p.25.
3. Cited in Sherronda J. Brown, *Refusing Compulsory Sexuality: A Black Asexual Lens on Our Sex-Obsessed Culture* (North Atlantic Books, 2022), pp. 152–154.
4. Emma Trosse, *Ein Weib? psychologisch-biographische Studie über eine Konträrsexuelle* (Max Spohr, 1897).
5. Cited in Brown, *Refusing Compulsory Sexuality*, pp. 152–154.
6. Lisa Orlando and Barbara Getz, 'The Asexual Manifesto' (1972), < https://app.box.com/s/p7ngvv3iueaj0hk7xadkwd92af2zx4yz > (accessed 13 December 2024).
7. Orlando and Getz, 'The Asexual Manifesto'.
8. *(A)Sexual*, dir. by Angela Tucker (Big Mouth Productions, 2011).
9. Impressive-Jaguar, 'AITA for Putting My Single Best Friends before My Married Ones All the Time?', *R/AmItheAsshole*, 2020, <www.reddit.com/r/AmItheAsshole/comments/eyqwy8/aita_for_putting_my_single_best_friends_before_my/> (accessed 4 January 2024).
10. Barbara Spycher, "Romantic love is preferred over friendship", *UniAktuell*, 2023 <https://www.uniaktuell.unibe.ch/2023/romantic_love_is_preferred_over_friendship/index_eng.html> (accessed 4 January 2024).

Chapter 2

1. 'Quickie: What is asexuality?', '*Dirty Mother Pukka with Anna Whitehouse*, podcast', 19 December 2023, <https://www.globalplayer.com/podcasts/episodes/7Drhcpm/> (accessed 6 June 2024).
2. Rebecca Epstein, Jamilia Blake, and Thalia González, 'Girlhood Interrupted: The Erasure of Black Girls' Childhood', SSRN, 2017 <https://genderjusticeandopportunity.georgetown.edu/wp-content/uploads/2020/06/girlhood-interrupted.pdf> (accessed 4 January 2024).
3. Sherronda J. Brown, *Refusing Compulsory Sexuality: A Black Asexual Lens on Our Sex-Obsessed Culture* (North Atlantic Books, 2022), p. 128.
4. Gail Dines and Carolyn M. West, '"White Girl Moans Black Lives Matter"', *Slate*, 9 July 2020, <https://slate.com/human-interest/2020/07/pornhub-black-lives-matter-genre-racism.html> (accessed 4 January 2024).
5. Angela Chen, *Ace: What Asexuality Reveals About Desire, Society, and the Meaning of Sex* (Boston: Beacon Press, 2020), p. 82.
6. Siggy, '2021 Ace Community Survey Summary Report', *The Ace Community Survey*, 2023, <https://acecommunitysurvey.org/2023/10/23/2021-ace-community-survey-summary-report/> (accessed 4 January 2024).
7. 'Aro Census 2020 Report', *AUREA*, 2020, <https://static1.squarespace.com/static/5cb6e4d565019f0c5aa6cf20/t/6155f54054f46f3d4568e6dc/1633023300767/Aro+Census+2020+Report.pdf> (accessed 15 December 2024).
8. Michael Paramo, 'The Asexual Community Is Predominately White. Why?', *Medium*, 25 October 2017, <https://medium.com/@Michael_Paramo/interrogating-the-whiteness-of-the-asexual-community-b5765a71f62b> (accessed 6 June 2024).
9. Sara Atske and Andrew Perrin, 'Home Broadband Adoption, Computer Ownership Vary by Race, Ethnicity in the U.S.', *Pew Research Center*, 16 July 2021, <https://www.pewresearch.org/short-reads/2021/07/16/home-broadband-adoption-computer-ownership-vary-by-race-ethnicity-in-the-u-s/> (accessed 6 June 2024).
10. Chen, *Ace*, p. 80.
11. Nancy J. Mezey, 'The Privilege of Coming Out: Race, Class, and Lesbians' Mothering Decisions', *International Journal of Sociology of the Family*, 34/2 (2008), pp. 257–276.

12. Stonewall, *Ace in the UK Report* (2023), <https://www.stonewall.org.uk/resources/ace-report> (accessed 14 March 2024).
13. Lillian Li, 'Coming out Stories in Media: Harmful, Overdone and Outdated – Daily Forty-Niner', *Long Beach Current*, 2 November 2021, <https://lbcurrent.com/opinions/2021/11/02/coming-out-stories-in-media-harmful-overdone-and-outdated/> (accessed 26 June 2024).
14. Chimamanda Ngozi Adichie, *The Danger of a Single Story*, TED, 2009 <https://www.youtube.com/watch?v=D9Ihs241zeg> (accessed 6 June 2024).
15. Yasmin Benoit, 'I Hate My TV Asexuality Documentary', 2018, <https://www.youtube.com/watch?v=ft8T5EDnjAo> (accessed 6 June 2024).
16. Lucy Knight, 'Heartstopper Author Alice Oseman: "If You Don't Have Sex and Romance, You Feel like You Haven't Achieved"', *The Guardian*, 19 November 2022, <https://www.theguardian.com/books/2022/nov/19/alice-oseman-author-heartstopper-sex-romance-asexuality> (accessed 20 June 2024).
17. Greg Hernandez, 'Tim Gunn's Revealing People Interview: "When I Was Seventeen, I'd Made a Serious Suicide Attempt"', *Greg in Hollywood*, 12 September 2010, <http://greginhollywood.com/tim-gunns-revealing-people-interview-when-i-was-seventeen-id-made-a-serious-suicide-attempt-37239> (accessed 11 December 2023).
18. Rene Lynch, 'Tim Gunn's 29 Years of Celibacy: Yes, It's Unusual, Expert Says', *Los Angeles Times*, 25 January 2012 <https://www.latimes.com/archives/blogs/nation-now/story/2012-01-25/tim-gunns-29-years-of-celibacy-yes-its-unusual-expert-says> (accessed 11 December 2023).
19. Rose Hartman, 'ASEXUALITY: Is everybody not doing it?', *Forum*, January 1979, p. 14.
20. Andy Warhol, *The Philosophy of Andy Warhol: From A to B and Back Again* (Penguin Classics, 2007), pp. 48–49.

Chapter 3

1. Sarah Vaughan, *Anatomy of a Scandal* (Simon & Schuster, 2017), pp. 23–26.
2. Sherronda J. Brown, *Refusing Compulsory Sexuality: A Black Asexual Lens on Our Sex-Obsessed Culture* (North Atlantic Books, 2022), p. 84.
3. Brown, *Refusing Compulsory Sexuality*, p. 152.

4. Lori A. Brotto, Morag A. Yule and Boris B. Gorzalka, 'Asexuality: An Extreme Variant of Sexual Desire Disorder?', *The Journal of Sexual Medicine*, 12/3 (2015), pp. 646–660, <https://doi.org/10.1111/jsm.12806> (accessed 26 June 2024).
5. Brown, *Refusing Compulsory Sexuality*, pp. 109–110.
6. Bella DePaulo, *Singled Out: How Singles Are Stereotyped, Stigmatized, and Ignored, and Still Live Happily Ever After* (Griffin, 2007), pp. 160–161.
7. Lynne Reid Banks, *The L-Shaped Room* (Vintage Classics, 2004), p. 296.
8. Elizabeth Brake, *Minimizing Marriage: Marriage, Morality, and The Law* (Oxford University Press, 2012), pp. 88–89.
9. Jack Julian, '7 Years after Deportation Saga, 79-Year-Old Finally a Permanent Resident', *CBC*, 13 February 2019, <https://www.cbc.ca/news/canada/nova-scotia/nancy-inferrera-permanent-residency-mildred-sanford-guysborough-1.5017153> (accessed 2 December 2024).
10. Angela Chen, *Ace: What Asexuality Reveals About Desire, Society, and the Meaning of Sex* (Boston: Beacon Press, 2020), p. 139.
11. Julian, '7 Years after Deportation Saga'.
12. 'Eight Reasons Women Stay in Abusive Relationships', *Institute for Family Studies*, 21 July 2016, <https://ifstudies.org/blog/eight-reasons-women-stay-in-abusive-relationships> (accessed 4 January 2024).
13. 'After Ray Rice News, Abuse Survivors Tell Their Stories on Twitter', *The Seattle Times*, 10 September 2014, <https://www.seattletimes.com/seattle-news/after-ray-rice-news-abuse-survivors-tell-their-stories-on-twitter/> (accessed 2 December 2024).
14. Jaclyn D. Cravens, Jason B. Whiting and Rola O. Aamar, 'Why I Stayed/Left: An Analysis of Voices of Intimate Partner Violence on Social Media', *Contemporary Family Therapy*, 37/4 (2015), pp. 372–385, <https://doi.org/10.1007/s10591-015-9360-8> (accessed 1 March 2024).
15. Cravens et al., 'Why I Stayed/Left'.
16. Amy Gahran, *Stepping Off the Relationship Escalator: Uncommon Love and Life: Volume 1* (Off the Escalator Enterprises LLC, 2017), p. 47.
17. DePaulo, *Singled Out*, p.6.
18. Amanda Kippert, 'The Woman Behind the Viral Hashtag #WhyIStayed', *DomesticShelters.Org*, 16 November 2022, <https://www.domesticshelters.org/articles/book-club/the-woman-behind-the-viral-hashtag-whyistayed> (accessed 3 January 2024).

19. 'BME Statistics on Poverty and Deprivation', *Institute of Race Relations*, 2024, <https://irr.org.uk/research/statistics/poverty/> (accessed 3 January 2024).
20. 'Poverty Rate in the United States in 2022, by Race and Ethnicity', *Statista* <https://www.statista.com/statistics/200476/us-poverty-rate-by-ethnic-group/> (accessed 3 January 2024).

Chapter 4

1. Siggy, '2021 Ace Community Survey Summary Report', *The Ace Community Survey*, 2023, <https://acecommunitysurvey.org/2023/10/23/2021-ace-community-survey-summary-report/> (accessed 4 January 2024).
2. Jessie V. Ford, '"Consensualish" – What about Sex That Is Unwanted, but Not Physically Coercive?', in *Council on Contemporary Families*, presented at the Defining Consent Online Symposium, 21 October 2019, <https://sites.utexas.edu/contemporaryfamilies/2019/10/21/defining-consent-symposium-2019-ford-consensualish/> (accessed 2 December 2024).
3. Zoe Williams, '"Raw Hatred": Why the "incel" Movement Targets and Terrorises Women', *The Guardian*, 25 April 2018, <https://www.theguardian.com/world/2018/apr/25/raw-hatred-why-incel-movement-targets-terrorises-women> (accessed 17 October 2024).
4. 'Poorcel', *Incel Wiki*, 2022, <https://incels.wiki/w/Poorcel> (accessed 18 October 2024).
5. Chris Capetown, *Sexual Market Value: The Cynical Truth about What It Is, How You Get It and How to Stop Yourself from Throwing Yours Away* (Blasphemy Books, 2016).
6. 'Asexual Men?', *Asexual Visibility and Education Network*, 6 July 2015, <https://www.asexuality.org/en/topic/121857-asexual-men/> (accessed 4 January 2024).
7. Joey Thurmond, 'Postscript: An Interview with Canton Winer', *Saveasdoc*, 23 October 2023, <https://joeythurmond.substack.com/p/postscript-an-interview-with-canton?utm_medium=email> (accessed 23 May 2024).
8. Nicole Andrejek, Tina Fetner and Melanie Heath, 'Climax as Work: Heteronormativity, Gender Labor, and the Gender Gap in Orgasms', *Gender & Society*, 36/2 (2022), p. 189, <https://doi.org/10.1177/08912432211073062> (accessed 18 October 2024).

9. Andrejek, Fetner and Heath, 'Climax as Work'.
10. 'DJ Khaled Said He Does Not Perform Oral Sex on Women Because "There Are Different Rules for Men"', *The Independent*, 7 May 2018 <https://www.independent.co.uk/arts-entertainment/music/news/dj-khaled-the-breakfast-club-oral-sex-interview-2015-a8337276.html> (accessed 18 October 2024).
11. Elizabeth A. Armstrong, Paula England, and Alison C. K. Fogarty, 'Accounting for Women's Orgasm and Sexual Enjoyment in College Hookups and Relationships', *American Sociological Review*, 77.3 (2012), pp. 435–62 <https://journals.sagepub.com/doi/full/10.1177/0003122412445802> (accessed 18 October 2024).
12. Bener Eshref, 'The White Hyper-Sexualized Gay Male: A Lack of Diversity in Gay Male Magazines', Thesis, University of British Columbia, April 2009, <https://open.library.ubc.ca/media/stream/pdf/42446/1.0103633/1> (accessed 2 December 2024).
13. Anna Pulley, 'Why Lesbian Porn Dominates 10 Years Of Pornhub Data', *Salon*, 17 September 2017 <https://www.salon.com/2017/09/17/why-does-lesbian-porn-dominate-milf-and-much-more-in-10-years-of-pornhub-data_partner/> (accessed 23 October 2024).
14. Philip Blumstein and Pepper Schwartz, *American Couples: Money, Work, Sex* (Morrow, 1983), p.195.
15. 'Why Won't the Lesbian Bed Death Myth Just Die?', *Cosmopolitan*, 12 April 2023, <https://www.cosmopolitan.com/sex-love/a43540867/lesbian-bed-death-myth/> (accessed 23 October 2024).
16. 'Debunking the Myth of "Lesbian Bed Death"', *Psychology Today*, 28 February 2023, <https://www.psychologytoday.com/gb/blog/all-about-sex/202302/debunking-the-myth-of-lesbian-bed-death> (accessed 23 October 2024).
17. Armstrong et al.
18. Ibid.
19. Canton Winer, '"My Gender is Like an Empty Lot": Gender Detachment and Ungendering Among Asexual Individuals' (OSF, 2023), <https://osf.io/nbr28> (accessed 4 January 2024).

Chapter 5

1. Hubert Izienicki, 'Netflix and Chill: Teaching Sexual Scripts in a Sociology Classroom', *Teaching Sociology*, 50/1 (2022), pp. 39–48, <https://doi.org/10.1177/0092055X211033633> (accessed 1 March 2024).

2. William Simon and John H. Gagnon, 'Sexual Scripts', *Society*, 22/1 (1984), pp. 53–60.
3. Jessie V. Ford, '"Consensualish" – What about Sex That Is Unwanted, but Not Physically Coercive?', in *Council on Contemporary Families* (presented at the Defining Consent Online Symposium, Columbia University, 2019), <https://sites.utexas.edu/contemporaryfamilies/2019/10/21/defining-consent-symposium-2019-ford-consensualish/> (accessed 3 December 2024).
4. Leslie Picca, 'But Was It Wanted? Young Women's First Voluntary Sexual Intercourse', *Journal of Family Issues*, 26 (2005), pp. 1082–1102, <https://doi.org/10.1177/0192513X04273582> (accessed 1 March 2024).
5. Kitty Drake and As told to Kitty Drake, 'This Is How We Do It: "We've Bought Lots of Sex Toys, and given Them Names, like Pets"', *The Guardian*, 18 November 2023, <https://www.theguardian.com/lifeandstyle/2023/nov/18/this-is-how-we-do-it-weve-bought-lots-of-sex-toys-and-given-them-names-like-pets> (accessed 4 January 2024).
6. Abbey Wright, 'Too Much Too Young: I Talked to 10,000 Children about Pornography. Here Are 10 Things I Learned', *The Guardian*, 13 September 2023, <https://www.theguardian.com/society/2023/sep/13/adults-are-terrified-of-talking-to-us-about-it-10-things-i-learned-from-children-about-pornography> (accessed 4 January 2024).
7. Emine Saner, '"I Was Scared after Watching": New Play Tackles Online Porn's Impact on Children', *The Guardian*, 1 May 2018, <https://www.theguardian.com/stage/2018/may/01/porn-tackroom-theatre-why-is-the-sky-blue> (accessed 4 January 2024).
8. German Lopez, 'John Oliver Takes on America's Disastrous Approach to Sex Education', *Vox*, 2015, <https://www.vox.com/2015/8/10/9126179/john-oliver-sex-education-last-week-tonight> (accessed 4 January 2024).
9. David Satcher, 'Opinion | Renew the U.S. Commitment to Sex Education', *Washington Post*, 22 May 2015, <https://www.washingtonpost.com/opinions/renew-the-us-commitment-to-sex-education/2015/05/22/8b86980e-fe53-11e4-833c-a2de05b6b2a4_story.html> (accessed 4 January 2024).
10. 'The Costs of Enforced Sexual Ignorance', *Center for American Progress*, 8 May 2008 <https://www.americanprogress.org/article/think-again-the-costs-of-enforced-sexual-ignorance/> (accessed 4 January 2024).

11. Linda Kay Klein, *Pure: Inside the Evangelical Movement That Shamed a Generation of Young Women and How I Broke Free* (Atria Books, 2018), p.75.
12. Wright, 'Too Much Too Young'.
13. David Sanderson, 'Boy Rapists Expect Girls to Cry during Sex, Says Activist Laura Bates', 13 August 2018 <https://www.thetimes.com/uk/crime/article/boy-rapists-expect-girls-to-cry-during-sex-says-activist-7z7r06lqr> (accessed 23 October 2024).
14. Hannah L. Fegley, 'The Danger of Assumed Realism in Pornography: Pornography Use and Its Relationship to Sexual Consent', 2013 <https://www.semanticscholar.org/paper/The-danger-of-assumed-realism-in-pornography-%3A-use-Fegley/150afbdf78454cbacdfdc4038e3e321136761af6> (accessed 4 January 2024).
15. 'Coining/Recoining Interaction Stance Terms: Asexuality', *Archive.Ph*, 2023 <https://archive.ph/osaCZ> (accessed 3 January 2024).
16. Angela Chen, *Ace: What Asexuality Reveals About Desire, Society, and the Meaning of Sex* (Boston: Beacon Press, 2020), p. 147.
17. Dr Emily Nagoski, *Come As You Are: The Bestselling Guide to the New Science That Will Transform Your Sex Life* (Scribe UK, 2015).
18. Ro White, 'The Gay B C's of Sex: S Is for Stone', *Autostraddle*, 5 January 2023, <https://www.autostraddle.com/stone-butch-definition/> (accessed 3 January 2024).

Chapter 6

1. Angela Chen, 'The Rise of the Three-Parent Family', *The Atlantic*, 22 September 2020 <https://www.theatlantic.com/family/archive/2020/09/how-build-three-parent-family-david-jay/616421/> (accessed 17 January 2024).
2. 'Why One Married Couple and Their Friend Formed a 3-Parent Family', 6 November 2017, <https://www.wbur.org/hereandnow/2017/11/06/three-parent-family> (accessed 25 January 2024).
3. 'Why One Married Couple and Their Friend Formed a 3-Parent Family'.
4. Louise Carpenter, 'Meet the Co-Parents', *The Guardian*, 15 December 2013, <https://www.theguardian.com/lifeandstyle/2013/dec/15/meet-the-co-parents-modern-families> (accessed 18 January 2024).
5. Bella DePaulo, *Singled Out: How Singles Are Stereotyped, Stigmatized, and Ignored, and Still Live Happily Ever After* (Griffin, 2007), p. 181.

6. Ibid., p. 177.
7. Nicola Slawson, 'Two Single Friends, One Radical Plan: Why I'm Having a Child with My Gay Best Mate', *The Guardian*, 6 January 2024, <https://www.theguardian.com/lifeandstyle/2024/jan/06/two-single-friends-one-radical-plan-why-im-having-a-child-with-my-gay-best-mate> (accessed 18 January 2024).
8. '7個廣州閨蜜合力造民宿 7 Girlfriends in Guangzhou Build a House to Live Together', dir. by 一条Yit, *YouTube*, 2019 <https://www.youtube.com/watch?v=Rqt2rZ99X4U> (accessed 18 January 2024).
9. Amy Gahran, *Stepping Off the Relationship Escalator: Uncommon Love and Life: Volume 1* (Off the Escalator Enterprises LLC, 2017), p. 243.
10. Ibid., pp. 3–4.
11. DePaulo, *Singled Out*, pp. 24–25.
12. Ibid., p. 8.
13. Melissa Persling, 'I Was Told I Was "Selfish" for Being Single at 38. But I Needed Those Years of Independence', *Yahoo Life!*, 15 December 2023, <https://ca.style.yahoo.com/told-selfish-being-single-38-121101641.html> (accessed 31 May 2024).
14. Andrew Lloyd, 'A 29-Year-Old Shared a Day in Her Life as a Single Woman with No Kids. When She Went Viral, She Was Flooded with Hate and Abuse for Her Choices', *Business Insider*, 8 September 2023, <https://www.businessinsider.com/single-no-kids-woman-viral-received-abuse-online-interview-2023-9> (accessed 31 May 2024).
15. Ibid.
16. Rachel Wearmouth, 'Unmarried Men Are "A Problem" For Society, Says Tory MP Iain Duncan Smith', *HuffPost UK*, 10 March 2017, <https://www.huffingtonpost.co.uk/entry/marriage-iain-duncan-smith_uk_59d3b8f9e4b04b9f92054af5> (accessed 31 May 2024).
17. DePaulo, *Singled Out*, pp. 127–128.
18. Ibid.
19. Ibid., pp. 28–35.
20. Ibid., pp. 35–37.
21. Bella DePaulo, *Single at Heart: The Power, Freedom, and Heart-Filling Joy of Single Life* (Apollo, 2023), p. 18.
22. Ibid., p. 232.
23. Ibid., p. 233.
24. Ibid., p. 252.

Chapter 7

1. Kimberley Smith, 'Charting Loneliness', *RSA Journal*, 165/1 (5577) (2019), pp. 38–41.
2. Sarah Johnson, 'WHO Declares Loneliness a "Global Public Health Concern"', *The Guardian*, 16 November 2023, <https://www.theguardian.com/global-development/2023/nov/16/who-declares-loneliness-a-global-public-health-concern> (accessed 24 October 2024).
3. Smith, 'Charting Loneliness'.
4. Richard Reeves, 'The Friendship Recession', dir. by Big Think, 2023 <https://www.youtube.com/watch?v=VpOan0hqdNA> (accessed 6 June 2024).
5. US Surgeon General, *Our Epidemic of Loneliness and Isolation*, 2023, p. 13, <https://www.hhs.gov/sites/default/files/surgeon-general-social-connection-advisory.pdf> (accessed 3 December 2024).
6. 'You with the Wide Eyes, Don't Lose Your Courage', *Tumblr*, 2023 <https://www.tumblr.com/bogkeep/706231655716864000/dont-get-me-wrong-i-love-being-aro-and-i-love> (accessed 6 June 2024).
7. 'Aromantics and Friendships', *Arocalypse*, 31 July 2020 <https://www.arocalypse.com/topic/3304-aromantics-and-friendships/> (accessed 6 June 2024).
8. Bella DePaulo, *Singled Out: How Singles Are Stereotyped, Stigmatized, and Ignored, and Still Live Happily Ever After* (Griffin, 2007), p. 258.
9. Natalia Sarkisian and Naomi Gerstel, 'Does Singlehood Isolate or Integrate? Examining the Link between Marital Status and Ties to Kin, Friends, and Neighbors', *Journal of Social and Personal Relationships*, 33.3 (2016), pp. 361–84. <http://journals.sagepub.com/doi/10.1177/0265407515597564> (accessed 6 May 2024).
10. Ibid.
11. Bella DePaulo, *Single at Heart: The Power, Freedom, and Heart-Filling Joy of Single Life* (Apollo, 2023), p. 145.
12. Bella DePaulo, 'Ditched by Friend Who Got Married: Can You Relate?' *Psychology Today*, 7 September 2011, <https://www.psychologytoday.com/gb/blog/living-single/201109/ditched-friend-who-got-married-can-you-relate> (accessed 5 June 2024).
13. Mihret Sibhat, 'I Grew up in a Culture That Embraced Physical Touch. Then I Came to America', *Los Angeles Times*, 2 September 2023, <https://www.latimes.com/opinion/story/2023-09-02/

queer-lgbtq-ethiopia-touch-sexuality-identity-united-states> (accessed 23 January 2024).

14. Mpho 'M'atsepo Nthunya and K. Limakatso Kendall, *Singing Away the Hunger: The Autobiography of an African Woman* (Bloomington: Indiana University Press, 1997), p. 69, <http://archive.org/details/isbn_9780253211620> (accessed 15 November 2024).
15. Brenna M. Munro, *South Africa and the Dream of Love to Come: Queer Sexuality and the Struggle for Freedom* (University of Minnesota Press, 2012).
16. Nthunya and Kendall, *Singing Away the Hunger*, p. 72.
17. Samir Chopra, 'Men and Intimacy, Physical and Conversational', *3QuarksDaily*, 12 March 2018, <https://3quarksdaily.com/3quarksdaily/2018/03/men-and-intimacy-physical-and-conversational.html> (accessed 3 December 2024).
18. Adam Smiley Poswolsky, *Friendship in the Age of Loneliness: An Optimist's Guide to Connection* (Running Press Adult, 2021).
19. Mark Greene, 'The Lack of Gentle Platonic Touch in Men's Lives Is a Killer', *Medium*, 20 July 2017, <https://remakingmanhood.medium.com/the-lack-of-gentle-platonic-touch-in-mens-lives-is-a-killer-5cc8eb144001> (accessed 30 October 2024).
20. Ibid.
21. Robert Strikwerda and Larry May, 'Male Friendship and Intimacy', *Hypatia*, 7 (2009), pp. 110–125, <https://doi.org/10.1111/j.1527-2001.1992.tb00907.x> (accessed 30 October 2024).
22. Ibid., p. 102.
23. Danu Anthony Stinson, Jessica J. Cameron, and Lisa B. Hoplock, 'The Friends-to-Lovers Pathway to Romance: Prevalent, Preferred, and Overlooked by Science', *Social Psychological and Personality Science*, 13/2 (2022), pp. 562–71, <https://doi.org/10.1177/19485506211026992> (accessed 6 June 2024).
24. Ibid., p. 569.
25. Ibid., p. 564.
26. Poswolsky, p. 78.
27. Ibid., p. 76.
28. Oliver Wainwright, 'Marmalade Lane: The Car-Free, Triple-Glazed, 42-House Oasis', *The Guardian*, 8 May 2019, <https://www.theguardian.com/artanddesign/2019/may/08/marmalade-lane-co-housing-cambridge> (accessed 6 June 2024).
29. Anita Chaudhuri and Jill Mead, '"We Have Brothers, Sons, Lovers

– but They Can't Live Here!" The Happy Home Shared by 26 Women', *The Guardian*, 24 August 2023, <https://www.theguardian.com/lifeandstyle/2023/aug/24/we-have-brothers-sons-lovers-but-they-cant-live-here-the-happy-home-shared-by-26-women> (accessed 6 June 2024).

30. Poswolsky, p. 216.
31. 'Over-50s Turn to House-Shares to Beat Rising Rents', *BBC News*, 20 August 2022, <https://www.bbc.com/news/business-62344571> (accessed 31 October 2024).
32. 'Meet the Housemates with a 68 Year Age Gap', *BBC News*, 23 December 2017, <https://www.bbc.com/news/uk-politics-42428782> (accessed 31 October 2024).

Chapter 8

1. D. H. Lawrence, *Lady Chatterley's Lover* (Penguin Books, 1932), p.22, <http://archive.org/details/in.ernet.dli.2015.38592> (accessed 7 June 2024).
2. Ibid, p. 313.
3. Louis Battye, 'The Chatterley Syndrome,' in *Stigma: The Experience of Disability* (G. Chapman, 1966).
4. Amber Raiken, 'Sofía Jirau Makes History as First Victoria's Secret Model with Down Syndrome', *The Independent*, 17 February 2022, <https://www.independent.co.uk/life-style/sofia-jirau-victoria-secret-downs-syndrome-b2017578.html> (accessed 7 June 2024).
5. Hannah Shewan Stevens, 'Stop Desexualising Disabled People like the Victoria's Secret Model with Down's Syndrome', *The Independent*, 27 February 2022, <https://www.independent.co.uk/voices/sofia-jirau-victorias-secret-downs-synrome-b2024418.html> (accessed 29 May 2024).
6. Stevens, 'Stop Desexualising Disabled People'.
7. Tom Shakespeare and Sarah Richardson, 'The Sexual Politics of Disability, Twenty Years On', *Scandinavian Journal of Disability Research*, 20/1 (2018), <https://sjdr.se/articles/10.16993/sjdr.25> (accessed 11 April 2024).
8. Angela Chen, *Ace: What Asexuality Reveals About Desire, Society, and the Meaning of Sex* (Boston: Beacon Press, 2020), p. 85.
9. Janna L. Fikkan and Esther D. Rothblum, 'Is Fat a Feminist Issue? Exploring the Gendered Nature of Weight Bias', *Sex Roles: A Journal*

of Research, 66/9–10 (2012), pp. 575–592, <https://doi.org/10.1007/s11199-011-0022-5> (accessed 4 October 2024).

10. Ibid.
11. Ibid.
12. Alicia Mccarvell, 'These Are Things That People Have Said about My Husband and I, Simply Because of Our Weight Difference', Instagram, 1 February 2021, <https://www.instagram.com/p/CKxEc8ynez0/?img_index=1> (accessed 31 October 2024).
13. 'Gabourey Sidibe Slams Fat Shamers for "Empire" Sex Scene: I Felt Sexy', *Inside Edition*, 2015 <https://www.youtube.com/watch?v=ZX7deTkNBnM> (accessed 31 October 2024); 'Gabourey Sidibe Responds Beautifully to "Haters" Who Shamed Her for Empire Sex Scene', *The Independent*, 2015 <https://www.independent.co.uk/news/people/gabourey-sidibe-responds-to-fatshamers-who-mocked-her-for-filming-sex-scene-on-hiphop-drama-empire-a6726996.html> (accessed 31 October 2024).
14. Zoe Strimpel, 'Bridgerton's Big Fantasy', *The Spectator*, 24 May 2024, <https://www.spectator.co.uk/article/bridgertons-big-fantasy/> (accessed 31 October 2024).
15. Paisley MacLeod, 'Sexualizing Desexualized Bodies: Fat Women and Sexual Objectification', *Footnotes*, 5 (2012) <https://journal.lib.uoguelph.ca/index.php/footnotes/article/view/6404> (accessed 7 June 2024).
16. Rachel Howe and Niwako Yamawaki, 'Weight-Based Discrimination of Rape Victims', 4 September 2013, <http://jur.byu.edu/?p=4406> (accessed 7 June 2024).
17. Your Fat Friend, 'Why Don't We Hear Fat Women's #MeToo Stories?', *The Establishment*, 15 May 2018, <https://medium.com/the-establishment/why-dont-we-hear-fat-women-s-metoo-stories-2e28f799b507> (accessed 7 June 2024).
18. Cool Cyat [@7rayof_sunshine], 'Discovering Plan B Doesn't Work When You're Overweight Explains Why I'm Laying on a Playmat Watching Sesame Street with My 9m Old', *Twitter*, 2021, <https://twitter.com/7rayof_sunshine/status/1476182185585655823> (accessed 7 June 2024).
19. Carolin Kost, Kimberly Jamie, and Elizabeth Mohr, '"Whatever I Said Didn't Register with Her": Medical Fatphobia and Interactional and Relational Disconnect in Healthcare Encounters', *Frontiers in Sociology*, 9 (2024 < https://link.springer.com/article/10.1007/s11199-

011-0022-5#:~:text=(1979)%2C%20followed%20by%20others,(normal%20and%20healthy)%20bodies%2C> (accessed 4 October 2024).

20. 'BMI in the BIPOC Community: Why It's Problematic', *EverydayHealth.Com*, 28 February 2024 <https://www.everydayhealth.com/weight/why-body-mass-index-bmi-can-be-problematic-for-the-bipoc-community/> (accessed 7 June 2024).
21. D. G. Aaron and F. C. Stanford, 'Is Obesity a Manifestation of Systemic Racism? A Ten-Point Strategy for Study and Intervention', *Journal of Internal Medicine*, 290/2 (2021), pp. 416–420, <https://doi.org/10.1111/joim.13270> (accessed 18 March 2024).
22. 'Why People Become Overweight', *Harvard Health*, 24 June 2019 <https://www.health.harvard.edu/staying-healthy/why-people-become-overweight> (accessed 18 April 2024).
23. Erin Shinners, 'Effects of the "What Is Beautiful Is Good" Stereotype on Perceived Trustworthiness', *Journal of Undergraduate Research*, 12 (2009), <https://www.researchgate.net/publication/255646074_Effects_of_The_What_is_Beautiful_is_Good_Stereotype_on_Perceived_Trustworthiness> (accessed 5 December 2024).
24. Solomon Asch, 'Forming Impressions of Personality', *Psychology* (1946) <https://www.all-about-psychology.com/solomon-asch.html> (accessed 1 November 2024).
25. Adrian Mehic, 'Student Beauty and Grades under In-Person and Remote Teaching', *Economics Letters*, 219 (2022), 110782, <https://doi.org/10.1016/j.econlet.2022.110782> (accessed 11 January 2024).
26. 'Attractiveness "Affects Jurors"', BBC News, 22 March 2007 <http://news.bbc.co.uk/1/hi/health/6478659.stm> (accessed 1 November 2024).
27. Timothy A. Judge, Charlice Hurst and Lauren S. Simon, 'Does It Pay to Be Smart, Attractive, or Confident (or All Three)? Relationships among General Mental Ability, Physical Attractiveness, Core Self-Evaluations, and Income', *Journal of Applied Psychology*, 94/3 (2009), pp. 742–755, <https://doi.org/10.1037/a0015497> (accessed 11 January 2024).
28. Ted Chiang, *Stories of Your Life and Others: Ted Chiang* (Picador, 2015), p. 297.
29. Genevieve L. Lorenzo, Jeremy C. Biesanz and Lauren J. Human, 'What Is Beautiful Is Good and More Accurately Understood: Physical Attractiveness and Accuracy in First Impressions of Personality', *Psychological Science*, 21/12 (2010), pp. 1777–1782.
30. Michael Herrmann and Susumu Shikano, 'Attractiveness and Facial

Competence Bias Face-Based Inferences of Candidate Ideology', *Political Psychology*, 37/3 (2016), pp. 401–417.

31. Lucy Webster, 'I Learned to Love My Disabled Body – Why Can't My Non-Disabled Friends Love Theirs?', *The Guardian*, 9 September 2023, <https://www.theguardian.com/lifeandstyle/2023/sep/09/i-learned-to-love-my-disabled-body-why-cant-my-non-disabled-friends-love-theirs> (accessed 19 April 2024).
32. Ben Quinn, 'French Police Make Woman Remove Clothing on Nice Beach Following Burkini Ban', *The Guardian*, 23 August 2016, <https://www.theguardian.com/world/2016/aug/24/french-police-make-woman-remove-burkini-on-nice-beach> (accessed 29 May 2024).
33. 'Man Attempts to Take off Woman's Headscarf on London Train', *The New Arab*, 22 February 2022, <https://www.newarab.com/news/man-attempts-take-womans-headscarf-london-train> (accessed 29 May 2024).

Chapter 9

1. Expert Participation, 'Equality Act 2010' (Statute Law Database) <https://www.legislation.gov.uk/ukpga/2010/15/contents> (accessed 7 June 2024).
2. 'Discrimination: Your Rights', GOV.UK <https://www.gov.uk/discrimination-your-rights/how-you-can-be-discriminated-against> (accessed 7 June 2024).
3. 'The Sexual Orientation Non-Discrimination Act ("SONDA")', Office of the New York State Attorney General, <https://ag.ny.gov/resources/individuals/civil-rights/sexual-orientation-non-discrimination-act-sonda> (accessed 27 March 2024).
4. 'Sexual Identity', Federal Anti-Discrimination Agency, <https://www.antidiskriminierungsstelle.de/EN/about-discrimination/grounds-for-discrimination/sexual-identity/sexual-identity-node.html> (accessed 14 November 2024).
5. Stonewall, *Ace in the UK Report.*
6. H.R.5 – 117th Congress (2021–2022) Equality Act, 2021, <https://www.congress.gov/bill/117th-congress/house-bill/5/text> (accessed 7 June 2024).
7. Stonewall, *Ace in the UK Report.*
8. Ibid.

9. 'Intrauterine Insemination', NHS, 2017, <https://www.nhs.uk/conditions/artificial-insemination/> (accessed 7 June 2024).
10. American Psychiatric Association, *Diagnostic and Statistical Manual of Mental Disorders: DSM-5*, 5th edn (2013).
11. Susan Bernstein, 'What Is Desire Disorder', *WebMD*, 2023, <https://www.webmd.com/sexual-conditions/desire-disorder> (accessed 7 June 2024).
12. APA, DSM-5.
13. World Health Organization, *The ICD-10 Classification of Mental and Behavioural Disorders: Clinical Descriptions and Diagnostic Guidelines* (2009).
14. Stonewall, *Ace in the UK Report.*
15. Mohammed Elnaeim, 'The "Deviant" African Genders That Colonialism Condemned', *JSTOR Daily*, 29 April 2021, <https://daily.jstor.org/the-deviant-african-genders-that-colonialism-condemned/> (accessed 13 December 2024).
16. Brabners, 'Void and Voidable Marriages', 12 October 2022, <https://www.brabners.com/insights/brabners-personal/void-and-voidable-marriages> (accessed 7 June 2024).
17. 'Annul a Marriage', GOV.UK, <https://www.gov.uk/how-to-annul-marriage> (accessed 7 June 2024).
18. Brabners, 'Void and Voidable Marriages'.
19. Thomas Mansfield Family Law, 'Difference Between Void And Voidable Marriage', 2024, <https://www.tmfamilylaw.co.uk/void-and-voidable-marriage/> (accessed 27 March 2024).
20. LawTeacher, 'Marriage and Nullity Case Summaries', 6 September 2021, <https://www.lawteacher.net/cases/marriage-and-nullity.php> (accessed 7 June 2024).
21. Marriage (Same Sex Couples) Act 2013 (Statute Law Database), <https://www.legislation.gov.uk/ukpga/2013/30/contents> (accessed 7 June 2024).
22. Siggy, '2019 Ace Community Survey Summary Report', *The Ace Community Survey*, 2021, <https://acecommunitysurvey.org/2021/10/24/2019-ace-community-survey-summary-report/> (accessed 7 June 2024).
23. '2022 National Survey on LGBTQ Youth Mental Health', *The Trevor Project*, <https://www.thetrevorproject.org/survey-2022/#anxiety-by-sexual-orientation> (accessed 14 November 2024).
24. Diane Taylor and Frances Perraudin, 'Couples Face "insulting"

Checks in Sham Marriage Crackdown', *The Guardian*, 14 April 2019, <https://www.theguardian.com/uk-news/2019/apr/14/couples-sham-marriage-crackdown-hostile-environment> (accessed 27 March 2024).

25. Zoe Playdon, *The Hidden Case of Ewan Forbes: The Transgender Trial That Threatened to Upend the British Establishment* (Bloomsbury Publishing, 2021), p. 185.
26. Bella DePaulo, *Single at Heart: The Power, Freedom, and Heart-Filling Joy of Single Life* (Apollo, 2023), p.1.
27. 'Singled Out: Discrimination for Living Alone', *Law Society of Scotland*, <https://www.lawscot.org.uk/members/journal/issues/vol-66-issue-03/singled-out-discrimination-for-living-alone/> (accessed 22 March 2024).
28. Lisa Arnold and Christina Campbell, 'The High Price of Being Single in America', *The Atlantic*, 14 January 2013, <https://www.theatlantic.com/sexes/archive/2013/01/the-high-price-of-being-single-in-america/267043/> (accessed 22 March 2024).
29. Wendy L. Morris, Stacey Sinclair and Bella M. DePaulo, 'No Shelter for Singles: The Perceived Legitimacy of Marital Status Discrimination', *Group Processes & Intergroup Relations*, 10/4 (2007), pp. 457–470, <https://doi.org/10.1177/1368430207081535> (accessed 22 March 2024).
30. Ibid., p. 463.
31. Ibid., p. 457.
32. Elizabeth Brake, *Minimizing Marriage: Marriage, Morality, and The Law* (Oxford University Press, 2012), p. 160.
33. DePaulo, *Singled Out*, p. 221.
34. Ian Jenkins, 'Children With Three Parents? A History of Multi-Parentage', *Psychology Today*, 22 February 2021, <https://www.psychologytoday.com/gb/blog/better-or-worse/202102/children-three-parents-history-multi-parentage> (accessed 7 June 2024).

Chapter 10

1. Högsta domstolen, 'Relationen Mellan Två Kvinnor Var Sådan Att Ett Parförhållande Enligt Sambolagen Förelåg', *Sveriges Domstolar*, 8 July 2022 <https://www.domstol.se/nyheter/2022/07/relationen-mellan-tva-kvinnor-var-sadan-att-ett-parforhallande-enligt-sambolagen-forelag/> (accessed 8 May 2024).

2. The Church of England, 'Prayers of Love and Faith', <https://www.churchofengland.org/prayer-and-worship/worship-texts-and-resources/prayers-love-and-faith> (accessed 7 June 2024).
3. Courtney G. Joslin and Douglas NeJaime, 'The Next Normal: States Will Recognize Multiparent Families', *The Washington Post*, 28 January 2022, <https://www.washingtonpost.com/outlook/2022/01/28/next-normal-family-law> (accessed 16 December 2024).
4. Ian Lovett, 'Measure Opens Door to Three Parents, or Four', *The New York Times*, 14 July 2012 <https://www.nytimes.com/2012/07/14/us/a-california-bill-would-legalize-third-and-fourth-parent-adoptions.html> (accessed 23 January 2025).
5. Ibid.
6. Ellen Barry, 'A Massachusetts City Decides to Recognize Polyamorous Relationships', *The New York Times*, 2 July 2020, <https://www.nytimes.com/2020/07/01/us/somerville-polyamorous-domestic-partnership.html> (accessed 22 May 2024).
7. Leidys Maria Labrador Herrera, 'Families, Plural', *Granma*, 19 May 2022, <http://en.granma.cu/cuba/2022-05-19/families-plural> (accessed 9 May 2024).
8. Image: Reddit user AcingOut, 2022, <https://www.reddit.com/r/asexuality/comments/yf2oap/surprised_and_happy_to_see_demisexuality/#lightbox> (accessed 6 December 2024).
9. 'Inclusive Equality Act Coalition', <https://www.inclusiveea.org> (accessed 13 December 2024).
10. Lauren Cahn, 'Every Word Coined the Year You Were Born', *Reader's Digest*, 7 November 2022, <https://www.rd.com/list/words-created/> (accessed 22 May 2024).
11. Margit Tavits and Efrén O. Pérez, 'Language Influences Mass Opinion toward Gender and LGBT Equality', *Proceedings of the National Academy of Sciences*, 116.34 (2019), pp. 16781–86 < https://www.pnas.org/doi/10.1073/pnas.1908156116> (accessed 22 May 2024).
12. *R/Asexuality*, 2020 <www.reddit.com/r/asexuality/comments/jk6q9z/rahul_kohli_i_first_knew_him_from_funhaus_then/> (accessed 7 June 2024).
13. Victoria Sanusi, 'Some People Are Pissed Off With American Apparel For Using The Term "Ally" On Its Pride Bag', *BuzzFeed*, 10 June 2016, <https://www.buzzfeed.com/victoriasanusi/some-people-are-pissed-off-with-american-apparel-for-using-t> (accessed 15 May 2024). Image: <https://www.refinery29.com/en-gb/2016/06/113563/

american-apparel-lgbtqa-bag-ally-asexual> (accessed 16 December 2024).

14. Falyn Stempler, 'Bumble Ad Has Users Deleting App in Droves after "offensive" Celibacy Campaign', *Daily Express US*, 14 May 2024, <https://www.the-express.com/lifestyle/life/137473/bumble-celibacy-ad-campaign-billboard> (accessed 15 May 2024).
15. 'Bumble Apologises for Anti-Celibacy Ad after Backlash', *BBC News*, 2024 <https://www.bbc.com/news/articles/cz4xx2rw0leo> (accessed 15 May 2024).
16. *Being Not Straight*, dir. by JaidenAnimations, 2022 <https://www.youtube.com/watch?v=qF1DTK4U1AM> (accessed 7 June 2024).
17. Elaine O. Cheung, Wendi L. Gardner and Jason F. Anderson, 'Emotionships: Examining People's Emotion-Regulation Relationships and Their Consequences for Well-Being', *Social Psychological and Personality Science*, 6/4 (2015), pp. 407–414, <https://doi.org/10.1177/1948550614564223> (accessed 6 July 2024).

Acknowledgements

There are so many people to thank for this book's existence. Thank you to my incredible agent, Judith Murray, for all her guidance and warmth. To my equally incredible editor, Erika Koljonen, and her team at Atlantic, who took a chance on me and the stories I had to tell.

To every one of the 1,900-odd aspec people who took the time to share their stories with me. Hope is a discipline, and you gave me 1,900 reasons to practice it.

To the academics and creators who gave me their time and their insights – in particular Canton Winer and Alice Oseman, who do so much to give aspec people a voice.

To Horatio Clare, who made me realise that I had a book to write in the first place. If he hadn't pushed me, this book might never have existed. Thank you, Horatio, for believing in me before I did.

To my family, who've rallied around me and surrounded me with love (especially my niblings, who are cooler than I will ever be).

To all my friends, who taught me just how powerful love can be. To Juno, Arabela, Thomas, Gwyn, Liz, and the rest of our Manchester crew, who cheered me on. To Zefir, Ali, and everyone who grew up with me across the internet – you helped me realise that my people were out there. To Jan, who explains the mysterious world of sex and dating to me with admirable patience, and who always lets me infodump about video game characters.

To Aryehi, my favourite human being and beloved college wife. Let's get hot chocolate and change the world.

And most of all, to the entire asexual and aromantic communities, who found me, shaped me, and inspired me. Thank you for your bravery, your defiance, and your joy.